T0329850

Counterculture Colophon

Post45 Florence Dore and Michael Szalay, Editors
Post•45 Group, Editorial Committee

Counterculture Colophon

Grove Press, the *Evergreen Review*,
and the Incorporation of the Avant-Garde

Loren Glass

Stanford University Press
Stanford, California

Stanford University Press
Stanford, California

© 2013 by the Board of Trustees of the Leland Stanford Junior University. All rights reserved.

No part of this book may be reproduced or transmitted in any form or by any means, electronic or mechanical, including photocopying and recording, or in any information storage or retrieval system without the prior written permission of Stanford University Press.

Printed in the United States of America on acid-free, archival-quality paper

Library of Congress Cataloging-in-Publication Data

Glass, Loren, author.
  Counterculture colophon : Grove Press, the Evergreen Review, and the incorporation of the avant-garde / Loren Glass.
  pages cm. — (Post 45)
  Includes bibliographical references and index.
  ISBN 978-0-8047-8416-0 (cloth : alk. paper)
  1. Grove Press—History—20th century. 2. Publishers and publishing—United States—History—20th century. 3. Literature, Experimental—United States—History and criticism. 4. Avant-garde (Aesthetics)—United States—History—20th century. 5. Counterculture—United States—History—20th century. I. Title. II. Series: Post 45.
  Z473.G74G57 2013
  070.50973'0904—dc23
  2012040241

Typeset by Bruce Lundquist in 10/15 Minion

published with the assistance of
Figure Foundation

For Barney Rosset (1922–2012)
And for my parents

Contents

Figures

Acknowledgments

First and foremost, I want to thank the students, faculty, staff, and administration of the University of Iowa. The generosity of the university administration began with a Dean's Scholarship in 2007 that, among other things, allowed me to purchase a full run of the *Evergreen Review* from 1957 to 1964, and peaked with a Faculty Scholarship that, among other amenities, provided me with three semesters off to conduct archival research and interviews. I offer my gratitude to the committee members who graciously decided to provide me with this support. My colleagues in the English Department and the Center for the Book also provided me with numerous opportunities to present my ongoing research. In particular, Kevin Kopelson, Matt Brown, and Naomi Greyser merit acknowledgment for facilitating these presentations, and Melanie Reichwald and Sonia Johnson deserve thanks for inviting me to deliver the keynote address at the Craft Critique Culture Graduate Student Conference in 2010. Two of my senior colleagues, John Raeburn and Ruedi Kuenzli, read an early version of the entire manuscript; I want to thank them for their insight and advice at that crucial juncture. As this project inevitably ranged across topics in which I lacked expertise, I needed the help of a number of scholars in reading over specific chapters. In particular, I would like to thank Heidi Bean and Jennifer Buckley for reading drafts of Chapter 2, Louis Siegel for reading an early draft of Chapter 4, and J. D. Connor for reading an early draft of Chapter 5. I also benefited from fruitful and frequent discussion with Kembrew McLeod, Harry Stecopoulos, Corey Creekmur, Charlie Williams, Sarah Fay McCarthy, Matthew Lavin, Michael Chasar, and Sonia Johnson.

I visited many archives in conducting the research for this book. My work began in the Grove Press Records housed at the Syracuse University Special Collections Research Center. I want to thank Sean Quimby, Nicolette Dobrowolski, Kathleen Manwaring, Nicole Dittrich, and Susan Kline for their patience and assistance. Susan was especially helpful in researching sales and print-run information at a time when I couldn't get to the archives in person. My work finished in the Barney Rosset Papers, acquired by Columbia University's Rare Book and Manuscript Library in 2010. Carrie Hintz very kindly allowed me to examine this collection before it had been fully processed. I also had the privilege to visit the archives at the Kinsey Institute for Research in Sex, Gender, and Reproduction, the Calder and Boyers Collection at Indiana University's Lilly Library, the Donald Allen Papers at University of California San Diego's Mandeville Special Collections Library, the Henry Foner Papers at New York University's Tamiment Library and Robert F. Wagner Labor Archives, and the Papers of William J. Brennan Jr. at the US Library of Congress. The librarians at all of these collections were invariably helpful and courteous, and I am grateful for the permission to use their archival materials. I also want to thank Astrid Rosset on behalf of the Estate of Barney Rosset for permission to quote from unpublished interviews and correspondence.

When I started this book, I had never conducted a formal interview, and I am forever indebted to the patience and enthusiasm of the many individuals who allowed me to learn on the job, as it were. Foremost among these is Barney Rosset, an experienced interviewee if there ever was one. Barney and his wife, Astrid, were gracious and cooperative during my two visits, and our discussions were invaluable not just for the information they provided about the history of Grove Press but also for the insights they enabled into the interpersonal dynamics of the remarkable community of people who worked there. These insights were widened and deepened by my conversations with Fred Jordan, Morrie Goldfischer, Nat Sobel, Jeanette Seaver, Herman Graf, Judith Schmidt, and Claudia Menza. I additionally want to thank Fred's son, Ken Jordan, for his support and enthusiasm. I also had an informative interview with Morgan Entrekin, current owner of Grove Press, and would like to thank him for taking time off his busy schedule to meet with me.

When I was in the midst of this project, I was fortunate enough to be invited to join the Post•45 Collective for their annual meeting in 2009 at the University of Missouri and then in 2010 at Brown University. Both meetings were invaluable in providing probing criticism of my project and an inspiring vision of the directions the study of postwar American literature and culture is taking. I want to thank the organizers of and participants in these meetings, including Andrew Hoberek, Deak Nabers, Abigail Cheever, J. D. Connor,

Amy Hungerford, Oren Izenberg, Michael Clune, Catherine Jurca, Debbie Nelson, Fred Whiting, Tom Cerasulo, Daniel Grausam, Florence Dore, and Michael Szalay. Michael and Florence also deserve thanks for convincing me to submit the manuscript to their Post•45 series with Stanford University. Their encouragement enabled me to bring the project to fruition.

At Stanford University Press, I would like to thank Emily-Jane Cohen and Emma Harper, whose patience and expertise were crucial in shepherding this project into its final stages. I also want to thank Stan Gontarski and Stanford's anonymous reader for their expert engagement with the manuscript and their useful suggestions for final revision.

And I would like to thank my family. In a sense, this book is about my parents, Ruth Minka and Marty Glass, who, like all participants in the Sixties counterculture, remember reading books published by Grove Press. My father read the entire manuscript as I was writing it, and his enthusiasm and support kept me excited about and invested in the project from its early stages. Finally, I want to acknowledge, with love and tenderness, my wife, Tara, and my two daughters, Nora and Becca.

Portions of this book have been published previously, and I am grateful for permission to reprint those materials here. Small sections from Chapter 3 appeared in *Naked Lunch at 50* (Southern Illinois University Press, 2009), edited by Oliver Harris, and in *Critical Inquiry* 32, no. 2 (Winter 2006); and a shorter version of Chapter 2 appeared in *Modern Drama* 54, no. 4 (Winter 2011). Finally, select portions of the Introduction and Chapter 3, along with small excerpts from Chapters 2, 4, and 5, appeared as a two-part series in the newly launched *Los Angeles Review of Books*, and I want to thank editors Tom Lutz and Evan Kindley for providing me with indispensable insights and suggestions at a crucial stage in the development of this project. In a book affirming the importance of editors in literary history, it is fitting that they should be recognized here as model practitioners of the profession without which nothing would get published.

Grove Press/*Evergreen Review* covers used by permission of Grove/Atlantic, Inc.

Introduction
From Avant-Garde to Counterculture

On October 4, 2009, I flew from Iowa City to New York to conduct interviews for this book. Everyone I contacted had agreed to meet with me except Barney Rosset. In a series of e-mails, his fifth wife, Astrid Myers, had firmly but politely resisted fixing a date, telling me that it all depended on how Barney was feeling. I had made all my travel arrangements, set to coincide with the fiftieth anniversary celebration of the publication of William Burroughs's *Naked Lunch*, without knowing whether I'd be able to interview the legendary owner of Grove Press, which had published Burroughs's masterpiece along with an entire canon of postwar avant-garde literature, and editor of the *Evergreen Review*, the premier underground magazine of the Sixties counterculture. I was eager to meet the man who bought the fledgling reprint house for three thousand dollars in 1951, built it up into one of the most influential publishers of the postwar era, and then was summarily fired after selling it to Anne Getty for $2 million in 1986. I checked into my room at the Chelsea Hotel, called Astrid, and succeeded in scheduling an interview for the following day.

I knew that Rosset liked martinis, so I bought a bottle of Bombay Sapphire gin at a liquor store around the corner from the East Village walk-up he shared with Astrid. Rosset was spry and loquacious; though his body was bent over with age, his motions were animated and he spoke with assurance. He emerged from behind the glass-brick partition separating the kitchen and living quarters from the long, narrow front room lined with bookshelves, and when he saw the blue bottle of gin, it immediately evoked the past. Without preamble or introduction, he launched into a lengthy memory of shipping out from New York through the Panama Canal and around Australia to Bombay. His ultimate destination was China, where he'd received a commission, through his father's government connections, as a photographic unit commander for the Army Signal Corps. At the opening of the voyage he'd been given a blue plastic canteen, which he filled with gin instead of water. By the time he arrived in Bombay, the plastic had melted into the gin, turning it blue. He drank it anyway.

It took more than ten minutes for Rosset to mention Grove Press, and when he did, it was in order to dismiss everything that had been written about it: "Something you have to understand about how Grove Press came about—nothing like what seems to be written down . . . It's really a big problem. People write about Grove . . . they think I came out of an egg or something."[1] I was later to discover that this has been an ongoing complaint. For Rosset, the roots of Grove Press penetrate deep into the soil of his childhood, and he dismisses any account that would attribute its success to others who worked with him or to larger historical and cultural forces. Rosset's reservations notwithstanding, this book will do both of those things: it will analyze Grove as a collective endeavor enabled by specific historical conditions. But Rosset was the president and owner, and his aesthetic tastes, political convictions, and entrepreneurial spirit were central to the identity of the company. It is thus appropriate that any history of Grove Press start with the story of Barnet Rosset Jr.

He did not come out of an egg. He was born and raised in Chicago, the only child of a Russian Jewish father and an Irish Catholic mother, and he attended the progressive (and private) Francis Parker School, which he credits with instilling in him the passionate left-wing convictions he maintained throughout his life. At Parker he made his first foray into radical publishing (along with his childhood friend Haskell Wexler) with a mimeographed newsletter called the *Sommunist* (a mash-up of communist and socialist), soon renamed *Anti-Everything*. His favorite writers were Nelson Algren and James Farrell. Chou En-lai was his hero. Rosset stood out at Parker—he was class president and captain of the football team—and its principal, Herbert W. Smith, recognized his promise. In a document obtained by US Army Intelligence (and then retrieved by Rosset himself through the Freedom of Information Act [FOIA]), Smith declares that Rosset is "one of the very best: a strong leader, a keen and habitual analyst; decided in his opinions without being intolerant of people who do not hold them; impetuous, courageous, and popular." The letter concludes: "Potentially, since he is an extremist, he is an outstanding fascist or a fair, sensitive democratic leader."[2]

In fact, Rosset saw himself as an enemy of fascism, and his greatest regret was that he was too young to fight in the Spanish Civil War. After graduation, he went to Swarthmore College, partly because its recruiter had been an ambulance driver for the Spanish Republicans and partly because he thought it was close to Vassar, the college his high school girlfriend attended. She broke up with him, and he found solace in reading *Tropic of Cancer*, purchased under the counter from the legendary Gotham Book Mart in New York City. "I didn't even notice the obscenity," Rosset told me; "I noticed two things: one, he'd had a terrible breakup with a girlfriend. And that struck home to me . . . And also Henry's anti-American stance: all Americans looked alike, talked alike . . . etc." As evidence, he gave me a copy of a paper he wrote at Swarthmore, "Henry Miller vs. 'Our Way of Life.'" Written on the eve of America's entry into World War II, when "drums are rolling" and "men are marching," the paper openly wonders what in "our way of life" is worth fighting for.[3] Noting that Miller, as an expatriate, might have a singular insight into this question, Rosset focuses on the author's comparison between Paris, where Miller found "greater independence" and became "a completely self-sufficient being," and New York, "a land of the dead" where he saw "only automatons."[4] Rosset approves of the critique but takes exception to Miller's individualism, arguing that "we must participate in action with our neighbors if we ever wish to achieve any of the freedom which Miller so covets." He concludes that "perhaps our salvation lies in all of us becoming artists."[5]

Rosset gave me a copy of this paper, which he had once used as evidence in court that his interest in Miller was not pecuniary, in order to refute yet another argument: mine. In an article for *Critical Inquiry*, "Redeeming Value: Obscenity and Anglo-American Modernism," I had argued that "the end of obscenity was also a triumph for modernist formulations of the literary, insofar as texts previously valued by an elite intelligentsia were finally being granted mainstream cachet."[6] Much of the article focused on Grove's battles against censorship in the 1960s, which I argued had brought late modernism into the mainstream; I intended this argument to be central to my book. Rosset would have none of it: "This is based much more on aesthetics," he argued, shaking his copy of my article in the air disdainfully, "to me it's like quibbling between Catholicism and Protestantism . . . None of them really interest me . . . I looked at *Tropic of Cancer* from a political, and social, point of view." But, as his conclusion affirms, Rosset wanted to make the freedoms Miller found in art available to everyone. With Paris as Rosset's primary resource, New York as his home base, and the booming American university population as his audience, his signal achievement with Grove Press and the *Evergreen Review* would be to take the avant-garde into the mainstream, helping to usher in a cultural revolution whose consequences are with us still.

Rosset got a B- on his Henry Miller paper and lasted less than a year at Swarthmore. He decided to run off to Mexico but made it only as far as Florida. He wandered back north and enrolled at the University of Chicago, before leaving again to attend UCLA, intending to study film, only to discover that the university did not yet have a film department. In the fall of 1942 he enlisted in the US Army. With a copy of *Red Star over China* close at hand, Rosset ran the only American film crew in the region. After the war, he returned to Chicago, joined the Communist Party (he left two years later, in 1948, after a visit to Czechoslovakia), and hooked up with a Parker schoolmate, the painter Joan Mitchell, a key figure in Grove's early history. Rosset followed Mitchell first to New York, where she introduced him to her circle of friends, the abstract expressionist painters who were in the process of revolutionizing the art world, and then to France, where the two were married. According to Rosset, witnessing Mitchell's development as a painter transformed his understanding of the visual arts: "If I have any taste today, or any emotion about art, and if the Grove book covers show any consistency, it's all thanks to Joan."[7] When they returned to New York in 1951, they began to drift apart but remained friendly; when Mitchell heard about Grove, she encouraged Rosset to purchase it.

At the time, Rosset was attending the New School on the GI Bill (taking classes from Wallace Fowlie, Alfred Kazin, and Meyer Shapiro, among others) and living off a stipend of eight hundred dollars from his father, who refused to give him access to the trust funds from which the stipend was taken. At twenty-nine, Rosset objected to being treated like a child, and he wrote to his father: "I am still in the position of a . . . minor, who receives a monthly stipend, who has no power in the [determining?] of its size, and who has no clear idea of where the money is coming from, how much of it there is, and who does not know if this river of gold will continue to flow."[8] Barney Rosset Sr., a highly successful investment banker, had never been in good health and died only three years later at the age of fifty-five, leaving his son as president of the Metropolitan Trust Company of Chicago. Rosset's father had specialized in government bonds, and, according to Rosset, "I suddenly had $50 million worth of these bonds and I knew almost nothing about them."[9] He noticed that the bonds were losing money, so he sold them all at a huge loss. In Grove's annual report for the year 1955, the Metropolitan Trust Company is valued at $1.5 million, which means, if Rosset's figures are correct, that he lost more than $48 million in a single year. The annual reports from the 1950s also affirm that Rosset essentially incorporated the bank into the publishing company, allowing him to operate at a loss without going under into the mid-1960s, when Grove began to make money. Rumors of Rosset's great wealth, which helped the company get credit in its early years, were founded in truth.

Rosset also began to acquire real estate on Long Island, starting in 1951 with a Quonset hut designed by Pierre Chareau, which he bought from Robert Motherwell for twelve thousand dollars; with his inheritance he expanded his holdings into more than a mile of oceanfront property in Southampton, purchased at forty dollars per foot. Rosset's Hamptons estate became a weekend social center for Grove employees and the writers and artists with whom they associated, and he provided vacation houses on the property for his closest associates. As Rosset remembers, "I moved a lot of people out there. I got a vision of all the Grove people living out there—and we did, or almost! I went and got houses that were abandoned, and we moved them on wheels and rebuilt them."[10] In the 1960s, when the press was mired in litigation across the country, he sold much of this land to keep the company afloat. If he had kept even a small piece of it, he would have remained a very wealthy man. But Rosset squandered his entire fortune on Grove Press; when I visited him, he was living in very modest circumstances. According to at least one obituary, he was almost broke when he died in March 2012 at the age of eighty-nine.[11]

By all accounts, then, Rosset was a reckless and impulsive man motivated by strongly held political convictions. He was also closely watched, and government surveillance of him dates to his years in the army. In 1943, US Military Intelligence, suspecting him of "disaffection," interviewed an informant who had been a classmate at the Francis Parker School.[12] The informant characterizes Rosset as "a headstrong individual, completely lacking in the spirit of compromise, refusing at all lengths to give up on his version of a particular issue." The informant continues that Rosset "was very radical in his views; that his views were definitely 'leftist' in character," and that he "was dissatisfied with the present organization of society and felt that the social organization that gives to people all the luxuries and comforts that he himself had and enjoyed is a corrupt one and should not exist." The informant comments extensively on Rosset's impulsiveness, noting that he "totally lacks sound judgment; he is incapable of appraising people, all of his impressions and judgments are based upon emotional reactions."[13]

Everyone I interviewed agreed with this appraisal. Fred Jordan, Rosset's longtime colleague and managing editor of the *Evergreen Review* throughout the 1960s, called Rosset "extraordinarily impulsive," adding that the company was "driven by Barney's moment-by-moment impulses."[14] Jeanette Seaver, widow of Grove's executive editor Richard Seaver, agreed that Rosset was "irrational," adding that he was also "very generous."[15] According to Herman Graf, who joined Grove as a salesman in the mid-1960s, Rosset "made most of his major decisions in seconds and spent the rest of his life regretting them."[16] Purchasing Grove Press was not one of those decisions.

Indeed, though Rosset developed a reputation for having an "iron whim," he in fact pursued his career in publishing with shrewd determination, and his instincts tended to be sound. He intuited that the obscure experimental dramatists whose work he acquired in the 1950s would become steady sellers once their reputations were established, and he realized early that the market for their printed work would be in the expanding American university system. He sensed that the regime of censorship established under the Comstock Act was collapsing and that challenging it could therefore become profitable. He saw the hypocrisies and contradictions of America's Cold War consensus in the 1950s and was therefore able to exploit the rise of student activism when that consensus began to unravel in the 1960s. And, possibly most important, he had exceptionally good instincts for finding other people who shared his vision and whose talent and expertise could help him realize it.

These people did not conceive of Grove as a business. As Fred Jordan told me, "If you take a publishing company to be a commercial enterprise, Grove never was." "It wasn't a business," his son Ken interjected. "It was a project driven out of passion, which Barney completely self-identified with." If Grove wasn't a business, what was it? "We just called it Grove. Because it was just its own thing," Ken replied. Jeanette Seaver had likened it to a family; Morrie Goldfischer, who had been in charge of promotion and publicity, repeatedly used the term "team" to describe Grove's core group. Nat Sobel, Grove's sales manager, told me that Rosset compared the company to a football team, adding, "I'm the quarterback, and I'm calling the signals." What about a rock band? "It's more like a band than anything else," Ken agreed. And then he added, "The relationship was not so much from one person to another. It was one person to Barney, and then Barney to everybody else." And Sobel confirmed, "If we had any personal relationship, it wasn't with each other; it was with Barney."

My interviews with Rosset's coworkers, all of whom remembered him with a combination of affection and aggravation, led me to conclude that Grove, before Rosset decided to take the company public in 1967, was what the sociologist Max Weber calls a "charismatic community," a small group of people who come together out of loyalty to a figure whose authority is based in his charismatic appeal. From 1960 to 1970, Grove Press was run not by Rosset alone but by a cadre of men and women who were unwaveringly loyal to him even as he made decisions that put the press economically at risk. Weber claims that "charisma rejects as undignified all methodical rational acquisition, in fact, all rational economic conduct," and Rosset's impulsive decision-making style and reckless disregard for money perfectly illustrates this quality of the charismatic leader, whose very irrationality is central to his appeal.[17]

Not surprisingly, most people who have written about Grove understand it as an expression of Rosset's personality. One of the first articles published about the company, "Grove Press: Little Giant of Publishing," characterizes it as "a dynamic expression of [Rosset's] own personal likes and tastes in literature ... Grove's editors are little more than extra-sensory ... extensions of the master's personal literary tastes."[18] And S. E. Gontarski, one of the few academics to write about Grove, affirms that Rosset "had personalized publishing, made it an extension of his own will and psyche."[19] Understanding Rosset as a charismatic leader, and Grove as a charismatic community, allows me to reframe this reductive (and seductive) interpretation and to understand Grove not as an expression of his personality but as a community enabled by it.

This community—which was to play a crucial role in the creation of the counterculture—has been neglected by literary and cultural histories of the 1960s. As James English attests, most cultural criticism and cultural history neglect the "middle space between acts of inspired artistic creation on the one hand and acts of discerning consumption on the other."[20] English focuses on the increasingly significant role of prizes in the circulation of literary prestige, but his claim applies equally to publishers and editors, whose role in generating literary value and meaning is equally important, if not always equally neglected. Like those who administer and fund prizes and awards, publishers function as gatekeepers, mediating the text's passage from author to reader and populating the expanding zone between them.[21]

Publishers, however, are only part of the story. As book studies pioneer Robert Darnton affirms, all books must pass through "a communications circuit that runs from the author to the publisher ... the printer, the shipper, the bookseller, and the reader."[22] Although I will not be dwelling at all the stops on this circuit—the printer and shipper do not play significant roles in the pages that follow—I will be emphasizing the multiple agents involved in establishing Grove's unique niche in the postwar field of cultural production. Rather than see this process in terms of a circuit, however, I choose to understand it as a network extending out from Rosset and his crew and linking authors, academics, editors, readers, and activists around the world. The Grove colophon became a kind of quilting point enabling this network to coalesce around a distinct set of aesthetic sensibilities and political affiliations.

The publisher's colophon is in fact one of the more undertheorized symbols in our cultural landscape. It started out as a "finishing touch" on the last page of a book, where the printer provided a description of the volume and the place and date of its manufacture. Gradually this material migrated to the title page, and in the twentieth century the term came to designate the publisher's emblem and to play a role analogous to that of the trademark or brand name in other industries. However, the unique nature of the book distinguishes the publishing industry from others and inhibits consumers from recognizing a colophon to the same degree they would a brand name like Coca-Cola or a trademark like the Nike Swoosh. As affirmed in "The Cult of the Colophon," an article that appeared in *Publishers Weekly* in 1927, establishing brand recognition is more difficult for publishers because they "have to promote one title after another, most of which can have but a few months' attention, while the producer of other merchandise markets the same product with the same appearance, year in and year out."[23] Thus, the article concedes that "while there is a small bookish public which really knows imprints, by far the larger number of book buyers do not carry along with them any remembrance of the publishers' name."[24]

"The Cult of the Colophon" discusses how modern publishers were attempting to enhance the visibility of their colophons through creative graphic design, and it concludes by noting that "modern art has not failed to influence the colophon," listing Norman Moore's work for Modern Library and Rockwell Kent's design for Random House as preeminent examples.[25] This emphasis on the aesthetics of the colophon accompanied an increased attention to jacket design, which also frequently borrowed principles and elements from modern art. Through a complex synergy of title selection, graphic design, and promotional rhetoric, modern publishers were attempting to garner the public recognition and customer loyalty that was already standard practice in other industries.

They were only modestly successful. As influential editor and cofounder of the *New York Review of Books* Jason Epstein noted twenty-five years later, "Publishers' imprints tend not to mean much to the people who buy books."[26] Despite the sustained efforts of copywriters and graphic designers, the identity of individual publishers remained, for the most part, of little concern to the book-buying public. Grove became the crucial exception to this rule. By focusing on a series of niches increasingly associated with the emergent counterculture, Grove developed a loyal following of writers and readers who bought books simply because they prominently displayed the Grove or Evergreen (and later Black Cat) colophon on the spine. The company was the central node in what could be called a colophonic network. If you owned books by Grove Press, if you read the *Evergreen Review*, you were hooked into this network.

In order to map this network, I've turned to Pascale Casanova, whose groundbreaking study *The World Republic of Letters* has generated considerable conversation and controversy, particularly since its translation into English in 2004. Casanova has little to say about publishers, but her ambitious thesis— that Paris has been the "Greenwich Meridian of Literature" for the past four hundred years—not only implicates them in the international game of literary competition that her book anatomizes but also foregrounds the networks through which Grove established its literary reputation in the United States.[27] A substantial proportion of the authors upon which Grove built its "avant-garde" reputation—most notably Samuel Beckett, Alain Robbe-Grillet, Eugène Ionesco, Henry Miller, and Jean Genet—were originally published in Paris, and Grove relied heavily on its French connections, and the prestige they afforded, in the first decade of its existence.

In this regard, *Counterculture Colophon* extends and elaborates the provocative thesis propounded by Serge Guilbaut in his important study *How New York Stole the Idea of Modern Art: Abstract Expressionism, Freedom, and the Cold War.* Focusing on the emergence, and astonishing success, of abstract expressionism in the years immediately following World War II, Guilbaut convincingly shows how New York City was able to appropriate the status of culture capital previously held exclusively by Paris. Abstract expressionism, Guilbaut affirms, became America's first internationally recognized avant-garde, permanently shifting the center of gravity of the art world.

Guilbaut concludes his study in 1951, the year of Leo Castelli's famous Ninth Street show, featuring paintings by Jackson Pollock, Willem de Kooning, Franz Kline, Helen Frankenthaler, Robert Motherwell, Ad Reinhardt, Robert Rauschenberg, and Joan Mitchell. Guilbaut sees the landmark show as "the symbol of both the triumph and the decadence of the avant-garde."[28] Rosset also bought Grove Press in 1951 and carried its entire stock of three titles to his apartment, also on West 9th Street, out of which he ran the company for the next two years. And 1951 is the year that Roy Kuhlman, a painter on whom Mitchell had been an influence, came to Rosset's apartment to show him some ideas for book cover design. Rosset was initially uninterested in his portfolio, but as Kuhlman was leaving, he accidentally dropped a twelve- by twelve-inch piece of abstract art he intended to pitch as a record cover to Ahmet Ertegun. Rosset immediately saw what he wanted. Kuhlman, whose aesthetic sensibilities had been formed by the abstract expressionist pioneers, owed a particular debt to the minimalist work of Franz Kline, as can be seen by a comparison between one of his early covers and a contemporaneous piece by Kline (Figures 1 and 2). Kuhlman was one of the first book designers to incorporate abstract expressionism into cover art, and his signature style, which made ample use of "negative space," provided a distinct look for Grove throughout the 1950s and 1960s.

If the success of abstract expressionism signaled the ascendance of New York in the international art market, literary consecration remained based in Paris, and Grove's story amply illustrates that city's persistence as an arbiter of cultural value in the postwar era. Grove effectively siphoned cultural capital from Paris to New York in the 1950s and 1960s, reprinting and translating authors it had acquired from Éditions de Minuit, Éditions Gallimard, Éditions du Seuil, and the Olympia Press, thereby establishing a reputation as the premier American disseminator of European avant-garde literature, especially drama. However, Grove championed the idea of an indigenous avant-garde as well, providing an early publication venue for the Beats, the New York school, and the Black Mountain school, publishing multiple scholarly studies of American jazz, adopting abstract expressionist designs for its book covers, and affirming the San Francisco Bay Area as itself a "cultural capital" in a burgeoning national scene.

For Guilbaut, the development of an indigenous avant-garde depended upon what he somewhat awkwardly calls the "De-Marxization" of the American intelligentsia and the purported political "neutrality" of the abstract expression-

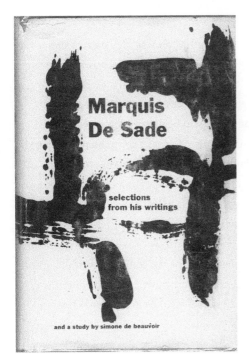

Figure 1. Roy Kuhlman's cover for *Marquis de Sade: Selections from His Writings* (1953).

Figure 2. Franz Kline, *New York, NY* (1953).
(Albright-Knox Art Gallery, Buffalo; Art Resources, NY; GPC)

ist aesthetic. In this way, abstract expressionist painting was part of the larger process of liberal consensus building during the Cold War that reconciled American intellectuals to the ideology of the American century. As Guilbaut affirms, "The depoliticization of the avant-garde was necessary before it could be put to political use."[29] By the 1960s, this consensus had begun to unravel, challenged by the rise of the New Left and the counterculture. A crucial component of this process, and in the emergence of the counterculture itself, was what one might call the "repoliticization" of the avant-garde and the increasing engagement of experimental artists with radical politics over the course of the 1960s. Grove Press was central to this effort to rearticulate the political to the aesthetic meanings of the avant-garde.

This effort did not rely on any coherent theory or philosophy of the avant-garde; rather, it inhered in a fundamental commitment to expanding the distribution of and access to what were understood to be avant-garde texts in the United States, which was the central, and successful, mission of Grove Press.[30] Grove entered the publishing industry at the height of the paperback revolution. Its most significant achievement was to establish and expand the circuits through which experimental and radical literature was distributed, particularly to the burgeoning college and university populations that were the seedbed of the counterculture, thereby effectively democratizing the avant-garde. This democratization involved both geographic dispersal—making avant-garde texts available in more places across the country and the world—and temporal absorption—closing the conventional lag between initial publication and critical consecration. By the end of the 1960s, the avant-garde had in essence become a component of the mainstream, and Grove Press, more than any other single institution, was responsible for this fundamental transformation of the cultural field, the consequences of which are still with us. This process determines the underlying structure of the narrative that follows.

New York

At one point in our second interview, Rosset made a sweeping gesture with his hand and said, "All of Grove Press's life was within about four blocks of here."[31] Indeed, Grove Press was a landmark in the downtown scene. In 1953, by which time the stock was straining the floors of his third-story walk-up, Rosset moved the company to a small suite of offices at 795 Broadway. In 1959, he relocated to 64 University Place; in 1964, to 80 University Place; and in 1969, he purchased an entire building on the corner of Mercer and Bleecker Streets. For the entirety of the long 1960s, Grove was located in the center of Greenwich Village, within walking distance of the Cedar Tavern, San Remo Café, Stonewall Inn, White Horse Tavern, Living Theater, Caffe Cino, Fillmore East, Cherry Lane Theater, Bitter End, Village Vanguard, Café Wha?, Strand, Eighth Street Bookshop, and the offices of the *Village Voice*. Grove's national function as a countercultural publisher was enabled by its central location in the institutional network of New York City's burgeoning downtown scene. Like these other famous institutions, Grove was not only a business; it was also a social nexus for the counterculture. Though Rosset himself moved to the Hamptons in the late 1950s, he frequently spent the night in the Village. Fueled by amphetamines and lubricated with alcohol, he often stayed up all night barhopping, flirting, and networking within blocks of the Grove offices. In the 1960s, he was a key player in a social scene that was also a cauldron of cultural dissidence, sexual experimentation, and political upheaval.

Though Grove was based downtown, its network extended the full length of Manhattan Island. Uptown was Columbia University, which was enjoying a surge of cultural influence as the academic wing of the New York Intellectuals. Columbia was the institutional home to many professors with close connections to Grove, including Donald Keene, Shincho Professor of Japanese Literature, who assisted in establishing Grove's extensive connections to Far Eastern literatures; and Eric Bentley, Brander Matthews Professor of Dramatic Literature, who edited the popular Grove Press edition of the work of Bertolt Brecht. Columbia was also the site of one of the most famous student occupations of 1968, closely followed in the pages of the *Evergreen Review*. The occupation was sparked partly by Columbia's vexed relationship with the adjacent neighborhood of Harlem, whose radical art and activism Grove helped publicize in the 1960s. Malcolm X founded the Nation of Islam's Temple Number Seven in Harlem in 1952. Harlem was also home to the legendary National Memorial African Bookstore, where Malcolm frequently spent time and where his autobiography and speeches, both published by Grove, sold in great numbers after his assassination at the Audubon Ballroom. In the later 1960s, Harlem became home base to the Black Arts movement, whose founder, Leroi Jones/Amiri Baraka, published a number of significant early works with Grove and who was a regular contributor to the *Evergreen Review*. And Harlem was the location of the Hotel Theresa, where Che Guevara and Fidel Castro stayed during their visit to the United Nations in 1960.

Grove had connections in the Cuban mission, published popular paperback collections of both men's speeches in the 1960s, and dedicated an entire issue of the *Evergreen Review* to Che after his death in Bolivia in 1967.

In Midtown, three recently established institutions immeasurably enhanced New York City's global stature in the postwar era: the United Nations, a massive complex dominating the East side, which injected Manhattan directly into the volatile geopolitics of the postcolonial era; Birdland, the legendary jazz club on West 44th Street where musicians such as Charlie Parker, John Coltrane, and Miles Davis launched their careers; and the Museum of Modern Art on West 53rd, which, through its savvy promotion of abstract expressionism, had just achieved the triumphant theft chronicled by Guilbaut. Grove had connections to, and was crucially influenced by, all three of these institutions in the 1950s and 1960s.

New York City was also home to a Jewish community that was on the eve of an unprecedented cultural apotheosis. The genteel anti-Semitism that had restricted Jewish access to higher education had lost its authority in the wake of the Holocaust, while at the same time numerous Jewish intellectuals fleeing Nazism had settled in New York, which had long been a destination for European Jewish immigrants. By the 1960s, Jewish writers and academics occupied the center of New York intellectual and cultural life, bringing European schools of thought into the American mainstream while also producing and defining what came to be understood as American literature and culture. When I asked Rosset if he identified as Jewish, he responded with disdain, saying he didn't see himself as Jewish *or* Catholic. "I didn't know which I disliked more," he quipped. "It made me a communist." Nevertheless, Rosset was perceived by many as Jewish, and most of the key players at Grove were New York Jews.

Fred Jordan, Rosset's right-hand man throughout the 1960s, was a Holocaust survivor. Jordan was born in Vienna on November 9, 1925, and his bar mitzvah was on Kristallnacht; it marked the end of his formal education. Soon after, he fled to England, where he became the cultural programmer for a small cell of fellow traveling Austrian Jews. Later in the war, he joined the British army as a member of the Glasgow Highlanders. He briefly returned to Vienna after the war, where he worked for the US Armed Forces newspaper. He arrived in the United States in 1949 with the intention of becoming a journalist. In 1956, Rosset hired him to handle the business end of things. Jordan shared Rosset's left-wing political sympathies and became deeply dedicated to realizing his vision for the press. And the two worked well together: Rosset was impulsive and intuitive, whereas Jordan was analytical and deliberate; the pairing of their personalities was crucial to the operations of the company.

As the company expanded, Rosset hired more New York Jews, including Morrie Goldfischer; Nat Sobel; Herman Graf; Myron Shapiro, who ran the book club; Jules Geller, who ran the educational division; and Harry Braverman, who was a prominent editor and jack-of-all-trades at the company on and off throughout the 1960s. All of these men came from traditions of left-wing Jewish activism and cultural entrepreneurship, with many having close ties to labor groups such as the Socialist Workers Party. Braverman and Geller's ties to the Monthly Review Press were particularly significant in developing Grove's list of radical political titles.

The industry into which these men were entering was also centered in New York City. All of the major American publishing houses—for example, Random House, New American Library, Dell, Doubleday, Knopf, and Scribner's—had been based in Midtown since the beginning of the twentieth century. In the early 1950s, the New York publishing world was on the verge of what John Tebbel has called "The Great Change," the era of conglomeration and consolidation during which book publishing, which had remained relatively insulated from the broader culture industry, was gradually absorbed by it.[32] Over the course of the 1960s and 1970s, most of the major Midtown publishing houses were bought by large publicly owned corporations that both capitalized and rationalized an industry that had remained a genteel backwater during the first half of the twentieth century. The New York publishing world had been an insular community of (mostly) men, all of whom knew each other and most of whom shared a commitment to literary culture that, they felt, distinguished their industry and their product from others. Many of these publishers, in particular the so-called new breed of second-generation Jewish immigrants such as Horace Liveright, Alfred Knopf, and Bennett Cerf, shared a sense of mission that led them to take risks with unknown authors and then to remain loyal to those authors once they had established themselves. Tebbel calls this earlier era the "Golden Age between the Wars," and under Rosset, Grove would in many ways be a holdover from it, an independent publisher committed to modernist standards of aesthetic evaluation without regard for the bottom line.[33] Like the new breed that preceded him, and consciously modeling his enterprise on James Laughlin's groundbreaking New Directions Press, Rosset was committed to bringing the latest in European experimental literature to the attention of an American reading public—a sense of mission that trumped any simple profit motive. Grove's location downtown emphasized the philosophical and political differences between Grove and the larger mainstream publishers that were ushering the industry into the era of late capitalism.

However, in one crucial respect, Grove depended on and grew out of the incorporation of the mainstream publishers, insofar as that process was driven by the paperback revolution of the postwar era, which, according to Kenneth Davis, "democratized reading in America."[34] Piggybacking on the distribution networks of mass-market magazines, and frequently featuring salacious and sensational cover art, most paperback books in the 1940s and 1950s were reprints either of bestselling hardcovers or of classics that were out of copyright. Initially, Rosset pursued this inexpensive route, developing his title list by reprinting classic texts such as Matthew Lewis's *The Monk* and Henry James's *The Golden Bowl*. But in the later 1950s, following the lead of Jason Epstein's groundbreaking Doubleday imprint Anchor Books, Grove began publishing original avant-garde texts as inexpensive "quality" paperbacks, which were quickly recognized in the industry as marking a new and significant stage in the paperback revolution.[35] As one writer for the *New York Times* remarked, the sudden success of the quality paperback evinced a "surprisingly large, if somewhat self-hidden, intelligentsia" in the United States.[36] In order to access this intelligentsia, Epstein had promoted and acquired his new imprint's authors through the *Anchor Review*, and Rosset adopted the same method. Thus, in 1957 Grove Press published the inaugural issue of the *Evergreen Review*, and in 1958 it launched the Evergreen Originals imprint. Through these two vehicles Rosset hoped to establish an identity for his fledgling enterprise. To achieve this goal, he needed to acquire contemporary authors, and to acquire such authors, he needed connections. And he made them, in Paris and across Europe. Grove became a conduit through which the cultural capital of European late modernism flowed into the United States, ballasting the emergence of an indigenous American avant-garde and generating a veritable canon of countercultural reading for the paperback generation.

Paris

Over the course of the 1950s Rosset established fruitful connections with most of the major publishing houses in Paris, including Maurice Girodias's Olympia Press, which was already well known across Europe for publishing

English-language pornography in its Traveler's Companion series, but which also published avant-garde and experimental literature. Grove also established ties with UNESCO, which afforded it a fruitful conduit to world literature, both classical and contemporary. From these sources Grove acquired the work of many of the authors with whom it would become closely identified in the ensuing decades, including Fernando Arrabal, Antonin Artaud, Régis Debray, Frantz Fanon, Eugène Ionesco, Alain Robbe-Grillet, Henry Miller, William Burroughs, Jean Genet, the Marquis de Sade, J. P. Donleavy, and Samuel Beckett.

Beckett, virtually unknown at the time, became Rosset's most important Parisian acquisition. The lifelong relationship the two established is one of the more underappreciated professional alliances in postwar publishing history. The unwavering loyalty between them hearkened back to Tebbel's "Golden Age," before huge advances and high-paid literary agents rendered such allegiances impractical. Rosset personally handled all of Beckett's literary rights in the United States, was adamant in encouraging the reluctant author to translate his own work, and hosted his only visit to the United States in the summer of 1964 to make *Film*, from a screenplay Rosset himself had commissioned. By 1957, Beckett's trust in Rosset to handle his affairs was implicit and complete, as he wrote: "I am incapable of understanding contracts. My 'method' consists, when they are drawn up by those in whom I have confidence, in signing them without reading them. Any contract drawn up by you, involving me alone, I shall sign in this fashion."[37] And Grove's role as Beckett's exclusive publisher in the United States provided it with high cultural cachet throughout the postwar era. It published all of his work and much of the early criticism that established the foundation of what became an academic industry, whose rapid growth ensured his place in the lucrative college curriculum of the booming postwar American university.

In reminiscences published in *Conjunctions* in 2009, Rosset credits two people with encouraging him to publish the Irish author: Sylvia Beach (a close friend of Joan Mitchell's mother, Marion Strobel Mitchell, who edited *Poetry* magazine) and his New School professor Wallace Fowlie, author of *Dionysus in Paris: A Guide to Contemporary French Theater*. According to Rosset, he gave Fowlie a copy of *Waiting for Godot*, and Fowlie, after reading it, guaranteed him that "Beckett will become known as one of the greatest writers of the twentieth century."[38] Rosset promptly informed Beckett that "what the Grove Press needed most in the world was Samuel Beckett."[39]

Rosset makes no mention in his reminiscences of Richard Seaver, who was equally instrumental, if not in Grove's initial acquisition of Beckett, then in managing the professional relations between them. Before Rosset became aware of Beckett, Seaver, a young University of North Carolina graduate working on a dissertation on James Joyce at the Sorbonne, had stumbled upon *Molloy* and *Malone meurt* in the display window of Éditions de Minuit. Knowing of Beckett's work on *Finnegans Wake*, he bought both books and, after reading through *Molloy* in one sitting, received "a shock of discovery" that marked the beginning of an extensive personal and professional relationship with the author and his work. Seaver mentioned Beckett's name to the Scottish exile Alexander Trocchi, who had just started a journal called *Merlin,* and Trocchi encouraged Seaver to write on Beckett for the fledgling journal.[40] One of the first critical appraisals of the postwar work on which Beckett's reputation would soon rest, "Samuel Beckett: An Introduction," appeared in the second issue.

Seaver and Rosset first met in the fall of 1953, when Rosset returned to Paris with his new wife, Loly, to meet Beckett, with whom he had just concluded a contract through Jerome Lindon of Éditions de Minuit. In Paris Seaver and Rosset began a relationship that became central to Grove's operations once Seaver returned to the States. Rosset told me, "If I'd ever had a brother, I wish it would have been him," and he spent years trying to convince Seaver to work for Grove. The two men, though they became very close, were also quite different. Seaver was from a WASP family in Watertown, Connecticut, clean-cut, athletic, and highly intelligent. He completed his dissertation, with honors, at the Sorbonne. Rosset, more of an outsider, lacked Seaver's discipline and focus; he attended four undergraduate institutions before receiving his BA from the New School in 1952. But the two men shared literary enthusiasms, and, according to Seaver's widow, Jeanette, Seaver recommended Eugène Ionesco and Jean Genet to Rosset. Genet, whom Rosset also met that year in Paris through his translator Bernard Frechtman, became crucial to Grove's radical image, first with his politically explosive theater and then with his homosexually explicit prose.[41]

In his article, Seaver calls Beckett "a prime example of that literary phenomenon which began some time during the last century and continues today, the writer in exile,"[42] and it was in self-conscious emulation of the Lost Generation that the "Merlin Juveniles," as Beckett called them, attempted to realize their literary aspirations in Paris. In addition to Trocchi and Seaver, the group at one time or another included the English poet Christopher Logue, the South African writer Patrick Bowles, and the American translator Austryn Wainhouse. All of them worshipped Joyce, whose *Ulysses* is praised in Trocchi's editorial statement opening the second issue as "a great work of genius" and a model for the type of writing the journal seeks to publish.[43] In this sense, *Merlin* was modeled on the now-legendary little magazines such as *transition* and the *Transatlantic Review*, which had launched the careers of so many modernists between the wars.

But, as Seaver notes in his introduction to the reissue of Trocchi's *Cain's Book*, which Grove had originally published and promoted in 1960 as a Joycean masterpiece, "Paris may have been our mistress, but the political realities of the time were our master."[44] And the master of political realities in Paris in the 1950s was, without question, Jean-Paul Sartre, whose pronouncements set the terms of engagement for literary and political dispute not only in Paris but around the world, and whose journal *Les temps modernes* provided the Merlin collective with their talking points. Seaver and Trocchi arranged to reprint articles from Sartre's magazine, and Seaver's next article for *Merlin*, "Revolt and Revolution," was his account of the famous break between Camus and Sartre over Francis Jeanson's review of *L'homme revolté* in *Les temps modernes*. Though Seaver opens with the challenge of commitment, averring that in a world of "categoric division, the position of the politically unaffianced is certainly ambiguous, perhaps even untenable," he himself scrupulously avoids affiliation in his scholarly summary of both the book and the ensuing break, concluding that "undoubtedly both men are sincere. There are certain elements of truth in both their arguments."[45] Seaver was a young and unknown American in Paris, and his objective was less to take sides in a dispute between two intellectual titans than to communicate accurately the philosophical underpinnings and historical contexts of the debate for an English-speaking audience. When Seaver joined Grove Press as an editor and translator in 1959, this was the role he played. He provided the press with scholarly gravitas and intellectual expertise; his connections to and knowledge of the French intellectual world were crucial to Grove's literary reputation.

Merlin may have helped launch Seaver's career, but it was not a moneymaking proposition. Like most little magazines, it was supported by private funds, in this case from Trocchi's American girlfriend, Alice Jane Lougee, who had a modest allowance from her family in Maine. A temporary solution to the collective's cash-flow problems arrived in the person of Maurice Girodias, who first commissioned the more fluent of the *Merlin* collective as translators and then, ultimately, as pseudonymous writers for hire of English-language pornographic titles conceived specifically for his Traveler's Companion series. Girodias, whom Trocchi introduced to Rosset, is a key figure in the early history of Grove Press, a pariah capitalist on the margins of modernism whose courage in publishing literature no one else would touch was matched by his unreliability in remunerating its authors.[46] Jeanette Seaver told me he was a "thief" and a "scoundrel" but also conceded that he was "a charming man." When I asked Rosset about Girodias, he told me they had "a deep relationship, and a very important one." Seaver, by contrast, called it "a fragile friendship."[47]

The parallels between the two men are noteworthy. They were born only three years apart, to wealthy Jewish fathers and Catholic mothers, and both were brought up without adherence to either religion. Indeed, Girodias took on his mother's last name to avoid being identified as a Jew during World War II. His father, Jack Kahane, was the founder and owner of Obelisk Press, original publisher of Henry Miller's *Tropic of Cancer*, for which the young Maurice designed the cover. Thus, both Rosset and Girodias forged an early link to Miller, who was crucial to their careers after the war, when each established a publishing house specifically designed to challenge the residual regimes of literary censorship. In this they were entering into a tradition of eccentric (and frequently Jewish) entrepreneurs of erotica on the avant-garde of the battle against censorship that, once won, rendered them superfluous. The Olympia/Merlin nexus represents the last incarnation of that symptomatic convergence of modernism and obscenity that centrally shaped the cultural field of the first half of the twentieth century.[48] Olympia's combination of highbrow obscurantism and pulp pornography provided the groundwork for Grove's title list, as the relaxation of censorship in the United States that Rosset almost single-handedly precipitated in turn enabled him to cannibalize most of Girodias's catalog from the 1950s.

In Paris, Rosset and Seaver tapped into two august traditions of the European avant-garde: experimental theater, with its origins in the Ubu plays of Alfred Jarry and the influential theories of Antonin Artaud, and obscenity, which had constituted the moral challenge of modernist masterpieces since the 1857 trials of *Madame Bovary* and *Fleurs du mal*. Grove virtually cornered the market on European experimental theater, publishing not only Beckett but also Ionesco, Harold Pinter, Artaud, Jarry, Arrabal, Brecht, Tom Stoppard, Joe Orton, Genet, and

Slawomir Mrozek. And Grove famously led the charge against the censorship of obscenity, precipitating landmark trials for its publication of *Lady Chatterley's Lover, Tropic of Cancer*, and *Naked Lunch* and then unearthing the entire field of clandestine pornography that had previously been available only through pariah publishers like Maurice Girodias and Samuel Roth.

In addition to Éditions de Minuit and Olympia, Grove benefited from its relationship with Gallimard, the most prestigious and well-established publisher in France. When Rosset was in Paris, Gallimard was already beginning to release its complete collection of the novels of Jean Genet, who, in the wake of his famous pardon by the French president in 1949, was in the process of his initial canonization. And Sartre, who along with Jean Cocteau had personally written to the president endorsing Genet's pardon, was just finishing his monumental psychobiography, *Saint Genet: Comedienne et martyr*, which had developed out of his introduction to the Gallimard edition and served to complete the consecration inaugurated by the pardon. The publication of the English translation of *Saint Genet* in 1961 enabled Grove to begin publishing Genet's homosexually explicit novels in the United States.

Also at Gallimard, though unknown to anyone at the time, a young female editor and veteran of the Resistance named Anne Desclos, who wrote under the pseudonym Dominique Aury, was completing a self-consciously Sadean fantasy of female submission that she had been secretly writing for her boss and sometime lover, Jean Paulhan, influential editor of Gallimard's house organ, the *Nouvelle revue française*. In 1954, her novel was published anonymously by Jean-Jacques Pauvert as *Histoire d'O*, generating feverish speculations in Paris as to its authorship. In the following year it was both charged with obscenity and awarded the prestigious Prix des deux magots. Ten years later, Grove caused a sensation when it published the novel in the United States, translated by Richard Seaver under the pseudonym Sabine d'Estrée.

The inaugural issue of the *Evergreen Review* in 1957 amply illustrates the success of Rosset's efforts to export Parisian cultural capital to New York. It features a cover photo and a portfolio by Harold Feinstein, the Brooklyn-born photographer already known for his scenes of New York City; the opening article is a translation of Jean-Paul Sartre's famous interview with *L'express* on the Soviet invasion of Hungary. This interview both provides the fledgling journal with the imprimatur of France's preeminent intellectual and situates the *Evergreen Review* at a moment of emergence for the post-Stalinist left. Indeed, Sartre's article is one of the first to introduce the term "New Left," only then coalescing as an identifiable political slogan in France and England, to readers in the United States. Grove Press and the *Evergreen Review* forged a crucial component of their political identity through their alliances with the New Left. This issue also features the first American publication of two works by Samuel Beckett, the short story "Dante and the Lobster" and the poetry selection "Echo's Bones." All of Beckett's major work over the next decade was introduced and advertised in the *Evergreen Review*. Finally, this issue of the review features University of California (UC), Berkeley English professor Mark Schorer's essay "On Lady Chatterley's Lover," which became his introduction to the landmark Grove Press edition of the suppressed erotic classic.

San Francisco

Grove complemented its reputation for publishing the latest in European avant-garde literature by tapping into the artistic scenes then emerging in the postwar United States. Rosset's key partner in this endeavor was Donald Allen, whom he had met in a publishing class at Columbia taught by the legendary Random House editor Saxe Commins. Allen coedited the first two volumes of the *Evergreen Review*, as well as *The New American Poetry*, brought out by Grove in 1960 and widely heralded, both then and now, as a key event for postwar American literature. Allen was a consummate editor, translator, and networker. Like Rosset, he was in the Pacific during the war. Upon returning, he attended graduate school at UC Berkeley, where he became involved with the Berkeley Renaissance. A taciturn midwesterner, gay, and something of a loner, Allen rarely showed up at the Grove offices. According to Rosset, "He couldn't stand anybody getting near him, emotionally," and "he wouldn't say hello to anybody" when he came to the office. Seaver's initial impression was that Allen was "scholarly, aloof, diffident."[49] Herman Graf, by contrast, called Allen, "brilliant, enigmatic, mysterious . . . and playful." He was crucial to the operations of the press and the initial design of the *Evergreen Review*, which he saw as "a kind of quarterly sized magazine that would have a longer shelf-life than the ordinary magazine."[50] In those groundbreaking first two volumes, Rosset and Allen reinforced Grove's reputation for obtaining the latest in European avant-garde literature, publishing Beckett's early poetry and prose, Ionesco's "There Is No Avant-Garde Theater," Robbe-Grillet's "A Fresh Start for Fiction," and Artaud's "No More Masterpieces"; alongside these pioneers of the Parisian avant-garde were American poets such as Frank O'Hara, Allen Ginsberg, Gregory Corso, Gary Snyder, Charles Olson, Lawrence Ferlinghetti, Robert Creeley, and Denise Levertov, as well as early prose by Jack Kerouac. The *Evergreen Review* was also a prominent venue for abstract expressionism, including one issue with a photograph of Jackson Pollock on the cover and a reminiscence by Clement Greenberg, and another featuring Frank O'Hara's interview with Franz Kline.

Allen was also instrumental in Grove's acquisition of novelists Jack Kerouac and John Rechy. He had been interested in Kerouac since editing "Jazz of the Beat Generation," Kerouac's contribution to New American Library's *New World Writing*. In July 1956, Allen wrote to Rosset that he was "feeling more and more strongly that Kerouac should be published" and therefore had "asked Sterling Lord to let me look at the MSS and present them to you—for I think there is a real chance that his novels would do well enough in Evergreen editions to justify taking him on."[51] Grove ultimately published *The Subterraneans, Dr. Sax, Satori in Paris, Lonesome Traveler, Pic,* and *Mexico City Blues,* which, piggybacking on the monumental popularity of *On the Road,* cemented its association with the Beats. Allen was even more important for Rechy, who had considerable difficulty completing *City of Night,* his semiautobiographical rendering of the life of a young hustler that became Grove's fastest-selling novel ever, affirming its commitment to the emergent genre of gay literature. Allen encouraged and assisted Rechy throughout the three-year process, publishing excerpts in the *Evergreen Review* and nominating him for the Formentor Prize.

In the late 1950s, Allen relocated to San Francisco, where he operated as Grove's West Coast representative throughout the 1960s. His West Coast connections would be crucial to the *Evergreen Review*'s legendary second issue on the San Francisco scene, the only issue Grove ever reprinted. Kenneth Rexroth introduced this issue, which featured poetry by Robert Duncan, Lawrence Ferlinghetti, Michael McClure, Jack Spicer, Gary Snyder, Philip Whalen, and, most famously, the first nationally distributed appearance of Allen Ginsberg's "Howl" (a mildly expurgated version, since Ferlinghetti's Pocket Poets edition was still on trial for obscenity in San Francisco). Allen sent a copy to Grove, which Jordan read aloud to Rosset over lunch at the Cedar Tavern. After he finished, he looked up and said, "This is the most radical thing I've read in America since I've come here." In his introduction, Rexroth calls the poem "a confession of faith of a generation that is going to be running the world in 1965 and 1975" and offers a "modest prophecy" that "Ginsberg will be the first genuinely popular, genuine poet in over a generation."[52] The first time most of these writers had appeared together in a nationally distributed publication was in this issue, which also features Jack Kerouac's "October in the Railroad Earth"; over the course of the 1960s almost all of them became closely affiliated with Grove and its house journal. Grove in turn became known as the "Beat" publisher on the literary scene, the go-to resource for the latest products of America's indigenous avant-gardes.

The second issue of the review was a big hit in the Bay Area. As Allen wrote back to Rosset, "Evergreen Review No. 2 went on sale here last Thursday. It is stacked up all over town, even in the cigar stores on the change counter! Ferlinghetti decided (against the advice of his lawyer) to stock it too: he's put it in the window and told me he sold 40 copies in the first two hours."[53] Jordan, who in his many sales trips across the country had helped build Grove's reputation on the West Coast, convinced Rosset that they should capitalize on the popularity of this issue by organizing an "Evergreen Book Week" in the spring of 1958 in coordination with the legendary Bay Area bookseller Fred Cody in Berkeley. The series of events scheduled over a three-week period was kicked off by a full-page ad in the *Daily Californian* headed "Cody's Salutes Evergreen Books" and announcing that "EVERGREEN BOOKS are a vital force on campus today."[54] The events of the first week—which included performances of Ionesco's *Victims of Duty* and *The Lesson*; a preview performance of Beckett's *Endgame*; two radio shows; numerous panel discussions with critics, editors, and English professors on both the UC Berkeley and Stanford campuses; and readings by Allen Ginsberg, Lawrence Ferlinghetti, and Robert Duncan—amply illustrate how Grove worked not only to associate its imprint with the latest in experimental literature but also to establish itself as a cultural force in the communities that both produced and consumed this literature in the United States, communities that would soon become epicenters of student revolt and countercultural revolution. As Rosset told me, the Bay Area "just adopted us, right from the beginning."[55]

In their news release for the second issue of the *Evergreen Review*, Grove announced that the writers included in the volume are "fast turning the Bay Area into the nation's cultural capital."[56] The events of the Evergreen Book Week explicitly interrogated the idea of a "San Francisco scene," with lectures and panel discussions on such topics as "The Art of Writing in the San Francisco Bay Area," "Prose Writing in the San Francisco Bay Area," and "The San

Francisco Renaissance: Fact or Fraud?" All the readings were by authors who had been published in the special issue. By combining these readings and discussions with performances of works by Ionesco and Beckett, Grove helped highlight the affinities between the European and American avant-gardes. Furthermore, the inclusion of editors, publishers, and professors along with authors on the scheduled panel discussions encouraged participants, mostly faculty and students, to understand the avant-garde as a cultural network, not just a list of titles.

In Berkeley, Cody's Books was establishing itself as a crucial institutional node in this network. Like City Lights in San Francisco, it specialized in paperback books, and its customer base was the faculty and students at UC Berkeley. In an account of his "Evergreen Salute" printed in *Publishers Weekly* on May 19, 1958, Cody claims he had "felt for some time that Evergreen Books make a special appeal to the University public served by the bookstore." For three weeks, Cody devoted his entire front-window display to promoting Evergreen Books, which Grove had provided him on consignment. And he emphasizes that his discussions with his customers not only about Evergreen and Grove but also about the book industry more generally were a crucial component of the campaign. Thus, he notes that "talk of what Grove was doing in the Evergreen Series led customers to discussion of other paperback lines and to a discussion of the 'revolution' in publishing brought about by paperbacks." He also notes that "new respect was gained for the store which had made the effort to organize a special promotion." Local paperback booksellers such as Cody's, which were cropping up in college towns across the country, became key nodes in Grove's countercultural network.[57]

Cody's display features the Evergreen colophon as a sort of visual pun, emphasizing its similarity to an arrow pointing downward, thereby directing the eye to the titles on whose covers and bindings it prominently appears (Figure 3). But the colophon itself is only one component of the visual language Grove deployed to generate brand identity and loyalty. As the prominent photos of Kerouac and Beckett affirm, Grove put its identifiably experimental stable of authors in the service of its brand recognition. Photos of both Beckett and Kerouac are featured prominently in many of Grove's advertisements over the course of the 1960s, as are images of Burroughs, Ionesco, Genet, and others. Unlike larger publishers, who worked to make their catalogs comprehensive, Grove acquired its authors almost exclusively from the avant-garde and the

Figure 3. Cody's Books display in Berkeley (1958). (Photographer unknown; GPC)

underground, providing a distinctive identity for its colophon that increasingly aligned it with the radical stirrings of the incipient student movement.

Kuhlman frequently incorporated the Evergreen colophon into his designs for this line. Thus, the cover for *The Subterraneans*, prominently displayed in the Cody's salute, plays on the Bay Area location of the narrative with a recognizable silhouette of the Golden Gate Bridge but then renders that silhouette as an abstract formal experiment in shape and color, distorting its symmetry and altering its hue. The off-balance green shades that bisect the bridge against the black background contrast with and foreground the blue lettering for the word *by* and the colophon that takes the place of the artist's signature in the bottom right corner, obliquely reminding us of the mediating role of the publisher in the production of the text (Figure 4). The colophon is similarly situated in Kuhlman's cover for Beckett's *The Unnamable*, which reflects the isolation of the novel's narrator with a central orange circle surrounded by concentric turquoise lines of uneven thickness against a black background (Figure 5). By the early 1960s, Kuhlman's style had become so recognizable that readers could identify a Grove Press book by its cover.

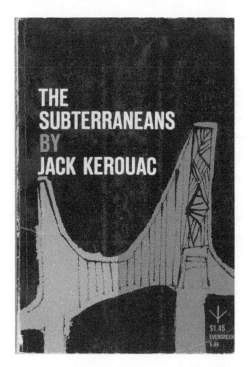

Figure 4. Roy Kuhlman's cover for the Evergreen edition of
The Subterraneans (1958).

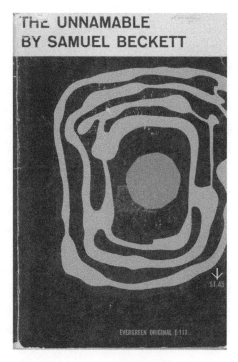

Figure 5. Roy Kuhlman's cover for the Evergreen edition of
The Unnamable (1958).

The Quality Paperback Generation

Grove organized its spring 1958 catalog around its new line of Evergreen Originals, announcing that

> though Grove Press has done some original publishing in paperback format before—most of Samuel Beckett's works first came to the attention of the American public in original EVERGREEN paperback editions—the launching of the new Spring list of ORIGINAL EVERGREENS represents a new emphasis on original books in "quality" paperbacks . . . Up to now the emphasis in the "quality" paperback field has been on reprints of old works. We at Grove Press feel the time has come for a major effort to make new works of a high level available to a larger audience through the lower prices afforded by paper covers.[58]

Grove launched the imprint as an experiment analogous to the avant-garde literature in its rapidly expanding catalog. In a 1958 circular to booksellers, boldly headed "An Experiment," Grove notes the industry's concern "over the shrinking market for new, original fiction" and attributes this shrinkage to "the wide gap between the prices of original hardbound fiction and paperback reprints." The circular proposes that the imprint will "bridge that gap" and requests that booksellers "display these books, talk about them, and report them to your local bestseller lists." The first of four titles listed in the circular is Jack Kerouac's *The Subterraneans*, which in the wake of the publication of *On the Road* had become a bestseller. A mere six months later, Grove ran an ad in the *New York Times Book Review* trumpeting its Evergreen Originals imprint as "an experiment in book publishing that worked!," listing *The Subterraneans'* "best sellerdom" as proof of success and offering new titles by Samuel Beckett and Alain Robbe-Grillet as the latest additions to the line.[59]

By 1962, the *New York Times*, in a special section of the *Book Review* dedicated to paperbacks, confirmed that the "quality" paperback revolution had, indeed, been a success: "Created only eight years ago to meet the curricular and extracurricular needs of academic communities, its popularity is now so widespread that it is being sold in virtually all the nation's 1,700 bookshops."[60] In that same year, Rosset returned to the Bay Area to speak in a lecture series, "The Popular Arts in American Culture," through the UC Berkeley extension. In his speech, he celebrates the paperback book for making reading "more popular, more voluntary, less dutiful" and specifies that the quality paperback has "done much to revitalize" bookstores, further noting that "many stores have opened just for them and new people trained in the craft of book selling. Certainly San Francisco and Berkeley are proof positive of these facts."[61]

The *Evergreen Review* in these early years was something of a "quality paperback" itself. It was identical in size and format, featured the same colophon, and was listed in Grove's catalogs along with its books. According to Rosset, "We just melted that right into our paperback line . . . We just slipped the magazine in as a book. To get distribution."[62] In a rare interview, Allen affirms that "we really thought of *Evergreen Review* in terms of a paperback . . . a quality paperback."[63] Initially, it featured no advertisements, though it did list the titles in the Evergreen imprint on both flyleaves, which by the second number exceeded one hundred, including plays by Beckett, Ionesco, Brecht, and Genet; Beckett's trilogy; Artaud's *The Theater and Its Double*; Robbe-Grillet's *The Voyeur*; and Olson's *Call Me Ishmael*. With the sixth issue, it began to include advertisements, focusing most prominently on other journals, such as the *Chicago Review* and the *Partisan Review*; other publishers, including many university presses; and numerous book clubs, including Marboro and the Readers' Subscription.

The Readers' Subscription, founded by Lionel Trilling, W. H. Auden, and Jacques Barzun in 1951 "to create an audience for books that the other clubs considered to be too far above the public taste," became a particularly important early outlet for Grove.[64] Reaching a mostly university-based membership of around forty thousand, the club was plagued by financial troubles and was sold off in 1963. Nevertheless, its influence exceeded its modest numbers; Marshall Best, writing for *Daedalus* in 1963, attested to the success of such book clubs, "which have not only increased the reading of better-than-average books among the existing audience, but also have brought to light a whole new public of sizable dimensions."[65] Grove made sure that this new public had access to the latest in contemporary avant-garde literature and drama, providing its members with an opportunity to join the underground.

This new public was mostly young and mostly in college. Subsidized by the GI Bill and the National Defense Education Act (NDEA), Americans entered college in unprecedented numbers in the postwar years. According to Louis Menand, undergraduate enrollment increased by almost 500 percent between 1945 and 1975, and graduate enrollment increased by an astonishing 900 percent.[66] Although the GI Bill has tended to receive more emphasis in the many accounts of this expansion, it was actually, as Menand affirms, the NDEA that "put the Federal Government, for the first time, in the business of subsidizing higher education directly."[67] Furthermore, as Menand crucially reminds us, "the strategic rationale for the postwar expansion of American higher education was technological and geopolitical . . . but the social policy rationale was meritocratic."[68] The NDEA was intended to broaden the talent pool in American colleges and universities, creating a student population that was not only larger but also more diverse than that of preceding generations.

In *The Marketplace of Ideas*, the title of Menand's chapter on this expansion (and the following contraction) is "The Humanities Revolution"; indeed, the humanities grew both in size and in cultural and social significance in the postwar era. The number of bachelor's degrees conferred in English increased by more than threefold between 1950 and 1972, while the number of advanced degrees (MAs and PhDs) more than quadrupled.[69] Modern languages, which the NDEA specifically targeted, saw comparable increases.[70] If the actual number of degrees granted in the humanities remained tiny relative to the size of the general population, the canon of texts and the habits of reading promoted by their recipients disseminated much more widely as the humanistic disciplines took on the mandate of "general education" that was part and parcel of the NDEA program. Furthermore, as Stephen Schryer has recently shown, students and scholars of literature and the humanities in the postwar era increasingly saw themselves as the cultural educators and ideological arbiters of the expanding "new class" of professional elites being educated in American universities.[71]

This generation is usually referred to as the baby boomers, but I prefer to follow Kenneth Davis in labeling Grove's readership the "paperback generation." As Davis affirms, the "'boomers' were the first generation to have paperbacks in the classroom. Unlike their parents and grandparents, they read their classics in soft covers, having been assigned reading lists filled with inexpensive paperbacks that they could *own*, not borrow."[72] Many of these paperbacks were so-called modern classics, illustrating and effecting the canonization of modernism in postwar American universities. For Fredric Jameson, this canonization was explicitly ideological, representing a cultural containment and domestication of high modernism's subversive energies into an ideal of aesthetic autonomy. However, as Jameson concedes, "The affirmation of the autonomy of the aesthetic is a contradictory one," and he offers Samuel Beckett as illustrating the late modernist exposure of "the failure of autonomy to go all the way and fulfill its aesthetic programme."[73] For Jameson, this is a "fortunate failure," generating a more accessible form of "middlebrow late modernist literature and culture" whose public "can be identified as the class fraction of college students (and their academic trainers), whose bookshelves, after graduation into 'real life,' preserve the souvenirs of this historically distinctive consumption which the surviving high modernist aesthetes and intellectuals have baptized as the canon."[74]

If such souvenirs survive as reminders of 1960s syllabi, these paperbacks were, during the 1960s themselves, something more. On the one hand, individual ownership was only one component of this generation's relationship to print, and in some ways a misleading one, since paperbacks were frequently shared as a form of collective property. On the other hand, assigned reading lists were only one delivery system whereby these books got into the hands of college students, whose loyalty to Grove Press extended into their "real life" outside the classroom. Indeed, the paperback generation was the last generation to identify itself by what it read; Grove Press nurtured a whole common culture of revolutionary reading in the 1960s. Here I follow Philip Beidler, who, in *Scriptures for a Generation*, affirms that the 1960s "was truly the last great moment of reading and writing in the West by an identifiable mass-cultural constituency, a moment of print-apocalypse, so to speak: materially, a true culmination of print production and distribution intersected with unprecedented consumer affluence and appetite; and spiritually, the last great moment of America's own faith in the Word as its basic article of political and educational reliance."[75] If Beidler's tone is a bit breathless here, he nevertheless indicates the degree to which private reading and public life were powerfully stitched together in the 1960s; to be in the Movement meant, at least partly, to be reading certain books, and many, if not most, of those books were published by Grove Press.

In 1961, Grove launched a new imprint, Black Cat (named after a nightclub in Frankfurt), calling it "the new mass-market line with the liveliest look in the field."[76] Smaller in format and lower in price than the Evergreen Originals, the Black Cat imprint was nevertheless also promoted as a "quality" line, featuring titles by the same authors and marketed prominently to colleges and universities. With these two imprints, Grove was able to establish itself, according to a 1962 article in *Paperback Trade News*, as "the largest publisher of original paperbacks in the nation."[77] But Grove, as we have seen, was already much more than this. It had by 1962 become the communications center for the emergent counterculture. Any writers or readers who felt marginalized by the mainstream came to feel that Grove Press represented their aesthetic tastes, social sensibilities, and political convictions. In the 1960s, the Grove colophon meant more than just avant-garde quality paperbacks; it was a signifier of countercultural sympathies, increasingly drawing radical authors, readers, translators, professors, lawyers, and activists into its expanding network.

Grove achieved this significance through focusing on a series of cultural and generic niches. *Counterculture Colophon* is therefore organized according to the categories in the company's catalog. Thus, each of the following chapters covers similar chronological ground, with the exception of the last chapter, which focuses on the feminist occupation of the press in 1970 and its consequent decline in the following decade. Structurally speaking, this book is recursive, with each chapter spiraling back through the 1960s along the lines mapped out by the niches in which Grove developed a name for itself. Together, they document the creation of a countercultural canon and the achievement of a cultural revolution.

The New World Literature

In the summer of 1949, at the Goethe Convocation in Aspen, Colorado, organized by University of Chicago chancellor Robert Maynard Hutchins, novelist and playwright Thornton Wilder proclaimed that Goethe, in predicting in 1827 that an epoch of world literature was at hand, had "spoke[n] too soon." Wilder announced that "it is now during the second quarter of the twentieth century that we are aware of the appearance of a literature which assumes that the world is an indivisible unit."[1] Wilder's examples of this world literature— T. S. Eliot, James Joyce, Ezra Pound—are predictably modernist, and the location and occasion of his speech, a conference in the United States organized by an influential theorist of higher education and proponent of the "Great Books" program, indicate the degree to which high modernism had by 1949 been embraced by the American university, effectively institutionalizing Wilder's version of Goethe's vision. Over the next two decades, as the university population expanded exponentially, this revised vision of world literature would come to inform the reading habits and cultural sensibilities of a considerable fraction of the American public.

Wilder's modernist elaboration of Goethe's romantic vision clearly implies a canon of texts based both in a certain idea of aesthetic value and in a certain consciousness of cultural diversity, but David Damrosch has recently reminded us that "world literature is not an infinite, ungraspable canon of works but rather a mode of circulation and of reading."[2] According to Damrosch, the category of world literature simply designates "literary works that circulate beyond their culture of origin."[3] Wilder's modernist definition, as illustrated by the Grove Press catalog, is the object of my analysis in this chapter, but I rely on Damrosch's more pragmatic definition for my method of analysis, which helpfully recognizes the importance of publishers, editors, and translators as crucial nodes in the network that enables this category to exist in the first place. Through close alliances with academics and translators across the country, Grove helped popularize a concept of world literature in the late 1950s that centrally informed the political investments of the counterculture in the 1960s.

Barney Rosset and his team at Grove were, like Wilder, steeped in European modernism, and many of the major writers they made available in the United States—Samuel Beckett, Alain Robbe-Grillet, Jean Genet—represented the final stages of the high modernism that had reigned between the wars and whose cultural capital had been Paris. But the political and cultural status of Europe had been transformed by the cataclysms of World War II. Grove's vision of world literature was also inflected by the decolonization of the European empires and the inception of the American century. From its beginnings, Grove worked to provide an American venue for the literature of the "new nations" rapidly emerging from the old empires, and of the so-called Third World more generally, making available many of the authors who formed the initial core of what later came to be known as postcolonial literature. In this sense, Grove can be understood as a central participant in what Casanova identifies as the third major stage in "the genesis of world literary space," which is marked by the entry of the new nations into international competition for literary recognition.[4] The resulting canon can be formulated as a version of what Mark McGurl calls "high cultural pluralism," literature that combines modernist formal experimentation with "a rhetorical performance of group membership."[5] McGurl sees high cultural pluralism as a mechanism whereby postwar American fiction accommodated and canonized US minority writers.

Grove's embrace of an expanded canon of world literature was enabled by the postwar mandate for cultural exchange elaborated by UNESCO, whose imprimatur appears on many of the texts discussed here. UNESCO's constitution, adopted in 1945, claims that "the wide diffusion of culture, and the education of humanity for justice and liberty and peace are indispensable to the dignity of man." It affirms that "a peace based exclusively upon the political and economic arrangements of governments would not be a peace which could secure the unanimous, lasting and sincere support of the peoples of the world, and that the peace must therefore be founded, if it is not to fail, upon the intellectual and moral solidarity of mankind."[6] The perceived urgency of this mandate at the inception of the atomic age is well illustrated by Archibald MacLeish's opening statement at the meeting of the American delegation to the organization's constituent conference in 1945, which emphasizes "the crucial importance of its success if the civilization of our time is to be saved from annihilation."[7]

As William Preston, Edward Herman, and Herbert Schiller confirm in their history of the vexed relations between UNESCO and the United States, "UNESCO's origin had been a utopian yet necessary invention in international cooperation, and the attempted elevation of educational and cultural relations to the forefront of world diplomacy was equally adventurous. Both represented the growing intensity of international contacts, as technology, communications, and economic interchange reduced the distance between the world's diverse populations."[8] Preston, Herman, and Schiller are predominantly concerned with the role of mass media in this globalizing process, but UNESCO was also heavily invested in promoting and enhancing the distribution of books around the world. In 1956, it published R. E. Barker's study of the international book trade, *Books for All*; and ten years later, Robert Escarpit's *The Book Revolution*, which opens with the claim that, due to innovations in paperback publishing, "over the last decade everything has been transformed—books, readers and literature."[9] In subsidizing and circulating studies such as Barker's and Escarpit's, UNESCO hoped to harness the energies and technologies of the paperback revolution in the service of cultural exchange.

Furthermore, as Christopher Pearson affirms in his fascinating study of UNESCO's architectural and artistic heritage, "The pan-national idealism that underlay its institutional activities found an immediate parallel in the ideologies of modern art and architecture" that informed its design and many of its cultural policies.[10] UNESCO, in other words, emerged at the "confluence of two ideas—international modernism and international cooperation."[11] In this sense, UNESCO's location in Paris is equally significant. As is clear from the published notes of Luther Evans, UNESCO's fourth director general, reporting on the meetings of the American delegation to the 1945 constituent conference, a consensus quickly developed that if the United Nations was to be located in the United States, UNESCO would have to be located elsewhere, and Paris, as a "natural cultural center," quickly rose to the top of the list.[12] When the British proposed the French capital as headquarters of the nascent organization, "Senator [James] Murray then went all out for Paris. Others followed in the same vein—Belgium, Mexico, China, Colombia, etc. The French were highly elated."[13] Aesthetically integrated into the cityscape, UNESCO would help Paris maintain its centrality to the circulation and consecration of culture during the period of decolonization.

Literary authorship in this cultural constellation attained a new stature of diplomatic statesmanship, conferring a mantle of ethical authority on figures of internationally recognized literary achievement. The modernist "exile" of the author, which between the wars had been resolutely apolitical and solitary (if not downright reactionary), attained a diplomatic significance as literary figures, officially or informally, took on the burdens of UNESCO's mandate to heal the world through cultural exchange. A number of important Grove authors during this period, including Nobel Prize winners Octavio Paz and Pablo Neruda, were themselves diplomats who were able to leverage their literary capital into political influence on the international stage.

To facilitate its vision of world literature, Grove employed a veritable army of translators who played a crucial role in negotiating the tensions between cultural elitism and cultural pluralism that informed its title list. As Casanova affirms, translation is a form of consecration that operates in two directions, depending on the relation between source and target languages. On the one hand, it is a mechanism whereby literary capital from the European center, principally Paris, can be diverted into the periphery; on the other, it enables texts written in peripheral languages to be recognized by literary authorities in the center. Grove worked in both directions, siphoning literary prestige from Paris to New York by translating figures such as Beckett, Robbe-Grillet, and Genet but also expanding international recognition for work written in Asia, Latin America, and Africa. Richard Howard, Bernard Frechtman, Ben Belitt, Lysander Kemp, and a host of other translators, many of whom were poets themselves and most of whom found their professional home in the American university system, not only translated key authors for Grove but also acted as liaisons and consultants in the international literary network that Grove helped build in the postwar era.

Most of Grove's translators can be positioned within what Lawrence Venuti, in his contentious history *The Translator's Invisibility*, analyzes as the modernist regime in English-language translation, which "seeks to establish the aesthetic autonomy of the translated text" through assimilating it to the modernist criteria of its target language.[14] Venuti's somewhat selective history mentions none of Grove's translators, but Paul Blackburn, the Poundian disciple who receives pride of place in *The Translator's Invisibility*, was well aware of Grove's importance when, in a 1962 article for the *Nation*, he ambivalently proclaims, "Now that colonialism has become an anachronism politically . . . it is as though we are witnessing the sack of world literature . . . by the American publishing business."[15] Citing a number of Grove's authors and translators, as well as the Mexican issue of the *Evergreen Review* that is discussed in detail later, Blackburn is cautiously optimistic, averring that "the mutual insemination of cultures is an important step toward what our policy makers think of as international understanding."[16]

Grove's cultivation of an international title list coincided with its innovation of the quality paperback, a conjunction that affected the cultural understandings of both categories. On the one hand, world literature, while maintaining the scholarly imprimatur of its translators and introducers, would be inexpensive and accessible, and Grove's translators explicitly targeted a broad English-speaking American public. On the other hand, Grove's Evergreen Originals took on the worldly and cosmopolitan cast of the contents they frequently contained. Thus, over the course of the 1950s, Grove established an identity as a source of affordable access to the latest developments in world literature. Kuhlman's abstract expressionist cover designs provided aesthetic continuity for the various literary products Grove offered. By packaging a wide variety of titles from all over the world under a uniform style of aesthetic innovation already associated with the postwar ascendance of the United States, Grove's Evergreen Originals, in their very format, accommodated the cultural pluralism of world literature to the cultural elitism of late modernism. And Grove aggressively marketed its international titles to an academic audience, announcing in one flyer circulated to colleges and universities that "Evergreen books have a particular interest for Humanities and World Literature courses. They represent an unusually wide range, from ancient classics of China to the latest novels from France" and boasting "the greatest number of individual titles being used this past year by Harvard University, the University of Chicago, and the University of California at Los Angeles."[17]

Two anecdotes, both set in Paris in the late 1950s, exemplify the network whose general shape I've just outlined. The first involves Khuswant Singh, the Sikh author and diplomat who in 1954 became a specialist in Indian affairs for the Department of Mass Communications at UNESCO. In 1955, Rosset, apparently not patient enough to acquire authors and then wait for them to win international prizes, decided to establish his own "Grove Press Contest for Indian Writers" in order "to further cultural relations between the United States and India," with an award of one thousand dollars to be given to "the best literary work in English to be submitted by a citizen of India."[18] The press received more than 250 submissions, from which a panel of two Indian and two American judges selected Singh's *Mano Majra*, a novel focusing on the violence and unrest in a small town on the newly established India-Pakistan border.[19]

The ensuing negotiations over the award and the novel's publication conveniently illustrate the institutional linkages through which Grove built its international reputation. Upon hearing that he had received the award, Singh wrote to Rosset, "I would very much like the presentation to be made by my own Director General, Dr. Luther Evans . . . It would do my ego a lot of good."[20] Rosset promptly wrote to Evans, the former librarian of Congress, who agreed to present the award, writing that "Mr. Singh's work will contribute to increasing mutual knowledge among peoples of one another's ways of life, which is one of the fundamental aims of UNESCO."[21] The award was presented to Singh on March 18, 1955, in the Louis XIV room of UNESCO House in Paris.

In his letter accepting the award, Singh suggested changing the title to *Train to Pakistan*, calling it a "cheaper title" that will "tempt reviewers to review, buyers to buy and even film companies to look upon it as a possibility. A train is a Freudian symbol which arouses a response at once."[22] Rosset preferred the original title, and the novel was initially published under both titles, though *Train to Pakistan* is the one that stuck (a movie was eventually made in 1998). Rosset also quickly secured translation deals with Gallimard and Verlag and granted British publication rights to Chatto and Windus. Grove then aggressively publicized the text as a "prize-winning novel" in both India and the United States. The story of Grove's acquisition and publication of Singh's novel economically illustrates the alignments between literary prestige, as conferred by the proliferating system of awards, and cultural exchange, as represented by UNESCO, that shaped the network in which Grove's vision of world literature circulated.

The second anecdote involves Richard Howard, the prize-winning American poet who translated key authors for Grove, including Alain Robbe-Grillet, Fernando Arrabal, and André Breton. In January 1959, Rosset sent Howard on a trip to Paris with an illuminating list of tasks. For the *Evergreen Review*, Howard was to solicit an article by Roland Barthes on "the current situation of the intellectual in France" and one by René Étiemble on "Red China." He was to study current productions of Arrabal's plays, with particular attention to "his use of the contemporary jazz idiom." He was to contact editors at Éditions de Minuit, Éditions du Seuil, and Gallimard concerning their latest projects. He was to visit Maurice Girodias of Olympia Press, partly to check up on the progress of the Lolita Nightclub (Girodias had achieved considerable notoriety for publishing Nabokov's novel as part of his Traveler's Companion series in 1955). And he was to look for a cartoonist.[23]

Howard's letters to Rosset provide insight into the formation of the network whereby Grove obtained most of its early access to an emergent international literary canon. He exults that he has "never had so many invitations to dinner, to lunch, to drinks, to talk . . . in all [his] life." He reports to Rosset that, based on his visits with Parisian publishers, "we have every reason to feel that the intellectual richesse of France will be showered upon Grove Press." And he exclaims that, in Paris, "Evergreen Review and Grove Press are perhaps the best known American manifestations of The Higher Culture." Finally, he notes that "there is a huge Jackson Pollock show [that] Frank O'Hara was here to hang."[24]

But Howard's most remarkable encounter is with Samuel Beckett, to whom Rosset had written a letter of introduction. Like almost everyone who writes about Beckett personally, Howard was smitten: "I was expecting that fierce, beautiful head that you use on your catalogue, but nothing had prepared me for the gentleness of his voice, the warmth of his welcome, and the fascination of his presence." The two, not surprisingly, discuss translation, with Beckett affirming that "he does not translate, he creates." Howard then recounts a remarkable story Beckett told him of a visit in 1940 to Valery Larbaud, the French author and translator of *Ulysses* under whose "patronage" Casanova places *The World Republic of Letters.* Larbaud was paralyzed as a result of illness, and Howard sees in this visit the genesis of the narrator of Beckett's *Unnamable*: "Surely the vision of that motionless, ignoble trunk babbling incoherent syllables . . . must have caught somewhere within Beckett's fierce head, his formidable heart," Howard provocatively speculates.[25]

Europe

The modernist credentials of Beckett—apprentice to Joyce, critic of Proust, continuously compared to Kafka—were impeccable. Rosset shrewdly anticipated that, like his modernist forebears, Beckett would make a good long-term investment. By 1955, he was already able to announce to Beckett, with whom he had become friends, "I am very happy to see this bubbling up of interest and my strong feeling is that your work is going to be more and more known as time goes by. There definitely is an underground interest here, the kind of interest that slowly generates steam and has a lasting effect."[26] In fact, Beckett was canonized with such unprecedented alacrity that Leo Bersani felt the need to ask, in his review of Martin Esslin's 1965 anthology of critical essays on the author, "Has Beckett . . . failed to fail?"[27] Bersani's review reveals how the academic industry that rapidly inserted itself into the interpretive space left open by Beckett's reticence effectively universalized his idiosyncratic literary response to the devastation and destitution of postwar Europe into an expression of "the nature of human existence itself."[28] Bersani finds it "somewhat disconcerting to read so many admiring, undaunted analyses of a significance for which Beckett implicitly expresses only boredom and disgust,"[29] but Esslin has a response to this understandable complaint. He asks in his introduction, "If there are no secure meanings to be established . . . what justification can there be for any critical analyses of such a writer's work?" He then lists a number of justifications, including elucidating "the numerous allusions" and uncovering "the structural principles." But both of these justifications rely for their ultimate utility on the third, which makes it the role of the critic to determine "the manner in which [Beckett's] work is perceived and experienced by his readers." For Esslin, "the critics' experience . . . serves as an exemplar for the reactions of a wider public; they are the sense organs of the main body of readers." Implicitly referencing the rocky initial reception of *Waiting for Godot* in the United States, Esslin explains that the critics' "modes of perception will be followed by the mass of readers, just as in every theater audience it is the few individuals with a keener than average sense of humor who determine whether the jokes in a play will be laughed at at all, and to what extent, by triggering off the chain-reaction of the mass of the audience."[30]

Esslin's collection displays a cultural confidence in the gate-keeping function of critics that derives, in somewhat circular fashion, not only from their consensus on Beckett's importance but also from the shared network of venues in which this consensus circulated. Their spectacular success in inverting Beckett's failure received the ultimate imprimatur three years later, when Beckett was awarded the Nobel Prize in Literature for, in the peculiar syntax of the Swedish Academy, "his writing which—in new forms for the novel and drama—in the destitution of modern man acquires its elevation." Karl Ragnar Gierow's speech, given in Beckett's absence, clarified this powerful logic of reversal. Conceding that "the degradation of humanity is a recurrent theme in Beckett's writing," Gierow goes on to ask, "What does one get when a negative is printed? A positive, a clarification, with black proving to be the light of day, the parts in deepest shade those which reflect the light source. Its name is fellow-feeling, charity."[31]

Gierow's photographic metaphor is revealing, since this humanist universalization of Beckett's themes tended to be reinforced by analogies to the visual arts. Esslin's collection exhibits this tendency by opening with Beckett's "Three Dialogues on Painting," which includes his famous assertion, offered as an appraisal of the Dutch painter Bram Van Velde but widely understood as an instance of critical self-reflection, that, in the absence of any coherent relation between artist and occasion, "to be an artist is to fail, as no other dare fail."[32] As the essays that follow reveal, it would be left to the critics to establish this relation, frequently by analogy to abstract painting. Grove's book design reinforced this analogy, as Kuhlman ensured that the covers for the individual paperbacks of Beckett's postwar trilogy sported the abstract expressionist designs he favored. Thus, the title *Molloy* jauntily tilts across the top of the cover, in black type framed by an irregular strip of white slanted against a black background. In the center, Beckett's name appears directly below an abstract design drawn in black lines of irregular thickness against a white background. The abstract, typographical, and thematic elements of the cover are brought together by the central geometric line drawing, which depicts two large black X's framed by adjacent rectangles (Figure 6). The cover reframes themes of constraint—the abstract design suggests bars or grids—as an image of formal free play. As an aesthetic object in and of itself, it encourages more generally the sublimation of thematic meaning into formal abstraction and stylistic virtuosity.

For the single-volume hardcover edition, offered as an alternate selection by the Readers' Subscription in 1959, Grove used the photo Howard mentions from its 1958 catalog cover, which appeared in advertisements and promotional materials throughout the 1960s. It features Beckett from the shoulders up, facing front but with his head slightly turned to the right and his forehead slanted forward, giving his direct gaze into the camera a vaguely menacing aura. He's wearing a turtleneck sweater and a tweed jacket, and his thick hair is combed straight up off his forehead and cut very short above his ears. His left ear is prominently visible, giving the sense that he is listening skeptically. He looks like a highly intelligent, and intimidating, college professor, buttressing Hugh Kenner's contention, in his early study of Beckett published by Grove in 1961 and excerpted in Esslin's anthology, that his work "plays ever bleaker homage

Figure 6. Roy Kuhlman's cover for *Molloy* (1955).

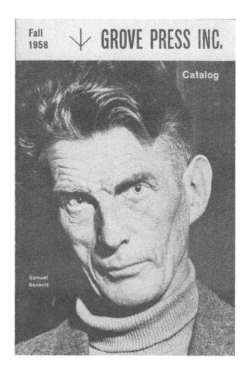

Figure 7. Grove Press catalog cover (Fall 1958). (GPC)

to the fact that ours is a classroom civilization, and that schoolmasters are the unacknowledged legislators of the race"[33] (Figure 7).

Since Beckett couldn't come up with a single title for the trilogy, Grove simply presents it on the jacket cover in yellow as *Three Novels by Samuel Beckett* to the lower left with the individual titles, also in yellow, to the lower right. The Black Cat paperback, which sold more than sixty thousand copies in its first five years, features simply *Three Novels by Samuel Beckett* in black, followed by *Molloy* in blue, *Malone Dies* in green, and *The Unnamable* in blue. Over the course of these serial iterations, Grove used all three of Kuhlman's styles—abstract, photographic, and typographic—to package Beckett's trilogy. And Beckett in turn ballasted Grove's reputation, grounding and legitimating the modernist standards that dictated its choices of international authors. His austere gaze appears authoritatively in many of its ads, and his name, conveniently early in the alphabet, always fronts any list of its titles. The combination is epitomized by the covers for the collected works that Grove issued in the wake of Beckett's Nobel Prize, all of which sport the now-classic photo in different colors.

Beckett also provided a model for the practice of translation that was so central, philosophically and economically, to Grove's international enterprise. Indeed, early correspondence confirms that Rosset should be given some credit for convincing Beckett to enter into the business of self-translation. In his first, and frequently cited, letter to Beckett, Rosset states emphatically, "If you would accept my first choice as translator the whole thing would be easily settled. That choice of course being you."[34] Beckett responded that he was willing to tackle *Godot* but that, concerning the novels, he would "greatly prefer not to undertake the job."[35] In his recently published memoirs, Seaver affirms Rosset's role in encouraging Beckett to take up the task, quoting him as saying, "I always felt Beckett had to be his own translator . . . but he resisted for a long time."[36]

As Paul Auster admiringly asserts in his "Editor's Note" to the Grove Centenary Edition of Beckett's complete works, "Beckett's renderings of his own work are never literal, word-by-word transcriptions. They are free, highly inventive adaptations of the original text—or, perhaps more accurately, 'repatriations' from one language to the other, from one culture to the other. In effect, he wrote every work twice, and each version bears his own indelible mark, a style so distinctive it resists all attempts at imitation."[37] Auster's shift from "adaptation" to "repatriation," from "language" to "culture," can be understood to indicate a certain "cultural turn" in the conventional understandings of translation, but he also invests the implied pluralism of this terminology with a model of modernist mastery indicated by the "indelible mark" of Beckett's authorship. Grove's translators were similarly split between an emergent cultural understanding of linguistic difference and a residual modernist understanding of literary value.

The difficult work of Alain Robbe-Grillet also solicited critical elucidation; unlike Beckett, Robbe-Grillet was eager to supply some of this elucidation himself. Robbe-Grillet claimed that he wrote the essays collected in *For a New Novel* because "I was not satisfied to be recognized, enjoyed, studied by the specialists who had encouraged me from the start; I was eager to write for a 'reading public,' I resented being considered a 'difficult' author," which situates him within the mandate for popularizing modernism that also motivated his American publisher.[38] His agent Georges Borchardt wrote to Grove about what became Robbe-Grillet's most popular book in the United States: "LA JALOUSIE has not yet been seen by any American publisher. I think *Grove* is just right for it, and it is just right for *Grove*."[39] And Grove indeed worked hard to promote both Robbe-Grillet's novels and his explanations of their technique, publishing a number of the essays in the *Evergreen Review* that were later collected in *For a New Novel*. The first, "A Future for the Novel," specifies the degree to which the "New Novel" implies a "New World": "Not only do we no longer consider the world as our own, our private property, designed according to our needs and readily domesticated, but we no longer even believe in its 'depth.'"[40] Robbe-Grillet's abandonment of "depth" allied his literary program with the visual arts, in particular film, to which he increasingly turned in the 1960s after the success of *Last Year at Marienbad*. Two issues later the *Evergreen Review* featured Roland Barthes's seminal essay on Robbe-Grillet, in which he affirmed that the author "requires only one mode of perception: the sense of sight."[41]

Barthes's essay formed one of the multiple paratexts inserted into the combined volume of *Jealousy* and *In the Labyrinth* that Grove published as a Black Cat paperback in 1965. According to Rosset, Robbe-Grillet, who had himself worked as an editor at Éditions de Minuit, had encouraged this repackaging of his most acclaimed novel during his US lecture tour, which the author claimed consisted of "forty universities and forty-three cocktail parties."[42] After the visit, Rosset wrote to Borchardt, "When Robbe-Grillet was here, we decided to do our own small format Evergreen containing JEALOUSY and IN THE LABYRINTH, plus a section of critical material by and about Robbe-Grillet, specifically aimed at the college market. This is what Robbe-Grillet wants, and so do we. We hope for an enlargement of the audience for Robbe-Grillet in this manner."[43] This academically pitched Black Cat mass-market version, appearing in the same year as *For a New Novel*, in fact features three critical introductions: Barthes's essay, a piece by the French critic Anne Minor, and one by University of Chicago professor Bruce Morrissette. These essays are followed by a map of the colonial villa in which the novel's action takes place, accompanied by a detailed legend, orienting and emphasizing the spatial logic of the narrative to follow. The texts of the two novels are then supplemented, as stated on the back cover, by "a bibliography of writings by and about the author." The back cover also prominently quotes an American reviewer's prediction that "Robbe-Grillet will take his place in world literature as a successor of Balzac and Proust." This paratextually packed "college" version of Robbe-Grillet's most famous novel, which sold more than forty-five thousand copies over the course of the 1960s, affirms the degree to which his work found a home in the American academy. It is not surprising, then, that Howard, Robbe-Grillet's American translator, also translated seminal work by Barthes and Michel Foucault, situating Robbe-Grillet in the advance guard for the army of French theorists who invaded the American university in the coming decades. Robbe-Grillet himself became a professor at New York University in 1971.

The final figure in Grove's triumvirate of Parisian late modernist literary innovators is Jean Genet, who modeled the passage from aesthetic to political revolution that informs the larger story of Grove Press in the 1960s. On the one hand, Genet was widely perceived, in the frequently excerpted words of Alex Szogyi's review of *Our Lady of the Flowers* for the *New York Times Book Review*, as "the foremost prince in the lineage of French *poètes maudits*."[44] Celebrated as heir to Baudelaire and Proust, Genet entered the English-speaking world with impeccable literary credentials, and his novels, once published, were widely celebrated as modernist masterpieces. On the other hand, the itinerant delinquency of Genet's youth, coupled with the impassioned political militancy of his later career, turned him into something of a stateless diplomat, as he leveraged his literary celebrity into a tireless advocacy for the oppressed. As a figure of sexual dissidence who persistently associated himself with the causes of ethnic and racial minorities, especially the Black Panthers and the Palestinian Liberation Organization, Genet anticipated the politics of difference that emerged from the social upheavals of the 1960s. More than any other single

Grove author, his career exemplifies the complex convergence of the aesthetic, sexual, and political meanings of "revolution" that linked Grove's early investment in European modernism with its later commitment to liberation movements around the world.

The philosophical framework within which this convergence was understood was resolutely existentialist, as Genet emerged onto the world stage in the enormous shadow of what Gerard Genette has called "the most imposing, or most inhibiting, example of philosophical support for a literary work," Sartre's monumental *Saint Genet: Comedienne et martyr*. Sartre's work began as a preface to Gallimard's edition of Genet's collected works but turned into a six-hundred-plus-page tome issued by George Braziller in the United States in 1961 as *Saint Genet: Actor and Martyr*, the same year Grove brought out its hardcover edition of *Our Lady of the Flowers*.[45] *Saint Genet*, from which Grove excerpted its prefaces to *The Maids*, *Our Lady of the Flowers*, and *The Thief's Journal*, ensured that Genet's development from thief to prisoner to poet to playwright to political radical, as well as the homosexual identity that subtends this development, would be understood dialectically, as willed appropriations of and identifications with an entire series of "others" against which the Western bourgeoisie defined itself.

Genet's entry into the English-speaking world was also enabled by a less celebrated figure, Bernard Frechtman, the American expatriate who translated all his major work, as well as much of Sartre's enormous corpus, including *Saint Genet*. Frechtman, a brilliant but emotionally unstable man with unrealized literary aspirations of his own, not only translated Genet's difficult work into English but also operated as his literary agent until their break in the mid-1960s, after which he descended into a deep depression that ended in suicide in 1967. Prior to their break, Frechtman had been a tireless advocate of Genet's genius, writing to Rosset in the early 1950s that "Genet—I haven't the slightest doubt about this—is the greatest living writer."[46] Frechtman also specified that translating Genet presented particular challenges: "You do realize that translating Genet is not like translating an ordinary book. I'm generally a very fast worker and have a certain routine for handling translations. But works by Genet, as you well know, are another matter. I cannot stand outside them, as I can when translating 'just another book.' I must, after a fashion, become the book."[47] Frechtman inserts himself as yet another double in the narcissistic hall of mirrors that constitutes Genet's Sartrian universe.

Significantly, Frechtman's break with Genet was precipitated by a dispute over their respective share in the revenues from the paperback deal that Grove made with Bantam Books in the mid-1960s. Rosset had delayed publishing Genet's sexually explicit novels until after his success in the trial of *Lady Chatterley's Lover*. Thus, the plays, written after the novels, were both published and performed in the United States before the novels became available. Even after his triumph with *Lady Chatterley*, Rosset was cautious with the explicit homosexuality of Genet's prose, first excerpting *Our Lady of the Flowers* in the *Evergreen Review* in 1961 and then issuing it as a hardcover, and a Readers' Subscription choice, in 1963. After this hardcover edition received the unanimous acclaim of American critics such as Susan Sontag, Richard Wright, and Wallace Fowlie, Grove sold the paperback rights in 1964 to Bantam, which reissued it as a Bantam Modern Classic in 1968, by which time it had gone through five print runs. This delayed publication meant that Genet's novels, while written in the 1940s, did not fully enter into the American cultural field until the 1960s, when they were rapidly canonized and widely circulated.

Beckett, Robbe-Grillet, and Genet represent the long twilight of the European male modernist as authoritative genius. All three men remain best known for their early work, which presents masculine protagonists in situations of impotence, confusion, and constraint, whose only dignity is granted through the stylistic virtuosity of their creators. While these thematic obsessions were frequently honored with celebrations of universality, they were also understood, with equal frequency, as representing the exhaustion not only of the modernist mandate to make it new but also of the entire Enlightenment project of epistemological mastery. The sense that the West had exhausted its ethical authority in the wake of a war that witnessed both the Holocaust and the atom bomb deeply informed Grove's investment in other cultural traditions. Its selection of these traditions was in turn informed by America's triumphant emergence from the war and the demands of its rapidly expanding university population for knowledge of the world the war had created.

Asia

In early 1953, Donald Allen began negotiations with Donald Keene, whom he had met and befriended in the Pacific during the war, over the publication of an anthology of Japanese literature. Allen described his vision to Keene as "a fairly large book, as complete as possible within such limits, and we'd like to present fairly long selections from the best Japanese writing together with informative prefatory notes that would somehow sketch in the history of Japanese literature. We aim to put together a book that will have some value as a textbook, we hope, but that will also appeal to the general reader."[48] Allen and Rosset also hoped that Keene could recruit Arthur Waley, by then the éminence grise of Oriental studies in the Anglophone world and translator of numerous works of classical Japanese and Chinese literature. But Waley, a "rather crotchety gentleman," according to Keene,[49] declined, telling Keene, "I don't feel inclined to come in on the anthology business."[50]

Keene, however, was enthusiastic about the anthology business. Like Rosset and Allen, he had become interested in East Asian culture from his experiences in World War II. Keene was a Columbia undergraduate studying with Mark Van Doren when the Japanese bombed Pearl Harbor. Since he could not imagine himself "charging with a bayonet or dropping bombs from an airplane," he decided to train as a translator and interpreter at the US Navy Japanese Language School in Boulder, Colorado, after which he honed his language skills as an intelligence officer in the Pacific.[51] After the war, he returned to Columbia to pursue graduate study in Japanese literature. He received his PhD in 1949 and taught Japanese literature at Columbia for the next fifty years, founding the Donald Keene Center of Japanese Culture and retiring only recently as the Columbia University Shincho Professor of Japanese Literature. Over the course of his long and illustrious career, he became one of the world's most respected scholars and translators of Japanese literature, and one of only three who were not Japanese to receive the title of Bunka Koro-sha (Person of Cultural Merit).

In 1955, Rosset and Keene decided to split the anthology in two: the first volume covered "the earliest era to the mid-nineteenth century," and the second was devoted to modern Japanese literature of the last century. In the preface to the second volume Keene felt compelled to account for the fact that both anthologies—one covering more than one thousand years; the other, less than eighty—were the same length. According to Keene, the "disproportion is largely to be explained in terms of the amount of literature which has poured from the printing presses in recent times."[52] In the introduction, Keene correlates this groundswell of literary production to the opening of Japan to Western influence, when "Japanese literature moved from idle quips directed at the oddities of the West to Symbolist poetry, from the thousandth-told tale of the gay young blade and the harlots to the complexities of the psychological novel."[53] Keene concludes with the prediction that, "as European traditions are finally absorbed, not only by the novels but by the drama and poetry as well, we can expect that the amazing renaissance of literature in Japan during the past half-century or so will continue to be one of the wonders of the modern literary world."[54] Keene's correlation of Japanese literary modernity with the absorption of "European traditions" indicates the degree to which the standards of Western modernism informed the developing canon of world literature in the postwar era. As he affirms in his introduction, Japan, like the rest of the world, had learned that "the industrial plant, democracy, economics, Symbolist poetry, and abstract painting all go together."[55] To visually affirm this series of equivalences, Grove used one of Kuhlman's abstract cover designs for the anthology (Figure 8).

The timing of Grove's publication of Keene's anthology was felicitous, as the newly formed Conference on Oriental-Western Literary Relations of the Modern Language Association had been lamenting the absence of affordable translations of Asian literature. In his review of the anthology for the conference's journal, *Literature East and West*, Glen Baxter of Harvard called it "the

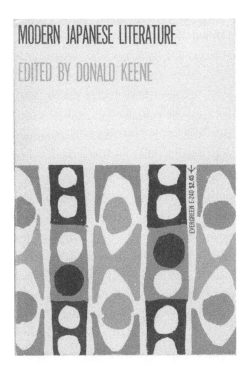

Figure 8. Roy Kuhlman's cover for *Modern Japanese Literature* (1956).

most satisfying anthology of the literature of any Asian country" and noted, in particular, that "thanks to UNESCO support Professor Keene has been in a position to decide what should be translated and then seek especially qualified persons to undertake it."[56] Over the course of the 1950s and 1960s, Grove published and distributed numerous translations and studies of Asian literature and culture, frequently in collaboration with UNESCO. In addition to translations by Keene and Waley, Grove published studies of Zen Buddhism, both by Japanese scholars such as Daisetz T. Suzuki and by American popularizers such as Alan Watts. Grove also became the American distributor for the London-based Wisdom of the East series, which had been founded in 1904 but received a renewed mandate in the postwar era. As its general editor, J. L. Cranmer-Byng, proclaimed, "Two great wars have done much to alter the map of the world and as a result, Asia is now assuming an important place in international affairs." Hewing close to the UNESCO mandate, Cranmer-Byng argues that this new situation requires that Westerners develop a familiarity with Asian culture, since "it is only through a sympathetic appreciation of Asia's cultural inheritance that foreigners will be able to . . . realize how great an extent their religion, philosophy, and poetry and art still mould the outlook of the peoples of Asia today."[57] In the late 1950s Grove also formed the East and West Book Club, offering a choice between *The Golden Bowl* and *The Anthology of Japanese Literature* free with a membership.

This developing East-West dialogue is abundantly evident in the pages of the *Evergreen Review*. The first issue to seriously engage Asian culture is volume 2, number 6 (Autumn 1958). Susan Nevelson's cover photo depicts a young Asian of uncertain gender dressed in black and holding a white dove. The inside cover features a full-page ad for Grove's lavish production of Ken Domon and Momoo Kitagawa's study, *The Muro-Ji: An Eighth Century Japanese Temple, Its Art and History*. And Daisetz T. Suzuki, just finishing a five-year stint as a visiting professor at Columbia University, contributes an essay analyzing the degree to which "Zen has entered internally into every phase of the cultural life of the [Japanese] people."[58] As an illustration, Suzuki offers the "one-corner" style of Japanese painting, characterized by "the least possible number of lines or strokes which go to represent forms."[59] Suzuki sees this style as an instance of the attitude "known as *wabi* in the dictionary of Japanese cultural terms"; and he explains, "*Wabi* really means 'poverty,' or, negatively, 'not to be in the fashionable society of the time.'"[60]

Suzuki's essay is followed by "Franz Kline Talking," a transcript of the abstract expressionist painter's conversation with Frank O'Hara, whose poem "In Memory of My Feelings" is also featured in this issue. O'Hara's introductory statement triumphantly announces, "The Europeanization of our sensibilities has at last been exorcized as if by magic . . . which allows us as a nation to exist internationally."[61] Kline discusses his "calligraphic style" in an international context, touching on a variety of painters he admires, including Hokusai, whose painting of Mount Fuji reveals how "his mind has been brought to the utter simplification of it."[62] Kline's monologue is followed by three reproductions of his calligraphic paintings, stark and simple black brushstrokes that clearly complement Suzuki's discussion of Zen aesthetics.

Gary Snyder's translation of the "Cold Mountain Poems" follows Kline's paintings. Though the poet Han-shan (Cold Mountain) was Chinese, Snyder introduces him as "a robe-tattered wind-swept long-haired laughing man holding a scroll" in a sketch featured in a Japanese art exhibit that came to the United States in 1953.[63] Snyder concludes, "He and his sidekick Shih-te (Jittoku in Japanese) became great favorites with Zen painters of later days—the scroll, the broom, the wild hair and laughter. They became immortals and you sometimes run into them today in the skidrows, orchards, hobo jungles, and logging camps of America."[64] Jack Kerouac dedicated *The Dharma Bums*, prominently advertised in this issue of the *Evergreen Review*, to Han-shan. As Kerouac and Snyder's presence here indicates, Grove's vision of an East-West dialogue was heavily inflected by the international interests and itineraries of the Beats.

In 1965, Rosset found a modern Japanese author who realized this Beat vision of world literature: Kenzaburo Oe, who had written a dissertation on John-Paul Sartre and whose favorite book was *Huckleberry Finn*. Oe was fluent in English, a passionate spokesman for the Japanese New Left, and an avid fan of Henry Miller; his international interests jibed perfectly with Rosset's. The two had become good friends by the time Oe visited the United States in 1968 to attend a Harvard summer seminar on *Huckleberry Finn* and *Invisible Man* and to promote *A Personal Matter*, which Grove had just published. In its "Authors and Editors" column, *Publishers Weekly* heralded Oe as "Japan's first 'modern' novelist, one whose literary ancestry is wholly Western."[65] In the flyleaf to *A Personal Matter*, Grove affirmed Oe as "the first truly modern Japanese writer," one who had single-handedly "wrenched Japanese literature free of its deeply rooted, inbred tradition and moved it into the mainstream of world literature."

The semiautobiographical plot of *A Personal Matter* illustrates the degree to which this vision of world literature was rooted in the geopolitics of the American century. Its hero, Bird, is a disaffected graduate student in English who longs to travel to Africa, but he has recently married and his new wife's pregnancy promises to put an end to his plans. The novel opens with Bird contemplating a map of Africa in a world atlas:

> Africa was in the process of dizzying change that would quickly outdate any map. And since the corrosion that began with Africa would eat away the entire volume, opening the book to the Africa page amounted to advertising the obsoleteness of the rest. What you needed was a map that could never be outdated because political configurations were settled. Would you choose America, then? North America, that is?[66]

With the noticeable absence of Europe, which was also undergoing somewhat dizzying geographic alteration, Bird's geopolitical musings conveniently lay out the postwar coordinates onto which Grove would map its vision of world literature: a formerly colonized African continent rapidly resolving into a turbulent mosaic of new nations; an American hemisphere renegotiating the scale and scope of the term "America"; and an "East" whose meaning to the "West" is being reconfigured by the US victory in the Pacific theater of World War II.

On Grove's publicity questionnaire for authors, in answer to the question, "What is the shortest statement you can make that aptly expresses [your book's] scope and theme?," Oe wrote: "The effort of a post-war youth of Japan for the genuine authenticity."[67] In his adolescent wanderlust, Bird bears some resemblance to Sal Paradise, but he diverges considerably in his successful discovery of the "authenticity" that Kerouac's avatars never fully achieve. After spending the entirety of the narrative in contemplation of abandoning his wife and disabled child to run off to Africa with his old girlfriend, Bird in the end decides to stay in Japan as "a guide for foreign tourists."[68] Instead of introducing himself to the world, he will introduce the world to Japan. In a draft of an essay entitled "How I Am a Japanese Writer," Oe insists, "If we want to find the authenticity of modern, Japanese literature, we must seek for it in the history of encounters with the occidental world, and especially we must seek for it in the history of encounters in which we Japanese played an active, not a passive, part."[69] Oe's novel, both in its plot and in its publication, can be understood as the implicit object of such a search. Oe was later awarded the Nobel Prize in Literature in 1994, one of five Grove Press authors to win this imprimatur of global literary reputation.

Africa

In the same year that Grove entered into negotiations with Keene over the anthology of Japanese literature, Rosset agreed to be Amos Tutuola's literary agent in the United States. In the late 1950s Grove published the three texts for which he remains most well known—*The Palm-Wine Drinkard, My Life in the Bush of Ghosts*, and *The Brave African Huntress*—while also exerting considerable effort to get his stories into American magazines. The books met with only modest success, and with the exception of a noteworthy inclusion in an Africa-themed issue of the *Atlantic Monthly* and a single story in the *Chicago Review*, American editors rejected Tutuola's apparently formless surrealistic stories. Rosset himself wrote to Tutuola in 1953, complaining, "Sometimes I think that the endings of your stories are rather weak. They might be more definite. We should know that the story has a beginning, middle and end. Also they (your stories) are sometimes too complicated. You start one story and then bring in another story, and the [reader] gets confused about what happened to the first story."[70]

Tutuola was initially understood in the United States as a sort of modernist manqué. As Selden Rodman affirms in his review of *The Palm-Wine Drinkard*, "If you like Anna Livia Plurabelle, Alice in Wonderland, and the poems of Dylan Thomas, the chances are you will like this novel, though probably not for reasons having anything to do with the author's intentions." Rodman adds that "Tutuola is not a revolutionist of the word, not a mathematician, not a surrealist. He is a true primitive."[71] This vision of Tutuola as unconscious modernist was reinforced by Kuhlman's covers for the Evergreen Original versions of his novels. The cover for *My Life in the Bush of Ghosts* echoes Kuhlman's designs for Beckett's trilogy, assimilating Tutuola's apparent primitivism to a modernist aesthetic (Figure 9). However, there are figural associations in Kuhlman's design that anticipate the more nuanced interpretations of Tutuola's work; the cover clearly references a television screen, commenting on the "Television-Handed Ghostess" who briefly figures in the text.

A more knowledgeable explanation of Tutuola's syncretism would have to await Grove's publication of the English translation of Janheinz Jahn's important study, *Muntu: The New African Culture* (1961). Jahn, coeditor of *Black Orpheus* and one of the most influential European scholars of African culture in the postwar era, opens his study with the portentous announcement that "Africa is entering world history."[72] For Jahn, this entry mandates a new approach to the

Figure 9. Roy Kuhlman's cover for the Evergreen edition of
My Life in the Bush of Ghosts (1954).

study of African literature. Deprecating earlier efforts to understand African writers in exclusively European terms, Jahn establishes that "the forced classification of neo-African authors into European literary groups . . . has done more harm than good to the understanding of their poetry." Jahn further affirms that, since African culture has "spread over several European languages," it is no longer logical to categorize literatures by national language. Once he analytically divorces nation from language, Jahn is able to claim, "Within African literature Tutuola is intelligible; within English literature he is an oddity."[73]

In his introduction, Jahn quotes extensively from Frantz Fanon, another important author whom Grove published only a few years later. When Grove published *Muntu*, Fanon's *Peau noire, masques blancs* had not yet been translated into English, but its prominent appearance here reveals the political volatility that roiled the calls for cultural exchange that motivated studies like Jahn's. Jahn cites Fanon's text to establish that "there is no universal standard for the evaluation of cultures" and to legitimate his study as an attempt to define and evaluate "neo-African" culture on its own terms.[74] By the time Grove published the English translation of *Neo-African Literature: A History of Black Writing* in 1968, Jahn was explicitly framing this cultural relativism geopolitically:

> The end of colonialism does not mean merely redrawing the political maps of Asia and Africa. The independence of the countries outside Europe which were formerly colonies is far from being only a political phenomenon; it tends to find expression in all spheres of life, especially the cultural sphere. If a true partnership is to be reached, the values hitherto centred on Europe need to be reappraised. For each member of a partnership should try to understand every other member on the basis of the fellow-partner's values—instead of taking his own standards as universally applicable.[75]

On the one hand, Jahn's insistence that Europe reappraise its values resonates with the widely shared sense that two world wars had fatally compromised its claims to ethical and political authority and that the literature of postwar Europe, as centrally illustrated by Beckett, affirmed this decline. On the other hand, Jahn's cultural relativism resonates with the UNESCO mandate, insisting on cultural exchange as a precondition to successful diplomatic relations. By this time, however, UNESCO's vision was widely seen as hopelessly utopian, and Fanon's program of regenerative violence had displaced Jahn's vision of cultural exchange.

America

In 1961, the year that Grove published *Muntu*, it also published Octavio Paz's now-classic study *Labyrinth of Solitude*, which famously announces, "For the first time, we are contemporaries of all mankind."[76] Paz's pronouncement echoes Jahn's claim about Africa entering world history, and he affirms that "Mexico's situation is no different from that of the majority of countries in Latin America, Asia, and Africa."[77] This perception of simultaneity was crucial to the very possibility of a truly international modernism; insofar as the conceptual coherence of an avant-garde depends upon a linear model of history, an international avant-garde requires that its constituent nations coexist at the same point on the same time line. This sense of global simultaneity began to emerge during the era of decolonization.

Written mostly in Paris, where Paz worked in the Mexican embassy after the war, and addressed partly to readers in the United States, where he had lived for a time during the war, *Labyrinth of Solitude* illustrates the coincidence of historical simultaneity and cultural difference that informed Grove's vision of world literature. In early 1961, Paz wrote to Rosset that US readers might be ready to reach a better understanding of his country as well as the larger geopolitical system within which their relations were transforming:

> I really do think this is the most opportune time for publication . . . I have the impression that, since the recent developments in Africa and specially in Cuba, the American people has started to be more conscious of what is called, in the burocratic jargon of our times, "underdevelopped" countries. My book is, in some ways, a portrait of one of those countries, an inquiry made by a native writer (underdeveloped or superdevelopped?).[78]

Paz was already acquainted with the United States from his tenure as a Guggenheim Fellow at UC Berkeley during the war, and he returned in 1961 at the invitation of the Institute of Contemporary Arts cultural exchange program funded by the Ford Foundation. Paz concedes in his opening chapter, "The *Pachuco* and Other Extremes," that many of the arguments he develops in *Labyrinth of Solitude* originally occurred to him during his stay in the States. Such a cultural context provides an important hemispheric sidelight on Paz's conclusion that, in the postwar era, "the old plurality of cultures . . . has been replaced by a single civilization and a single future" and that "world history has become everyone's task, and our own labyrinth is the labyrinth of all mankind."[79]

In his preface to the *Borzoi Anthology of Latin American Literature*, editor Emir Rodríguez Monegal cites Paz's claim to contemporaneity and dates the boom in Latin American literature to 1961. He chooses this year not because of the US publication of *Labyrinth of Solitude* but because of another event that also involved Grove Press: the co-awarding of the newly established International Publisher's Prize to Jorge Luis Borges and Samuel Beckett. As José David Saldívar affirms in *The Dialectics of Our America*, this simultaneous recognition gave "our American literature . . . its rightful place."[80]

It is worth dwelling briefly on the significance of this now defunct prize, which is oddly absent from James English's otherwise excellent study, *The Economy of Prestige*. Established by six publishers, Weidenfeld and Nicolson (United Kingdom), Gallimard (France), Einaudi (Italy), Seix Barral (Spain), Rowohlt (Germany), and Grove (United States), the prize was to be given to "an author of any nationality whose existing body of work will, in the view of the jury, be of lasting influence on the development of various national literatures."[81] The publishers themselves established committees that both chose submissions and constituted the jury. The winners were then rewarded with translations into the native languages of the publishers, which by the next year had expanded to eleven. According to Grove's press release, "The aim of the prize ... is to provide the largest possible international audience for the winning author."[82] In other words, to win the prize was to be immediately catapulted into the realm of world literature. In his letter inviting Alfred Kazin to be on the selection committee, Rosset ambitiously affirms that the prize is "similar to something like the Nobel Prize, excepting that we hope it will benefit a writer still in his most creative years and bring world attention to someone who is perhaps not known outside his own country."[83]

Grove's committee included Kazin, Donald Allen, William Barrett, Jason Epstein, and Mark Schorer. Although the committee was free to choose any published writer, the top three nominees were Samuel Beckett, Henry Miller, and Jean Genet, all Grove Press authors. According to Rosset's recollection, the initial voting was split between English- and non-English-speaking committees, which meant that Beckett also had the support of the Weidenfeld committee, which included Angus Wilson and Iris Murdoch. Borges was endorsed by the Einaudi committee, which included Carlo Levi, Alberto Moravia, Pier Paolo Pasolini, and Italo Calvino; the Seix Barral committee, which consisted almost entirely of Catalan dissidents, including José Castellet, Juan Petit, and Antonio Vilanova, plus Octavio Paz; and the Gallimard committee, which included Michel Butor, Roger Caillois, Raymond Queneau, Jean Paulhan, and Dominique Aury. As Seaver affirms in his memoirs, "There was a clear division between north and south, the Germanic languages on the one hand and the Romance on the other."[84] Awarding the prize to both Borges and Beckett was a compromise, certainly deserving of the historical significance it's been granted by historians of the Latin American boom. Insofar as both authors had already been consecrated in Paris, their co-award can be seen as marking that city's persistence as a cultural capital in a postwar literary landscape increasingly dominated by Anglophone and Hispanophone publishing industries.

Borges himself famously commented, "As a consequence of that prize, my books mushroomed overnight throughout the world."[85] Borges's work in the postwar era was likewise understood in international terms. As Anthony Kerrigan affirms in his translator's introduction to the Grove Press edition of *Ficciones* (1962), the "work of Jorge Luis Borges is a species of international literary metaphor."[86] For Kerrigan, Borges's encyclopedic knowledge transfers "inherited meanings from Spanish and English, French and German, and sums up a series of analogies, of confrontations, or appositions in other nations' literatures."[87] Borges's work, in other words, structurally transcends the national literary traditions based in individual European languages. Borges himself, in an essay included in the New Directions anthology of his work, *Labyrinths*, which was issued in the same year as *Ficciones*, deprecated "the idea that a literature must define itself in terms of its national traits" and instead announced that Argentines, like Jews, "can handle all European themes, handle them without superstition, with an irreverence which can have, and already does have, fortunate consequences."[88] But he also recognized the belatedness of this appropriation in its relation to the cosmopolitan modernism on which it piggybacks. In his own prologue to the first section of *Ficciones*, he satirically laments: "The composition of vast books is a laborious and impoverishing extravagance. To go on for five hundred pages developing an idea whose perfect oral exposition is possible in a few minutes! A better course of procedure is to pretend that these books already exist, and then to offer a résumé, a commentary."[89] Borges's proto-postmodern aesthetic self-consciously subordinates itself to high modernism. Instead of writing a new magnum opus, Borges describes imaginary ones that play on the extravagant claims made for those that do exist. In this sense, *Ficciones* can be further imagined as a series of prefaces—Jason Wilson calls them "essay-cum-short-story-cum-book reviews"—not only to the imaginary texts that they comment upon but to the wave of literary experimentation that they will inspire.[90] Furthermore, as librarian and bibliophile, Borges marks an era when world literature can still be understood in terms of the circulation of printed texts.

Borges foregrounds what one might call the paratextual politics of world literature; his short descriptions of much longer works both illustrate and parody the degree to which translated literature tends to mandate prefatory protocols, particularly when geared toward an academic audience. Ben Belitt, who translated the work of Federico García Lorca and Pablo Neruda for Grove, acknowledged as much when he collected his translator's prefaces into a book entitled *Adam's Dream: A Preface to Translation*, published by Grove in 1978. Donald Allen had solicited Belitt as a possible translator for Lorca's *Poet in New York* in 1952, and Belitt responded favorably, noting "the impressive record that your imprint has created for itself in its initial publishing commitments. It seems to me your combination of fastidious choice and public usefulness is already a unique one."[91] In the transcribed "conversation" with Edwin Honig that makes up the opening chapter of *Adam's Dream*, Belitt credits Allen with the "uncanny facility of sensing what are generally called 'vogues' or waves in the making, and later turn out to be total landslides of taste."[92] Belitt backdates the beginnings of the Latin American boom to his bilingual edition of Lorca's modern poetic sequence of surrealist impressions written during the poet's brief visit to the East Coast during the Depression. In his translator's foreword, reprinted in *Adam's Dream*, Belitt affirms that "it was to American readers in the broadest sense of the term . . . that the poem was initially addressed by its publishers in Mexico, Argentina, and New York . . . Today, *A Poet in New York* remains an indispensable book for readers of the two Americas."[93] The positioning of this text by a Spanish poet in the hemispheric context of the "two Americas" was reinforced by the frequent critical references to the influence of Walt Whitman, to whom Lorca dedicates an ode late in the sequence, and to the possible influence on Allen Ginsberg, whose "Howl" it arguably anticipates. The initial printing of *A Poet in New York* sold more than thirty-five thousand copies.

Belitt's major achievement for Grove during these years was a sequence of anthologies of the poetry of Pablo Neruda, who was awarded the Nobel Prize in Literature in 1971 and whom Rodríguez Monegal introduces as "the greatest Latin American poet since Rubén Darío."[94] Neruda's itinerant career and international reputation undoubtedly helped realign the meanings of "America" in the postwar era. As with Lorca, this realignment ran through Whitman, to whose work Neruda's was frequently compared. In his translator's foreword to *Selected Poems*, the first of four Neruda collections he assembled for Grove, Belitt affirms that Neruda's vision is "like Whitman's" and further elaborates that the poet's ambitious *Canto general* (*General Song*) is, "like *Moby Dick* and *Leaves of Grass*—whose cadences should convey it to American ears—a *progress*: a total book which enacts a total sensibility."[95] In the introduction to his collection of critical prefaces, Belitt clarifies how this hemispheric sensibility trumps and transcends the discourse of "three worlds" that dominated the 1960s, offering instead a cosmopolitan vision of "the literature of one world and a single community of tradition, rather than a symptomatic 'third' of it."[96] Grove organized a big party at its downtown offices for Neruda, an early hero of Rosset's, when he came to New York to attend the International Progressive Education Network (PEN) conference in 1966, the year in which he also received a citation as an Honorary Fellow of the Modern Language Association. At a well-attended reading at the Young Men's Hebrew Association's (YMHA) Poetry Center, his first in the United States, Archibald MacLeish emphatically introduced Neruda as "an *American* poet," while Selden Rodman titled his review of the reading for the *New York Times* "All American."[97]

Neruda's international significance was enhanced by his global itinerary. During his years as a Chilean diplomat, Neruda lived first in Rangoon, Java, Ceylon, and Singapore, after which followed posts in Buenos Aires, Barcelona, Madrid, and Mexico City. After the war, he was briefly a Communist Party senator in Chile, but when the party was outlawed in 1948, he went into exile. He spent the next four years traveling across Europe, Asia, and the Soviet Union, returning to Chile in 1952, where he remained until his death in 1973. By the time Neruda's poetry became popular in the United States, he was already a figure of considerable international stature and experience. The titles of his two major poetic sequences—*Residence on Earth* and *General Song*—reflect the global scope of his life and reinforce the correlation between political and poetic diplomacy that coincided closely with the international vision of Grove Press.

Grove's decision to publish bilingual editions of Spanish-language poetry translated by North American poets (it also issued a bilingual edition of the Peruvian poet Cesar Vallejo's *Poemas humanos*, translated by Clayton Eshleman) projected in material and textual form some of the complexities of a hemispheric literary field divided by both language and geopolitics. Belitt asserts that, in bilingual translations, "the binder's seam is there to remind us that the translation of poetry is not a systematic plagiarism of the original, under cover of a second language: it is an act of imagination forced upon one by the impossibility of the literal transference or coincidence of two languages, two minds, and two identities, and by the autonomy of the poetic process."[98] For Belitt, this autonomy should be granted to both the original and the translation. Thus, he wrote to Rosset, regarding his translations of Lorca, "I would like to make it clear that the English text is a creative undertaking whose authorship is attributable to me in the same sense that 'my own' poems are attributable to me."[99] The "binder's seam," then, becomes a highly complex site of mediations and separations. It both marks and bridges the division between languages, affirming the impossibility of literal translation while simultaneously enabling the autonomy of literary translation. It also, significantly, allows Belitt to lay claim to the English translations without occluding the integrity of the Spanish originals.

This tension between autonomy and appropriation is abundantly evident in the special issue of the *Evergreen Review* published in the winter of 1959, "The Eye of Mexico." Donald Allen had originally arranged with Paz to be guest editor, but after he had selected the contributors, Paz became too busy and recommended Ramón Xirau of the Centro mexicano de escritores to take over. Xirau was in fact from Barcelona but had migrated to Mexico after the Spanish Civil War. He had studied in Paris and lectured in the United States under the auspices of the Rockefeller Foundation, which had also provided the initial funding for the Centro, originally established by the American novelist Margaret Shedd. Xirau became subdirector and editor of its bimonthly English-language bulletin. In addition to issuing the newsletter, the Centro provided fellowships to Mexican and US writers, as well as labor and subvention for translations between Spanish- and English-language literature.

"The Eye of Mexico" opens with an excerpt from *Labyrinth of Solitude* and includes prose by Juan Rulfo and Carlos Fuentes, poetry by Jaime Sabines and Manuel Durán, paintings by José Luis Cuevas and Juan Soriano, and an essay by anthropologist Miguel León-Portilla, "A Náhuatl Concept of Art." The poetry is translated by Paul Blackburn, Lysander Kemp, Denise Levertov, and William Carlos Williams, who, like Belitt, were "more concerned with re-creation in English than with completely literal translation."[100] The Spanish originals are not included. The issue also provides a directory of Mexican bookstores and art galleries, ads for Mexican restaurants in Manhattan, and a back-cover ad for Aeronaves de México. Grove arranged for a front-window display in the Aeronaves offices, located at the heavily trafficked corner of 5th Avenue and 42nd Street, featuring artwork by Cuevas and Soriano and a blow-up of the journal's cover. Aeronaves agreed to fly a small group of Mexican authors and artists to New York for a cocktail party in their offices celebrating the issue, and Grove offered issues in quantity at cost for the airline to distribute on its flights. According to *Publishers Weekly*, Grove sold out its initial printing of twenty thousand in less than a month.

The contents of the "Eye of Mexico" issue are framed by articles and reviews that place it in a more complicated global frame. It opens with "The Continuing Position of India," a long piece by Anand (Arthur) Lall, India's ambassador to the United Nations. Lall was one of the judges in Grove's Indian literature contest and had become friendly with Rosset, who agreed to insert this piece into the Mexican issue at the last minute. This "special statement on India's foreign policy" defending Nehru's position of nonalignment begins before and ends after the contents of the special issue, inevitably reminding readers of the larger Cold War context within which this hemispheric dialogue is taking place. More specifically, it emphasizes the degree to which Cold War–era cultural exchange would be facilitated by diplomatic figures such as Lall and Paz, who was Mexico's ambassador to India from 1962 to 1968. Paz then resigned from the diplomatic service in opposition to Mexico's suppression of the student protests in Tlatelolco, which he wrote about in *The Other Mexico*, also published by Grove. By then, the rhetoric of cultural exchange that Grove promoted in the late 1950s and early 1960s had been supplanted by a rhetoric, and practice, of political revolution.

The special-issue contents of "The Eye of Mexico" are followed by a section of news and reviews. One of the texts reviewed is Paz's *Anthology of Mexican Poetry*, which, as reviewer James Schuyler notes, was "published by agreement between Unesco and the Government of Mexico."[101] This volume, initially issued by Indiana University Press and then reprinted by Grove in 1985, features a preface by C. M. Bowra that, the flyleaf affirms, is intended "to emphasize the essential solidarity of creative artists in different nations, language, centuries, and latitudes, and to point out the fundamental identity of emotions to which the genius of the poet can give a form at once lasting and beautiful." But Schuyler is less interested in Bowra's "official bull" or Paz's "informing" introduction than he is in the task of the translator, Samuel Beckett, whose labors he lauds as "a Horowitz performance of gift and skill."[102]

Beckett haunts "The Eye of Mexico," as Schuyler's brief appraisal of what S. E. Gontarski calls "the single most neglected work in the Beckett canon" is followed by Richard Howard's translation of Maurice Blanchot's landmark review of Beckett's trilogy, "Where Now? Who Now?"[103] In this somewhat unexpected New World context, Blanchot's review creates a felicitous apposition between Beckett's masterwork and the final lines of Paz's excerpted chapter: "The Mexican does not transcend his solitude. On the contrary, he locks himself up in it. We live in our solitude like Philoctetes on his island, fearing rather than hoping to return to the world. We cannot bear the presence of our companions. We hide within ourselves . . . and the solitude in which we suffer has no reference either to a redeemer or a creator."[104] Beckett's narrator can figure both as a reduction of Paz's solitude to its purest generic state—and indeed, Beckett's trilogy was frequently framed in precisely these "universal" terms—but also as a specification of the writer's predicament in the twilight of modernism.

If, in the postwar European context, this predicament solicited the strained silences and solitudes of Beckett's austere universe, in the New World context late modernist exhaustion blossomed by a sort of dazzling dialectical reversal into an explosion of aesthetic opportunities, abundantly illustrated by Donald Allen's landmark anthology *The New American Poetry*, issued by Grove in 1960. I conclude with this foray into a more conventionally organized anthology in order to point out the degree to which the project of postwar American literature was implicated in and inflected by the global literary field illustrated by Grove's international title list. Most of the poets included in the volume, which was the first to lay out for a popular readership the now canonical—and significantly geographical—designations of the Black Mountain College, the San Francisco Renaissance, and the New York school, appeared as well in the pages of the *Evergreen Review*, frequently as both translators and poets. While the exclusive US origins of the poets included in the volume itself seem almost blithely to disregard the hemispheric model endorsed by Grove's simultaneous investment in Spanish-language literature, the international scope of Allen's

Figure 10. Roy Kuhlman's cover for *The Art of Jazz* (1959).

projects for Grove during these years dictates that we grant some dialectical nuance to its contents.

Allen calls the poets in his anthology "our avant-garde, the true continuers of the modern movement in American poetry" and further claims that "through their work many are closely allied to modern jazz and abstract expressionist painting, today recognized throughout the world to be America's greatest achievement in contemporary culture."[105] In this same period Grove published a number of pioneering studies of American jazz, including translations of André Hodeir's foundational *Jazz: Its Evolution and Essence* (1956) and *Toward Jazz* (1962), as well as important anthologies edited by Nat Hentoff, Albert McCarthy, and Martin Williams, who also wrote a regular column on jazz for the *Evergreen Review*. These titles, all heavily promoted in quality-paperback format, feature some of Kuhlman's most characteristically abstract expressionist covers (Figure 10), evoking his designs for both Beckett and Tutuola. Allen's goal for his anthology was to make "the same claim for the new American poetry, now becoming the dominant movement in the second phase of our twentieth-century literature and already exerting a strong influence abroad."[106] Allen places his anthology within the late modernist matrix, offering his cross section of postwar poets as an American contribution to an international scene. And it was a huge success; as Rosset affirms in an unpublished interview, "That book became the standard, the landmark book, and it sold and sold. It taught poetry to a whole generation of young kids."[107]

Publishing Off Broadway

The early performances of Samuel Beckett's *Waiting for Godot* are landmarks in the history of modern theater. Roger Blin's succès de scandale at the Théatre Babylone in Paris on January 5, 1953; Alan Schneider's debacle at the Coconut Grove Playhouse in Miami on January 3, 1956 (billed as "the laugh sensation of two continents," and starring Tom Ewell and Bert Lahr, the play confounded the audience, who came expecting a light comedy); Herbert Blau's triumph at San Quentin on April 19, 1957: all have become legendary events that anchor any study of Beckett's dramatic work.[1] Much less has been written about an equally significant event in the history of this epoch-defining play: Grove Press's publication of a one-dollar Evergreen paperback edition in 1956. Spurred by the play's Broadway debut, when it was sold in the lobby of the John Golden Theater, it eventually sold more than two million copies, becoming an iconic American paperback and one of the bestselling plays of all time.

W. B. Worthen, one of the few critics who has considered the significance of plays as printed texts, affirms that "Beckett's plays are an essential part of the modern drama's seizure of the page," particularly because Beckett's authority over permissions to perform them was exercised with such high modernist imperiousness and exactitude.[2] The authority of the printed play in Beckett's case anchors the authority of the auteur as source and adjudicator of the conditions and conventions under which the play can be performed. As a profoundly literary figure, in many ways the last modernist genius, Beckett has been a crucial model for the authority of the modern playwright as *writer*, as producer of the printed text that determines the parameters of performance.

Nevertheless, as Worthen concedes, "Theatre is particularly inimical to print, as print culture tends to derogate both manuscript and oral forms of transmission as lapses from the ideal, transparent, neutrality of mechanical reproduction."[3] This resistance to print was particularly true of the so-called theater of the absurd, whose postwar ascendance dates to the debut of *Godot,* influenced as it was by the antiliterary theories of Antonin Artaud. Artaud, whose international influence and reputation expanded considerably with the publication of Grove's English translation of *The Theater and Its Double* in 1958, famously decried "the idolatry of fixed masterpieces which is one of the aspects of bourgeois conformism," proclaiming that "it is in the light of magic and sorcery that the *mise en scène* must be considered, not as the reflection of the written text."[4] Artaud was also instrumental in replacing the authority of the playwright with that of the director, whom he saw becoming "a kind of manager of magic, a master of sacred ceremonies."[5]

As James Harding affirms in the introduction to his important anthology *Contours of the Avant-Garde,* "The theatrical avant-garde has consistently defined itself vis-à-vis a negation not only of the text and mimesis but also of author-ship and author-ity and of . . . academic institutions" more generally.[6] Artaud, unsurprisingly, is a recurrent and representative figure in Harding's collection, which emerged as a response to Bonnie Marranca's critique of the text-centered curriculum in academic theater studies, "Theatre at the University at the End of the Twentieth Century," published in *Performing Arts Journal* in 1995. The essays in Harding's anthology illustrate the degree to which debates over avant-garde theater tend to adopt Artaud's opposition between print and performance, an opposition that, in turn, maps onto the tension between playwright and director. In this chapter, I focus instead on the relationship between publisher and reader, a relationship that presents the printed text in complementary, rather than antagonistic, relation to live performance. As a publisher, Grove worked to market printed plays as supplements to performance for those who could attend one, and as substitutes for performance for those who couldn't. Its texts were designed, as much as possible, to invoke the experience of seeing the play live, frequently in direct reference to specific performances. Its success in this endeavor was crucial to the reception and interpretation of avant-garde drama in the postwar United States.

Grove's achievement as a publisher of experimental drama complicates Julie Stone Peters's groundbreaking history of the relations between print and performance in European theater prior to the twentieth century, which concludes with a brief discussion of *Krapp's Last Tape.* Peters argues that in the twentieth century, attention shifted from "the difference between the presence of live spectators and the remoteness and privacy of the reader in the study" to "the theatre's place, on the one hand, in the industry of mass spectatorship and, on the other, in a culture in which one's most intimate relationship might be, in the end, with a machine."[7] But Grove's marketing and design of avant-garde scripts reveal that the dialectic between public performance and private reading extended well into the twentieth century. Postwar experimental theater positioned itself in stark opposition to the culture industries and, Beckett's experiments with radio and tape recording notwithstanding, remained philosophically and politically committed to liveness, especially in the happenings and street theater of the 1960s., Furthermore, the conceptual difficulties of much avant-garde theater were commonly elucidated by American academics in terms of modernist literary technique, mandating that such plays be read as a necessary supplement to seeing them live, and the popularity of experimental theater on college campuses created a large audience for these scripts. As the exclusive publisher of Beckett, Eugène Ionesco, Harold Pinter, Kobo Abe, John Arden, Fernando Arrabal, Brendan Behan, Ugo Betti, Friedrich Durrenmatt, Jean Genet, David Mamet, Slawomir Mrozek, Joe Orton, Sam Shepard, Boris Vian, and many others, Grove cornered this market, in the process acquiring an identity as the "off Broadway of publishing houses."

Grove's connections to off-Broadway theater were enhanced by its downtown location, close to the Cherry Lane, Village Gate, St. Mark's Playhouse, and Living Theatre. In 1967, Grove also began producing off-Broadway playbills after Showcard, the company that usually designed them, refused to print one for *MacBird!*, Barbara Garson's Shakespearean parody of the Johnson and Kennedy administrations. In that same year, Rosset acquired a theater at 53 East 11th Street. Although it eventually became mainly a venue for screening experimental film, the Evergreen Theater made history with the triumphant New York debut of Michael McClure's *The Beard*, which had been shut down for obscenity in San Francisco. Finally, starting in 1968, the *Evergreen Review* began regularly publishing essays and theater reviews by John Lahr, whose father, Bert Lahr, had famously played Estragon in the American debut of *Waiting for Godot* and who was already an influential new voice in modern theater criticism. *Up against the Fourth Wall: Essays on Modern Theater*, a collection of the groundbreaking work he wrote for the magazine, was printed as an Evergreen Original in 1970.

The Evergreen Originals imprint was foundational for Grove's identity as a publisher of avant-garde drama, and its printed plays had a far more lasting impact than its direct forays into the downtown theater scene. Though it was initially developed as a format for original fiction, Grove quickly adapted it to include original drama as well, as the May 8, 1960, ad in the *New York Times Book Review*, "Off Broadway's Most Sensational Hits—in Book Form," makes abundantly clear. The titles listed include Jack Gelber's *The Connection*, Beckett's *Krapp's Last Tape*, Genet's *The Balcony*, and Ionesco's *Four Plays*. In the ad, Grove calls these "the plays that are making theater history" and encourages readers to "discover their meaning as well as their excitement by reading them for yourself, in EVERGREEN ORIGINAL PAPERBACKS." Grove adapted this imprint to present avant-garde theater as a specifically literary, and resolutely international, genre that needed to be read in order to be fully understood.

Grove was assisted in this task by a stable of academic critics who, while maintaining an investment in performance, emphasized the "literary" qualities of contemporary drama. Wallace Fowlie, the Harvard-educated professor of French who taught at Bennington, Chicago, Yale, and the New School before spending most of his career at Duke University, encouraged Rosset to publish Beckett in the early 1950s; in his influential study of postwar French drama, *Dionysus in Paris*, Fowlie heralded the arrival in France of a "new type of supremely literary playwright."[8] Martin Esslin, the English theater critic whose work as a producer for the BBC in the 1960s was centrally responsible for popularizing experimental drama (and who eventually settled at Stanford University), emphasized in his classic study *The Theatre of the Absurd* that the plays in this "school," whose name he coined, are "analogous to a Symbolist or Imagist poem."[9]

Academics such as Fowlie, Esslin, Richard Coe, Ruby Cohn, Eric Bentley, and Roger Shattuck, all of whom worked with Grove over the course of the 1950s and 1960s, helped chart this genealogy from the modernist literature of the first half of the twentieth century to the experimental theater of the second half, thereby establishing the literary antecedents of the theater of the absurd for the English-speaking world. Coe wrote monographs on Beckett, Ionesco, and Genet, all of which Grove published in the 1960s; Cohn wrote one of the earliest dissertations on Beckett in 1959 and edited Grove's *Casebook on "Waiting for Godot"* in 1967. Bentley was responsible for the American reception of Bertolt Brecht and became the general editor of the Grove Press edition of his plays, issued over the course of the 1960s. Shattuck's *The Banquet Years: The Origins of the Avant-Garde in France, 1885 to World War I*, originally published in 1955, became a standard reference on the origins of the French avant-garde; he was guest editor of an early issue of the *Evergreen Review* on 'pataphysics in 1960 as well as coeditor of Grove's *Selected Works of Alfred Jarry* in 1965.

In their biographically oriented studies, these critics frequently emphasized poetry as an apprenticeship to drama, positioning the early poems of these dramatists as crucial to an appreciation of their later plays. Furthermore, by establishing an analogy between experimental theater and modernist poetry, they affirmed the necessity of reading both the plays themselves and their own commentary in order to understand fully the significance of these difficult texts.

. . .

Rosset knew that Grove would have to market these plays *as* literary texts, and from the beginning he thought of *Waiting for Godot* as a book. He convinced Beckett not to publish the first act in *Merlin*, arguing that "EN ATTENDANT GODOT should burst upon us as an entity in my opinion."[10] On the same day, Rosset wrote to Alexander Trocchi, affirming that he would like to see "the play first appear in its entirety in a handsome book."[11] A few months later, Rosset described the book he envisioned to Jerome Lindon: "Our edition will include the play GODOT, plus a page or two of biographical material at the back of the book—as well as photographs of the production (assuming we can obtain them). The book's jacket will also tell about Beckett and will also contain his photograph, along with quotations from French reviews of his work." And he affirmed that "we have decided to go ahead with publication of GODOT regardless of the status of the play's production here."[12]

Initial sales of the cloth edition were, unsurprisingly, modest; according to Rosset's recollections Grove printed one thousand copies and sold about four hundred in the first year, one of which ended up in the hands of actor Bert Lahr, delivered by messenger from the offices of producer Michael Myerberg. Lahr was befuddled by the play, asking his son, the future drama critic, "You're a student— what does it mean?"[13] Lahr eventually accepted the role, and the name recognition he brought to the play helped promote the paperback Grove published in 1956, the year of the play's debut in the United States. After the famous failure in Miami, Rosset wrote to reassure Beckett: "Certainly all is not lost—the printing of the inexpensive edition forges ahead."[14] And Beckett was on board from the beginning, writing to Rosset, "By all means a paper bound edition, I am all for cheaper books."[15]

Meanwhile, in the *New York Times*, Myerberg made a public appeal for seventy thousand intellectuals to come see the play in order to avoid a repeat of the

Miami debacle. Not only did Myerberg agree to sell the cheap paperback in the lobby of the theater but he also arranged for symposiums to be held with the actors during the Broadway run. Later that year, Myerberg wrote to Beckett to report on the success of these discussions:

> Of particular interest were the four symposiums we held during the run. They were extremely well attended and displayed a keen interest in the play. A rather startling development here is that four-fifths of our audience are young—under 24, and even boys and girls 17 and 18 are storming the box office for the cheaper seats. At no time have we had cheap seats available at a performance. The youngsters had a complete and ready acceptance of the play, and quite a lot to say about its meaning, which seemed clear to them and had entered into their lives intellectually and emotionally.[16]

Grove tapped into this youthful and impecunious audience over the next two decades, in the process making *Waiting for Godot* one of its bestselling paperbacks. Grove also helped to domesticate the notion of the "absurd," which had begun as a pointedly pessimistic response on the part of European artists and intellectuals to the cataclysmic devastation of World War II but, spurred by the ubiquitous existentialism of John-Paul Sartre and the proliferating scholarship of American academics, developed in the 1960s into a more affirmative ethical orientation, with Beckett as its figurehead.

Rosset realized early on that the college-student audience would be central to *Godot*'s success, and he convinced Dramatists Play Service to reduce the royalty rate for amateur productions: "We are in close contact with the potential audiences for the play and we know that they consist in the main of university students who may well not be able to afford more than a minimum royalty . . . The whole successful history of this play is the strongest evidence of the necessity for allowing it to be played before very small groups who may also have very limited means."[17] Grove aggressively marketed the paperback edition of the play to these "very small groups," offering them on consignment to student productions and to every bookstore at any college or university where the play was being performed. And it was performed extensively across the country, as Henry Sommerville affirms: "Between 1956 and 1969, amateur performances of *Waiting for Godot* were given in every state except Arkansas and Alaska. On average, during each of these years, the play was performed by North American amateurs in thirty-three cities spread across 18 states and one Canadian province."[18]

The design of the Evergreen paperback of *Waiting for Godot* is clearly intended to match in austerity and simplicity the meager decor of its initial production in Paris, the cast and credits for which are listed following the text of the play. The cover photo, selected by Beckett himself, depicts in black and white the heavily backlit silhouettes of Vladimir and Estragon, their hands barely touching, strolling toward the spindly tree that stands to the right. The title and author's name, all lowercase, run across the top in simple white type against a black background (Figure 11). Inside the book, ample use is made of white space to further emphasize the sparse environment in which the play's characters find themselves. The title, now in all caps, is spread over the initial recto and verso pages, unevenly spaced both horizontally and vertically, as if the text itself were aimlessly wandering. On the verso page, all in lowercase italics, unjustified, are four lines—*"tragicomedy in 2 acts / by samuel beckett / grove press / new york"*—resolutely if modestly linking publisher to author and text (Figure 12). On the next recto page the names of the cast are listed, centered vertically and horizontally. Across the top of the following recto page, unevenly spaced like the title, runs the announcement of "ACT I," below which, left justified, we see the simple setting: "A country road. A tree. / Evening." In the text of the play that follows, only the verso pages are numbered sequentially in bold black type, as if it is the space across recto and verso, rather than the individual pages, that is being read through. The dialogue is left justified to the immediate right of the speech prefixes, expanding the amount of white space on the page, and foregrounding the alternation of speakers while simultaneously alienating them from their speech, which appears as an autonomous centered column (Beckett insisted on using the speakers' full names, since "their repetition, even when corresponding speech amounts to no more than a syllable, has its function in the sense that it reinforces the repetitive text").[19] The back cover features an austere photo of Beckett, the left side of his face almost entirely in shadow, accompanied by laudatory reviews of the play and a brief blurb ranking him with Kafka and Joyce.

While it anticipates the design Grove used for Beckett's other plays, *Waiting for Godot* came out before Grove launched the Evergreen Originals imprint; the first Evergreen Original Beckett play was *Endgame*. The cover photo, from Roger Blin's production, is an uncompromisingly bleak black-and-white shot of Hamm in his chair against a black background, the handkerchief over his face bleached to bright white with the bloodstains in the center vaguely coalescing

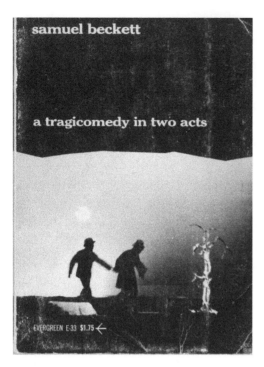

Figure 11. Roy Kuhlman's cover for the Evergreen paperback of *Waiting for Godot* (1954).

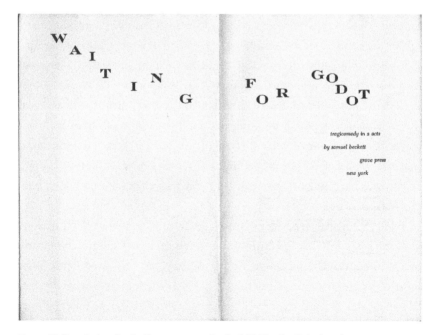

Figure 12. Frontispiece for the Evergreen paperback of *Waiting for Godot* (1954).

into an expressionless skull-like face. The text of *Endgame* is far more compressed than that of *Godot*, with the italicized stage directions considerably smaller in point size than the dialogue, which wraps around the speech prefixes. The text, then, gives a sense of the claustrophobic interior in which the action of the play unfolds.

Grove complemented these efforts to re-create typographically a sense of the play's setting and mood with a campaign to convince audiences that it was necessary to read it. Initially, Grove capitalized on the befuddlement of critics by claiming that reading the play could clarify its meaning, promoting it as "the play the critics didn't understand" and encouraging audiences to "read it before you see it," which became a tagline in the campaign for this and other plays.[20]

Grove attributed both the difficulty of the play and the necessity of reading it to the poetic quality of Beckett's dialogue. The back cover of *Endgame* features a lengthy blurb by Harold Hobson of the *Sunday Times*, emphasizing that "Mr. Beckett is a poet: and the business of the poet is not to clarify but to suggest; to employ words with auras of association, with a reaching out toward a vision, a probing down into an emotion, beyond the compass of explicit definition." When Grove distributed *Endgame* through the Readers' Subscription, the scholar Vivian Mercier used this designation of Beckett as poet in an essay included in the catalog, "How to Read Endgame." The play was sold along with a recording of its performance, and Mercer urged readers to listen to it first, because "I want you to *experience* the play before you interpret it. Listen to what the play *is* before you start asking yourself what it *means*; that is what the practiced reader always does with poetry, and Samuel Beckett remains a poet whatever he is writing."[21]

Many readers wanted help in becoming "practiced" and wrote to Grove in droves asking myriad questions about the larger significance of these plays. Beckett, of course, was notoriously reticent about the meaning of his work, so Grove responded to the queries with a boilerplate letter that suggested resources that would become central to interpreting the play. The letter began in this way: "Mr. Beckett prefers not to discuss his work. If you would like some help in understanding Mr. Beckett's work, you might refer to any number of critical works that have appeared."[22] The letter also frequently noted that "Grove Press publishes a short book on Beckett, entitled SAMUEL BECKETT, by Richard Coe, which sells for 95 cents." Grove published Coe's book in 1964, Hugh Kenner's first book on Beckett in 1961, and Ruby Cohn's *Casebook on "Waiting for Godot"* in 1967, along with a series of critical studies of Beckett, Ionesco, Genet, and others over the course of the decade.

The academic industry that rapidly grew around Beckett's work amply compensated for his silence, and Grove published many of the key critical texts that helped frame his significance for his American audience. This industry ensured that Beckett would early become a staple in college courses, not only in English but also in religious studies and philosophy departments. Grove marketed aggressively to this academic audience, going so far as to propose courses on Beckett and the theater of the absurd consisting entirely of Evergreen paperbacks. By this time, responsibility for the college catalog was in the hands of ex-union organizer and *Monthly Review* contributor Jules Geller, who explained his plans to Donald Allen in October 1967: "Rather than plan the publishing of 'textbooks'—an obscene form of book publishing as it's commonly practiced— I am working on fitting our Evergreen and some Black Cat books in groups for certain courses, and promoting them in these groups as a more modern and more interesting way to teach a given subject. This is working out very well."[23]

Cohn's *Casebook*, which Grove recommended along with Coe's monograph, Alec Reid's *All I Can Manage, More Than I Could: An Approach to the Plays of Samuel Beckett* (1969), and Michael Robinson's *The Long Sonata of the Dead: A Study of Samuel Beckett* (1969) for a course entitled "The Vision of Samuel Beckett," conveniently illustrates the process whereby the initial performance contexts of the play and its controversial reception were assimilated into the readerly practice of academic interpretation. Cohn's introduction begins by affirming that "*Waiting for Godot* has been performed in little theaters and large theaters, by amateurs and professionals, on radio and television," but she quickly shifts to the claim that "*Waiting for Godot* has sold nearly 50,000 copies in the original French, and nearly 350,000 in Beckett's own English translation." She warns that these numbers "help you to know the best-seller, the smash hit, but only the individual can know a classic which is a work that provides continuous growth for the individual," grounding the value of the play in a resolutely literary and readerly register. She concludes her opening paragraph: "Paradoxically for our time, *Waiting for Godot* is a classic that sells well," implicitly recognizing the Evergreen paperback as the embodiment of the play's success.[24] The structure of the anthology then replicates this trajectory, starting with the section "Impact," which excerpts reviews and accounts of early performances, and concluding with "Interpretation," which excerpts the type of academic analysis, much of it published by Grove Press, that crucially depends on the printed text. The course itself places Beckett in the company of Proust, Joyce, Kafka, and Sartre; in addition to *Waiting for Godot, Endgame*, and the trilogy, it includes Beckett's early study of Proust, which had already become a common resource for academic interpretation of Beckett's work. Grove's course proposal, then, attests to its crucial role in enabling the initial development of the academic industry that quickly emerged around Beckett's work and to the way this industry reciprocally helped Grove establish *Waiting for Godot* as required reading across the college curriculum.

Waiting for Godot and *Endgame* also appear in Grove's 1970 college catalog on the syllabus for a more eclectic course proposal called "The Absurd as Reality." The other playwright included in this course is Eugène Ionesco, and Grove's marketing of his plays provides additional insight into how Grove translated drama whose performance conventions were inimical to print into bestselling Evergreen Originals. Ionesco's plays are much busier than Beckett's, involving elaborate and frequently cluttered sets as well as bizarre costumes and makeup, so Grove couldn't take the minimalist approach that worked with Beckett. Furthermore, unlike Beckett, Ionesco was generous with his opinions about his work specifically and contemporary drama more generally, so Grove had the opportunity to present the playwright's views more directly to the American public.

The strategy of marketing the printed text in conjunction with student performances was replicated with Ionesco, whose plays were also popular on college campuses. During initial negotiations with Gallimard in 1958, Rosset explained the success of this arrangement regarding *Godot*: "At this time, we have sold 30,000 copies of Samuel Beckett's WAITING FOR GODOT and a good part of these sales came to us through amateur productions. A special group handles the amateur production rights to this play, and we cooperate with them in a mutually agreeable manner."[25] Some years later, Rosset had to clarify to Gallimard himself the nature of the paperback Evergreen Originals that were sold in this manner: "It is not really equivalent to a 'livre de poche,' since it is a full-sized book, selling for approximately $1.95. We have found that the major market for the Ionesco works is in the academic fields, and most of the books are purchased by professors and students."[26]

The first Ionesco Evergreen Original was *Four Plays* (1958), whose design and format significantly contrast with those of *Waiting for Godot*. The very inclusion of four plays in one volume—*The Bald Soprano, The Lesson, Jack, or The Submission,* and *The Chairs*—both mitigates against the idea of a singular masterpiece and contributes to the sense of clutter between the covers. Instead of a photograph from a production—the conventional design for playscript covers—Grove used one of Kuhlman's typographic designs, featuring simply a large, black number "4" against an orange background, with a thin strip of white along the left border in which appear the titles of the individual plays in orange. The white background of the border extends into the orange background of the number "4" in horizontal bars of uneven length and dimension, reinforcing the sense of busyness and blurred boundaries (Figure 13). The text itself includes no blank pages and minimal white space. The dialogue wraps around into the speech prefixes, further filling the space of each page. The four plays in this volume complement this sense of clutter, featuring proliferations of prattle and props. Starting with Ionesco's first play, *The Bald Soprano,* famously inspired by an English-language primer, and ending with *The Chairs,* whose elaborate set becomes increasingly congested, the text of *Four Plays* feels chaotic and confusing.

Figure 13. Roy Kuhlman's cover for the first Ionesco Evergreen Original, *Four Plays* (1958).

Richard Coe, in his study of the playwright, argues that Ionesco "raised language from the status of a secondary medium to the dignity of an object-in-itself,"[27] and this objectification is immediately evident in *The Bald Soprano*, which consists entirely of banal clichés without reference to plot, story, or character. This play in particular seemed to call for innovative book design, and in 1965 the French graphic artist Robert Massin, working with photographs of the revival performance directed by Henry Cohen, produced a radically experimental text of the play that Grove reissued in the United States. As the promotional flyer affirms, the book was meant to re-create graphically the experience of the play's performance: "Like Ionesco's play itself, it manages to break every rule of conformist book design with a tour de force of explosive image and symbol. All criteria of margin allowance, type combination, spacing and legibility are violated. Yet it brings the action of the play into electrifying life as though each spread were a frame from a flickering silent film arrested momentarily in startling black and white."[28] Grove tried to market this deluxe edition as a gift book in 1966, trumpeting in the press release: "NEW EDITION OF IONESCO'S PLAY THE BALD SOPRANO USES PHOTOS AND TYPE IN A UNIQUE WAY TO CONVEY ON PAPER THE QUALITY OF A LIVE PERFORMANCE,"[29] but, as Fred Jordan wrote to Marshall McLuhan in 1967, "For some reason I am not fully able to understand, sales on the book have been disappointing."[30]

An elaborately illustrated oversized hardcover, the Massin edition of *The Bald Soprano* is a remarkable work of art, but its commercial failure affirms the success of the more modest and affordable design of the Evergreen Original, which had no real equivalent in the Parisian book market. Neither a *livre de poche* nor an objet d'art, the Evergreen Originals format fused economic affordability and aesthetic quality without being seen as middlebrow. Although the design of these inexpensive paperbacks was meant to give a sense of performance conventions, this correlation could not, as with the Massin edition, compromise their affordability, which was crucial to the democratic ideology of their marketing. Thus, Grove promoted *Four Plays* in the same way as Beckett's work, arguing that the printed text provided the opportunity for readers to determine the plays' significance for themselves. The ad in the *Times* asked readers, "Are Eugene Ionesco's plays 'pretentious fakery' or 'amusing and provocative'? Make up your mind—read 4 Plays by Eugene Ionesco."[31] Although he didn't sell as well as Beckett, Ionesco nevertheless became a reliable author for Grove: *Four Plays* sold more than ten thousand copies per year throughout the 1960s.

Grove also used Ionesco's own pronouncements about the freedom of the artist to bolster its campaign. Ionesco wrote extensively about the theater, and Grove's publication of his *Notes and Counternotes* in 1964 played an important role in framing his reception in the United States. In the preface, Ionesco apologizes for the repetitiveness of the collection, explaining, "I have been fighting chiefly to safeguard my freedom to think, my freedom as a writer."[32] And he extends this freedom to his audience, proclaiming in his ambivalent response to the success of *Rhinoceros* in the United States: "A playwright poses problems. People should think about them, when they are quiet and alone, and try to resolve them for themselves, without constraint."[33] Ionesco presents a complementarity between the collective and chaotic confusion of seeing the play and the solitary and quiet contemplation afterward, clearly an ideal context in which to read the Evergreen Original.

Within the literary field of the United States the theater of the absurd generated a mandate not only to read the plays before or after or instead of seeing them but also to read an expanding canon of commentary intended to frame the meanings of these difficult texts. No Grove Press playwright carried a heavier paratextual burden than Jean Genet, whose reception in both France and America was guided, if not determined, by Jean-Paul Sartre's gargantuan study *Saint Genet*, ensuring that Genet's work would initially be understood in terms of the reigning philosophy of existentialism, which formed a kind of interpretive frame around the entire theater of the absurd. Furthermore, Sartre's opus was written before Genet turned to theater; thus, its focus on his poetry and prose, on his becoming a writer, ballasted his literary credentials and bolstered the common interpretation that he was a poet who had turned to the theater.

Rosset was introduced to Genet's work by Bernard Frechtman, who, according to his partner at the time, Annette Michelson, "invented Genet for the English-speaking world."[34] Frechtman wanted Grove to begin with *The Thief's Journal*, which he called "one of the profoundest books of this century,"[35] but Rosset, after seeking legal advice, wrote back that "the Genet book would absolutely be banned and criminal proceedings invoked, and they would probably be successfully invoked to the extent of a jail sentence."[36] In the early 1950s, publishing Genet's prose unexpurgated would have been foolhardy even for Rosset, so he wisely decided to start with the plays, effectively inverting Genet's reception in France. After some wrangling, Frechtman accepted this decision.

The Maids, with an introduction by Sartre and a copyright in Frechtman's name, was issued as an Evergreen paperback in 1954. Sartre's introduction, originally an appendix to *Saint Genet*, reads the play in terms of the thematic concerns of the novels that form the literary focus of the second half of his monumental study, establishing them as crucial for understanding the play and laying the groundwork for their eventual publication by Grove in the 1960s after the legal triumph with *Lady Chatterley's Lover*. Sartre understands the play in classically existentialist terms, arguing that "the maids are relative to everything and everyone; their being is defined by absolute relativity. They are *others*. Domestics are pure emanations of their masters and, like criminals, belong to the order of the Other, to the order of Evil."[37] Sartre's philosophical terminology became crucial not only to framing Genet's reception in the United States but also to understanding the broader historical and political developments with which his work was increasingly associated.

As were those of Beckett and Ionesco, Genet's plays were popular on college campuses, and Grove replicated the practice of encouraging theater departments to sell the paperback in conjunction with their performances. In the late 1950s, both Harvard and Yale put on productions of *Deathwatch*, and Wellesley did a production of *The Maids*. Grove prepared a boilerplate letter that opened in this way: "We were wondering if you would be interested in selling copies of our $1.45 edition of THE MAIDS and DEATHWATCH, in the theatre on the evenings of your performance. This has been very successfully done by other groups which have produced the play."[38] Another version elaborates: "Often people are interested in reading a play right after seeing it."[39]

The characters and settings in these first plays—maids, prisoners, and, in *The Balcony*, a brothel—were at best ancillary to the sensibilities of most Americans who saw or read them. Not until the publication of *The Blacks* in 1960, followed by its triumphant and controversial three-year run at the St. Mark's Playhouse starting in 1961, did Genet become thoroughly assimilated into the American cultural and political scene. In his introduction to *The Maids*, Sartre had noted that mistresses create maids in the same fashion that "Southerners create Negroes";[40] the publication and performance of *The Blacks* provided the opportunity for Americans, both black and white, to contemplate this claim and, in a larger sense, to gauge the relevance of Sartre's philosophical premises for their own most immediate social and political concerns.

The Blacks appeared on the American scene well before civil rights had given way to Black Power, before the term "Negro" had ceded its prominence to "black" in the volatile vocabulary of race relations in the United States. Rosset had originally intended to entitle it "The Negroes," as he emphasized to Frechtman in late 1959: "We've had a great deal of discussion about the title and feel that it absolutely must stay as THE NEGROES. We do not feel that THE BLACKS has as much bite nor is as acceptable."[41] Frechtman was adamant in his refusal: "The title *must* be THE BLACKS. THE NEGROES is absolutely out of the question . . . Negroes is a purely neutral and even scientific term. It could be used in the title of an anthropological or sociological work."[42] Eventually Richard Seaver communicated Grove's concession: "We give in. Reluctantly and contre coeur . . . THE BLACKS here has a rather ugly connotation rather than the bite you mention."[43] In the end, the publication and performance of *The Blacks* in the United States arguably contributed to the terminological shift from the purportedly neutral term "Negro" to the more aesthetically and politically loaded "black."

More than any other play Grove published, *The Blacks* was inextricably yoked to a specific American performance, photos from which were generously distributed throughout the paperback reissue of the play, which sold more than eighty thousand copies over the course of the 1960s. The cover photo features Roscoe Lee Browne in the role of Master of Ceremonies Archibald Absalom Wellington, his hand raised as if conducting a symphony. Above him looms the "Court," five black actors in garish outfits and grotesque white masks. In contrast to the stark black and white of the cover photo, the title across the top features three colors: "The Blacks" in black; "a clown show" in orange; and "by Jean Genet" in purple, as if implying that the aesthetic form of the play is in tension with its philosophical premises (Figure 14). There are no blank pages in the text, nor is there any paratextual material besides Genet's provocative instruction that the play "is intended for a white audience." In addition to Browne, the original New York cast featured James Earl Jones, Louis Gossett Jr., Cicely Tyson, and Maya Angelou Make; the interspersing of their photos throughout the text creates a fascinating tension between the generic anonymity of the masks that illustrate the play's purportedly existential philosophy of race relations and the idiosyncratic specificity of the faces that soon became highly recognizable in the American media, partly as a result of the publicity around this play.

Print and performance are deeply interdependent in *The Blacks*, both within the plot—which persistently foregrounds its scriptedness—and in the critical controversies around it, in which the disputants seem scripted into roles determined by their race. The play itself, of course, comments on this interconnection

The Blacks: a clown show by Jean Genet

Figure 14. Roy Kuhlman's cover for *The Blacks* (1960).

between race, writing, and role playing, since its central conceit is a performance by blacks of white fantasies about blackness. Thus, early in the play Archibald admonishes the character of Village (played by James Earl Jones): "You're to obey *me*. And the text we've prepared."[44] One of the early photos features Village's ambiguous declaration of hate to Virtue (played by Cicely Tyson), during which Archibald makes the conducting motions depicted on the cover, "as if he were directing Village's recital," according to Genet's footnote.[45] The subtle transit between the footnote and the cover photo, between Genet the playwright and Browne the actor as Master of Ceremonies, generates a tension between actors and script that illuminates the terms in which the play was discussed at the time.

This tension was the central subject of Norman Mailer's review of *The Blacks*, spread over two issues of the *Village Voice* in May 1961 and then reprinted in *The Presidential Papers* in 1964. Revisiting the racial essentialism of "The White Negro," Mailer asserts that the actors are members of the "Black Bourgeoisie" who "cannot know because they have not seen themselves from outside (as we have seen them), that there is a genius in their race—it is possible that Africa is closer to the root of whatever life is left than any other land."[46] Further elaborating that "the Negro tends to be superior to the White as an entertainer, and inferior as an actor," Mailer concludes that the cast was too inhibited and self-conscious to fully inhabit Genet's incendiary dialogue. In the next issue of the paper Lorraine Hansberry offered both Mailer and Genet as examples of "the New Paternalism" and reminded *Voice* readers that *The Blacks* must be understood as "a conversation between white men about *themselves*."[47] Furthermore, she vociferously defended both the actors and the acting, proclaiming that she knew most of them to be "part-time hack drivers, janitors, chorus girls, domestics" and that she found "the acting, almost without exception, brilliant."[48]

In its self-conscious reprise of the dispute between Mailer and Baldwin over "The White Negro," the disagreement between Mailer and Hansberry feels scripted, as if both were playing roles of which they were becoming weary, preventing either of them from fully engaging the challenges of Genet's play. It is thus informative to contrast their conventional exchange with Jerry Tallmer's review of *The Blacks*, which appeared alongside Mailer's. Tallmer, cofounder of the *Voice* and contributing editor to the *Evergreen Review*, chose to review the play in the form of a dramatic dialogue between Village and Virtue, allowing him to comment more immanently on the complex rhetorical structures of Genet's text. Significantly, Tallmer opens by appropriating Genet's prefatory comment, which was not included in the showbill for the play and therefore would be familiar only to those who had read it: "One evening an actor asked me to write a play for an all-black cast. But what exactly is a black? First of all, what's his color?"[49] Then Tallmer begins:

> VILLAGE: If we are not what they think us, neither shall we avoid being invented, being evacuated, by their thoughts. What then are we?
> VIRTUE: Blacks, Clowns, Phantasms, of Jean Genet.
> VILLAGE: What exactly is Jean Genet? First of all, what's his color?
> VIRTUE: White.
> VILLAGE: What color is that?
> VIRTUE: Pink, orange, yellow, black. Black as the ace. Black as sin. Black as diamonds. Black as the black semen of hatred. Black as genius. Black as the black chambers of masterpiece.[50]

Tallmer's review begins by inverting Genet's comment, routing the opening question back through the playwright and seemingly anticipating the color dynamic of the Evergreen paperback that incorporated photos from the New York production. Tallmer uses the same formal mimicry to comment on the identity of the actors:

> VILLAGE: Do you speak as a white?
>
> VIRTUE: As a Negro and a performer. Is not each of us—are not you—a Negro and a performer?
>
> VILLAGE: I am Deodatus Village, rapist of the unraped, murderer of the unslain. I am a performer. Deodatus James Earl Jones Village.
>
> VIRTUE: A Negro?
>
> VILLAGE: A young American Negro. My name is Jones.[51]

Tallmer's dialogic response to *The Blacks* comments more cogently than Mailer's or Hansberry's on the complex racial and rhetorical dynamics of the cast's position in the New York production. And Tallmer concludes by claiming that such dialogue is only the beginning of a new rhetoric of revolution: "In the new swamps, the new colonialism. Slaves, criminals, Negroes, put on your masks; clowns, take your places. What does not yet exist must now be invented. It begins; it is only the beginning."[52] While Mailer and Hansberry's exchange looks back to the context of the 1950s and the beginnings of the civil rights movement, Tallmer's appropriation of Genet looks forward to the alliance in the later 1960s between the New African Nations and the Black Power movement, an alliance in which both Genet and Grove Press played a role.

The early and sustained prominence of Beckett, Ionesco, and Genet in Grove's list of contemporary dramatists attests both to the persistent power of Paris as a cultural capital in the immediate postwar era and to the quality of the literary connections Rosset and company had there. After Paris, the most significant European capital of dramatic innovation was undoubtedly London, and Grove also established an impressive list of playwrights from the United Kingdom, including Brendan Behan, John Arden, Alan Ayckbourn, Joe Orton, and Tom Stoppard. The most successful and influential of this list was certainly Harold Pinter, whose collected works Grove began issuing under their mass-market Black Cat imprint in the 1970s. As the introduction to the first volume of the *Complete Works of Harold Pinter*, Grove chose "Writing for the Theatre," the transcript of a speech Pinter gave at the National Student Drama Festival in Bristol in 1962, which was reprinted in the *Evergreen Review* in 1964. Commenting on the contrasting critical responses to his first two major plays, Pinter dryly and dismissively opens: "In

The Birthday Party I employed a certain amount of dashes in the text, between phrases. In *The Caretaker* I cut out the dashes and used dots instead . . . So it's possible to deduce from this that dots are more popular than dashes and that's why *The Caretaker* had a longer run than *The Birthday Party*."[53] Pinter's comment is intended as a dig at his critics, who "can tell a dot from a dash a mile off, even if they can hear neither,"[54] but his wry dismissal of the relation between punctuation and performance can't help having a rhetorical boomerang effect in retrospect, given the importance of pauses in his plays. As Worthen affirms, "In the first decade of Pinter's real celebrity, the material idiosyncrasies of Pinter's printed text drove the understanding of Pinter's dramatic writing," and no idiosyncrasy was more prominent than Pinter's famous pauses that, as Worthen further elaborates, tend to assimilate the plays into a temporality associated with "certain kinds of reading."[55]

For Worthen, Pinter's pauses function within a larger literary temporality that is explicitly poetic since, as Martin Esslin affirms, Pinter "is a poet and his theatre is essentially a poetic theatre."[56] For both Worthen and Esslin, Pinter's poetics are those of the modernist lyric, precise and pregnant with hidden meanings that can become legible through close critical attention to their arrangement on the page, and usually with the help of a critic who can explain, as Esslin notes in the preface to his book-length study of the dramatist, "much that is puzzling, obscure, and evokes a desire for elucidation."[57] This correlation between Pinter's plays and modernist poetics receives further affirmation from his self-fashioning as an author. As he continues in his speech, "The theatre is a large, energetic, public activity. Writing is, for me, a completely private activity, a poem or a play, no difference . . . What I write has no obligation to anything other than to itself."[58] Given such dedication to the autonomy of the writer, it is not surprising that Varun Begley has recently suggested that Pinter supplant Beckett as "the last modernist."[59]

The antinomy between private writing and public performance is folded into the setting and substance of most of Pinter's early plays, almost all of which take place in the sorts of constrained domestic spaces where reading and writing frequently occur. Indeed, as Begley affirms in his interpretation of the significance of the newspaper in Pinter's work, everyday reading, as opposed to "poetic" reading, is frequently thematized as a component of the action in his plays. Both *The Birthday Party* and *The Room*, published together as an Evergreen Original in 1961, open with a principal male character reading, only partially attending to the dialogue of the principal female character. Significantly, then, the opening pauses in these plays indicate a man reading while his wife speaks. *The Birthday Party* begins with the following lines between Meg and her husband, Petey, who is sitting at the kitchen table reading a newspaper:

MEG: Is that you, Petey?

Pause.

Petey, is that you?

Pause.

Petey?[60]

The Room opens with an almost identical scene between the couple Rose and Bert, in which Rose addresses a long monologue to Bert as he sits silently reading a magazine. In this scene, instead of simply indicating pauses, Pinter inserts extensive stage directions detailing Rose's actions as she prepares Bert's meal. This scene was chosen as the cover photo for the Evergreen Original. It is a low-angle, black-and-white close-up of Bert sitting at the table with Rose, her face partly in shadow, leaning over him; between the two of them is propped the magazine with the title *The Last of the Mohicans*, presumably serialized, just showing over the edge of the table that juts into the foreground of the shot. Above their heads the background is entirely black (Figure 15).

As the design of this edition indicates, Grove chose to introduce Pinter's peculiar sensibilities—what quickly became known as the "Pinteresque"—through a dialogue between typographic and photographic representation. Since most of Pinter's early plays take place in domestic interiors, they are particularly conducive to the photographic frame, whose rectangular shape conveniently mirrors the geometry of the room. In *The Birthday Party & The Room* a sequence of photos follows the text of each play, replicating in condensed visual stills the action the reader has just followed in print. Frequently these photographs represent silences in the text; the first photo from *The Room* is a frontal shot of Bert sitting at the table, the magazine propped in front of him, as Rose pours him a cup of tea (Figure 16). The third photo depicts a subtle alteration of the action described in the printed text. It shows Rose, alone, in the process of concealing the magazine in her shawl (Figure 17). Based on its order in the sequence, one can deduce that this photo represents her solitary actions between Bert's departure and the arrival of Mr. and Mrs. Sands, which Pinter describes at some length:

He fixes his muffler, goes to the door and exits. She stands, watching the door, then turns slowly to the table, picks up the magazine, and puts it down. She stands and

listens, goes to the fire and warms her hands. She stands and looks about the room.
She looks at the window and listens, goes quickly to the window, stops and straightens
the curtain. She comes to the centre of the room, and looks towards the door. She goes
to the bed, puts on a shawl, goes to the sink, takes a bin from under the sink, goes to
the door and opens it.[61]

If *The Room*, in its pure reduction to a single interior space, epitomizes Pinter's settings, the surreptitious transit of a serialized American novel across the photographic reproductions of this space reveals how Grove worked to replicate its complexities in textual form. Pinter's printed dialogue tends to hover over or penetrate into silences that indicate modes of everyday reading that significantly contrast with the type of attention solicited by the dialogue. The selection of photographs for this text foregrounds this dynamic, ensuring that Pinter's pauses will be pregnant with the practice of reading in mind, a practice that, increasingly, was inculcated in the college classroom.

. . .

Figure 15. Roy Kuhlman's cover for the Evergreen Original edition of
The Birthday Party & The Room (1961).

Figure 16. Vivian Merchant and Michael Brennan in Harold Pinter's *The Room* (1960). (Royal Court Theatre, London; photograph by John Cowan)

Figure 17. Vivian Merchant in Harold Pinter's *The Room* (1960). (Royal Court Theatre, London; photograph by John Cowan)

Grove's resolutely international list of dramatists was weighted toward the European, but it did not neglect contemporary American drama, particularly with the now-legendary Living Theatre only a few blocks away. Grove published one of its first real successes, Jack Gelber's *The Connection* (1960), a plotless play-within-a-play that centers on a group of addicts in an apartment as they wait for the dealer to arrive. As Kenneth Tynan notes in his introduction, "Its theme is akin to that of *Waiting for Godot*" but with a higher level of explicit self-reflexivity about its status as a performance.[62] The cast includes a producer, director, and author, as well as two photographers who move in and out of the audience. It also includes periodic performances by jazz musicians.

Grove made ample use of photographs in its print edition. Kuhlman's controversial cover features a close-up of the character Leach leaning over a table shooting up, with smoke curling in the background (Figure 18). Photos are generously distributed throughout the text, some across both recto and verso pages, many including the photographers and musicians (Figures 19 and 20). The photos function analogously to the musical interludes in the performance

Figure 18. Roy Kuhlman's cover for *The Connection* (1960).

Figure 19. Musicians in Jack Gelber's *The Connection* (1959). (Living Theatre, New York; photograph courtesy of John Wulp)

Figure 20. Photographers in Jack Gelber's *The Connection* (1959). (Living Theatre, New York; photograph courtesy of John Wulp)

(recordings of which were available through Blue Note records), encouraging the reader to experience pauses in the lackadaisical action. Most of the photos are dark and grainy; many of them prominently feature the stage lighting. Thus, they create a paradoxical combination of verisimilitude and self-reflexivity. On the one hand, the front cover is startlingly realistic, and the murkiness of the photos in the text reinforces the underground atmosphere of the action. On the other hand, the presence of photographers reminds the reader that this is a performance about a performance, the kind of metalevel theatrical experience that became a signature of the Living Theatre.

In the ensuing years, the Living Theatre performed *The Connection* across Europe, generating a cultural countercurrent to the stream of European avant-garde drama appearing in the United States in the postwar era. The Living Theatre itself was deeply influenced by the European avant-garde. Both Julian Beck and Judith Malina had been inspired by the theories of Antonin Artaud, and in the 1950s the struggling repertory company had staged work by absurdist forebears Alfred Jarry, August Strindberg, and Luigi Pirandello. They also staged a number of productions by another of Grove's more important dramatic acquisitions, Bertolt Brecht, whose mentor, Erwin Piscator, had also been a strong influence on Malina.

Unlike Beckett, Ionesco, Genet, Pinter, Gelber, and the many other young and relatively unknown playwrights Grove published and whose careers it was therefore able to nurture from the beginning, Brecht was dead by the time Grove established itself as a publisher of contemporary drama, and he already had a towering reputation reaching back into the modernist era. Furthermore, the condition of his literary estate was a crazy quilt of textual variants and conflicting copyright claims. The key figure in Grove's acquisition and marketing of Brecht was Eric Bentley, Brander Matthews Professor of Dramatic Literature at Columbia University and drama critic for the *New Republic*. As a translator, editor, and critic, Bentley, who had also been a personal friend of Brecht, introduced his work to the English-speaking world after the playwright's death. Bentley first approached Rosset and Donald Allen in the mid-1950s, suggesting that they devote an issue of the *Evergreen Review* to Brecht. Allen thought that such an issue would have too narrow an appeal and instead suggested "a one volume selected Brecht, *his own* theory and some of the plays . . . the kind of one vol. that students would have to have, etc. Bentley would be a good editor."[63] Grove published the hefty *Seven Plays by Bertolt Brecht* in 1961, and Bentley, in close coordination with Fred Jordan, continued on as the general editor of the never-completed Grove Press edition of the *Works of Bertolt Brecht*.

The year 1961 was a turning point for Brecht's career in English. In addition to the Grove publication of *Seven Plays*, the *Tulane Drama Review* devoted an entire issue to his work, including the first English translation of his essay "On the Experimental Theater." Also in 1961, Anchor Books released a mass-market version of Martin Esslin's *Brecht: The Man and His Work*. Grove issued its own Evergreen Pilot study of Brecht by Ronald Gray. Together, these publishing events laid the groundwork for the popular availability of English translations of Brecht's work that Bentley envisioned for the Grove Press edition.

Grove emphasized the scale and scope of *Seven Plays* in its ads, calling it "one giant volume of the lyrical, cynical, grim, comic plays of Bertolt Brecht."[64] Crucial to the design of this near six hundred–page tome was a selection of Brecht's early work, before his conversion to Marxism. The inclusion of these plays allowed Bentley to frame Brecht as an absurdist forebear, in essence reverse-engineering his appeal. As the flyleaf affirms, the volume features "the great early plays in which critics have found the beginnings of that Theater of the Absurd which we associate with the names of Beckett and Ionesco." This design also enabled Bentley to argue in the introduction that, despite Brecht's political transformations and the collaborative nature of most of his work, his oeuvre has the unity and coherence necessary to place him in the ranks of his modernist contemporaries.

Brecht's plays, according to Bentley, are essentially poetic since, as he argues in his introduction, Brecht "remained the Poet as Playwright."[65] Esslin agreed that "Brecht was a poet, first and foremost."[66] For both Bentley and Esslin, Brecht's poetic sensibility unites a corpus that would otherwise lack coherence, since Brecht resisted authoritative written versions of his plays and collaborated so extensively on their composition and production as to solicit sustained charges of plagiarism and exploitation. Nevertheless, Bentley insists, "In the Brecht theatre, though others made contributions, he himself laid the foundation in every department: he was the stage designer, the composer, and the director. The production as a whole, not just the words, was the poem. It was in essence, and often in detail, *his* poem."[67] Drama is collaborative; poetry is solitary. In order to establish Brecht as a modernist auteur, Bentley projects the latter onto the former. As we have already seen, this logic pervaded the positioning of Grove's list of major playwrights; it allowed the dramatist to claim the autonomy of the poet and provided a reason to read the plays.

Seven Plays—as well as the entire Grove Press edition of Brecht's works—was itself a highly collaborative and complicated endeavor. In addition to Bentley's translations of *In the Swamp, A Man's a Man, Mother Courage, The Good Woman of Setzuan,* and *The Caucasian Chalk Circle* (with Maja Apelman), it includes Frank Jones's translation of *Saint Joan of the Stockyards* and Charles Laughton's version of *Galileo.* Each play has its own title page, detailing its copyright and permission status (only *Galileo* has a copyright in Brecht's name). Bentley's introduction, subtitled "Homage to B. B. by Eric Bentley," based on his Christian Gauss seminar on Brecht from the previous spring, is characteristically scattered and feisty, in essence a series of polemical observations and interventions intended to jump-start "a real discussion of Brecht."[68] Bentley's commentary on Brecht's collaborative methods is as revealing about him as they are about his subject. Bentley notes: "It has not escaped attention that, following the title page of a Brecht play, there is a page headed: *Mitarbeiter—* Collaborators. It has only escaped attention that these names are in small type and do not appear on the title page of the book or, presumably, on the publisher's royalty statements."[69] It is impossible not to notice that the title page of *Seven Plays* prominently features Bentley's name but doesn't mention the many translators and editors who assisted him in his task. These names appear in the acknowledgments, which conclude with the following lines: "Finally, I wish to thank Mr. Barney Rosset. There's a lot of prattle in America about enterprise. Barney Rosset, so far as my personal acquaintance goes, is one of the few enterprising Americans."[70]

This enterprise came to partial fruition over the course of the 1960s, as Grove issued a variety of Brecht's plays as part of the Grove Press edition of the *Works of Bertolt Brecht,* under Bentley's general editorship. Most of these plays were published as mass-market paperbacks under Grove's Black Cat imprint, reflecting an aspiration toward a popular audience appropriate to Brecht's political vision.[71] The proliferation of cheap paperback editions of his plays—pocket parables, as it were—alongside their frequent production by college and university drama departments over the course of the 1960s, illustrates the degree to which Bentley's domestication of Brecht for an English-speaking public was based in a dialectical interplay between reading and spectatorship.

In his introduction to *Seven Plays,* Bentley calls "epic theatre" a "misnomer" for Brecht's work, partly because he thought the term diminished appreciation of Brecht's "lyric" talents but also because Brecht had failed to find a public adequate to his aspirations.[72] A few years later, Grove published a play by a much younger German playwright who, according to Brecht's mentor Erwin Piscator, fulfilled both the formal and political objectives of a modern epic theater. Rolf Hochhuth's *The Deputy*, a lengthy free-verse moral melodrama indicting Pope Pius XII for his silence on the Holocaust, generated a firestorm of controversy from its debut in West Berlin on February 23, 1963. Since it was too long to be feasibly performed in a single evening, its German publisher issued the print edition on the same day as its debut. From its initial appearance, *The Deputy* was a play that demanded to be read.

The German debut of *The Deputy* was directed by Piscator, whom Brecht had earlier credited with "the most radical attempt to endow the theatre with an instructive character."[73] In his introduction to the print edition, Piscator called *The Deputy* "an epic play, epic-scientific, epic-documentary; a play for epic, 'political' theater, for which I have fought more than thirty years; a 'total' play for a 'total' theater."[74] This impassioned introduction appears as the first chapter in Eric Bentley's edited volume for Grove, *The Storm over "The Deputy,"* the foreword to which bombastically claims that the controversy over this play "*is almost certainly the largest storm ever raised by a play in the whole history of the drama.*"[75] Bentley goes on to explicitly compare this response to the relatively restricted audience for Brecht's plays: "Who more than [Brecht] wished to speak to the whole modern world on burning issues that concern everyone? Yet the most one can say for the audience of *Mother Courage*, even where the play has been received most enthusiastically, is that it interests a rather considerable minority group."[76]

Grove did its best to exploit the controversy that accompanied this play across Europe when it hosted Hochhuth's visit to the United States for its American premiere (in an abridged version) at the Brooks Atkinson Theater in February 1964. Grove arranged for a press conference in the Grand Ballroom of the Waldorf-Astoria, where Hochhuth appeared with Fred Jordan at his side, as well as for a television interview with Hannah Arendt. The play ran for 316 performances, and the hardcover, released simultaneously with the premiere, was prominently reviewed in the *New York Times Book Review*, the *New York Review of Books*, and *Bookweek*. At 352 pages, including Hochhuth's 65-page appended "Sidelights on History" documenting the veracity of his portrayals, *The Deputy* is almost as long as *Seven Plays*, dictating that it would rarely be performed in full.[77] Thus, while its very length contributed to its claims to "epic" scale, it also determined that this scale could be fully appreciated only by reading it. In its ads, Grove specified that "this is not an acting version, but Rolf Hochhuth's complete historical drama, which would take about eight hours to perform entirely, and from which every stage version has been adopted. Only by reading THE DEPUTY in this form can you realize the full depth and power of one of the most significant works to come out of postwar Europe."[78] This substitution of "work" for "play" indicated the difficulty in classifying this text. As the flyleaf affirms, *The Deputy* is "ostensibly a play, but transcend[s] the framework of the stage." This "transcendence" is immediately evident in the opening stage directions, which include such editorial interjections as "it would seem that anyone who holds a responsible post for any length of time under an autocrat . . . surrenders his own personality" or "it seems to be established, therefore, that photographs are totally useless for the interpretation of character."[79] The lengthy text that follows looks like a cross between a George Bernard Shaw play and an epic poem. Set with minimal white space, the text fills every page, with stage directions frequently extending over five or six pages.

Critics were divided on the aesthetic value of this text, which, with the exception of one character, a Jesuit priest who voluntarily commits himself to Auschwitz (where the last act takes place) after he is unable to convince the pope to publicly condemn the Final Solution, is highly documentary in character, hewing closely to historical persons and events. As such, *The Deputy* depicts in stark immediacy events that precipitated the theater of the absurd but that are rarely directly referenced in it. More specifically, in attacking the pope, *The Deputy* directly engages the challenge that the Holocaust posed for the moral and institutional power of Christianity. Thus, *The Deputy* penetrated directly into the mainstream, in contrast to the "considerable minority" that discussed Beckett or Brecht, explicitly challenging the beliefs and allegiances of millions of people in a popularly accessible form and format (the mass-market edition, distributed by Dell, sold more than two hundred thousand copies). It is little surprise that the bibliography appended to Bentley's edited volume runs to almost twenty pages, with many entries from Catholic and Jewish dailies.

Though none of Brecht's plays generated the scale and scope of immediate controversy that followed the performance and publication of *The Deputy*, the "considerable minority" that read them ultimately ensured their longevity, whereas Hochhuth's incendiary drama, and the "storm" over it, has vanished into relative obscurity—surely because it never entered into the college curriculum. This symptomatic division between drama as a direct intervention in current events—indeed, as an "event" in and of itself—and drama as a literary genre studied in the classroom is elegantly illustrated in the contrasting legacies of two plays Grove published in Black Cat editions in the late 1960s.

In August 1965, student activist Barbara Garson, speaking at an antiwar rally in Berkeley, accidentally called the president's wife "Lady MacBird Johnson." Inspired by her felicitous slip of the tongue, Garson over the next few years penned a full-length Shakespearean parody of the Kennedy and Johnson administrations, based on *Macbeth* but making ample use of other of Shakespeare's plays. In 1966, a draft of *Macbird!* was printed by the Independent Socialist Club of Berkeley and began circulating among Movement intellectuals on both coasts, generating considerable buzz in countercultural circles. Given that the borrowed plot dictated that the title character successfully plan the assassination of his predecessor, John Ken O'Dunc, Garson had difficulty interesting mainstream publishers in *Macbird!*, so her husband founded the Grassy Knoll Press explicitly for the purpose of issuing the play. By January 1967, the play had gone through five printings of more than 105,000 copies.

The play debuted at the Village Gate Theater on January 19, 1967, featuring Stacy Keach in the title role. Showcard, the company that produced off-Broadway playbills, refused to print one for the performance. Grove, which had already obtained publishing rights from Grassy Knoll, stepped into the breach. Later that year, Rosset bought Showcard, and for the rest of the 1960s Grove became the principal producer of playbills for off-Broadway performances, further enhancing its connections in the downtown scene and its reputation as a publisher and promoter of radical theater. The play generated considerable controversy and critical accolades, including gushing endorsements from Dwight McDonald, Richard Brustein, Eric Bentley, and Jack Newfield.

Macbird! was meant to intervene in its moment, and it paralleled current events so closely that Garson had to continue revising as new developments arose. The opening scene in a hotel corridor of the Democratic National Convention refigures the three witches as "a student demonstrator, beatnik stereotype," a "Negro with impeccable grooming and attire" (played by Cleavon Little), and "an old leftist, wearing worker's cap and overalls."[80] The opening lines, spoken in turn by the three witches—"When shall we three meet again? /

In riot! / Strike! / Or stopping train?"—indicate the political immediacy of the action that follows. While that action tracks the structure of *Macbeth*, many of the most memorable lines, as well as the conclusion, in which Robert Ken O'Dunc (played by William Devane) arranges for the three witches to perform a play revealing Macbird's guilt, are cribbed from *Hamlet.*

Thus, Polonius's advice is twice parodied in speeches by the old leftist, who in the second scene recommends, "Neither a burrower from within nor a leader be, / But stone by stone construct a conscious cadre. / And this above all—to thine own class be true / And it must follow, as the very next depression, / Thou canst not be false to revolution";[81] in the last act he revises his advice: "But this above all: to thine own cause be true. / Set sentiment aside and organize. / It is the cause. It is the cause . . . "[82] Hamlet's soliloquy is wonderfully satirized in a speech by Adlai Stevenson's character, the Egg of Head, who wonders, "To see, or not to see? That is the question. / Whether 'tis wiser as a statesman to ignore / The gross deception of outrageous liars, / Or to speak out against a reign of evil / And by so doing, end there for all time / The chance and hope to work within for change."[83] Not surprisingly, he opts for the former.

The play's resolution is also borrowed from *Hamlet*, with Robert Ken O'Dunc conceding that he is "no Prince Hamlet nor was meant to be," encouraging the three witches to perform a play in Macbird's convention hotel room that reveals his guilt. The witches agree to perform but refuse to follow his script, as the second witch avers, "Man, we write our *own* lines. Screw your script."[84] In the next scene, he performs a minstrel show with the chorus: "Ober de nation / Hear dat mournful sound / Chickens coming home and roosting / Massa's in the cold cold ground."[85] The play ends with Washington in flames and the Ken O'Dunc monarchy restored. Grove's Black Cat paperback sold more than 250,000 copies in 1967.

If *Macbird!* appropriates Shakespeare toward immediate political ends, Tom Stoppard's award-winning *Rosencrantz and Guildenstern Are Dead*, originally performed in 1966 at the Edinburgh Fringe Festival and then issued as a Black Cat paperback by Grove in 1967, had more long-term literary and philosophical objectives, making it more appropriate to the college curriculum. Realizing this potential, Grove's education department issued a free study guide to accompany the play. The guide opens with a number of promotional blurbs, the first of which, from Clive Barnes's review for the *New York Times*, is also featured on the play's back cover. The last line—"Mr. Stoppard is not only paraphrasing *Hamlet*, but also throwing in a paraphrase of Samuel Beckett's *Waiting for Godot* for good measure"—succinctly sums up the guide's strategy, which reveals the degree to which the formal and thematic experimentation associated with the theater of the absurd had, over the course of the 1960s, been assimilated by the sensibilities of the paperback generation. Following the blurbs, the guide presents a letter from a Macalester College English professor attesting to the success of a paper assignment on *Hamlet* and *Rosencrantz and Guildenstern Are Dead*. After three pages of excerpts from papers this professor received, Grove announces an essay contest on the same topic, to be judged by its editorial board. Grove promoted the contest aggressively, announcing in a press release: "*ROSENCRANTZ AND GUILDENSTERN ARE DEAD* ADOPTED FOR CLASSROOM USE FROM COAST TO COAST; GROVE SPONSORS ESSAY CONTEST FOR STUDENTS."[86] The promotion was a success, with *Rosencrantz and Guildenstern Are Dead* exceeding 150,000 copies in sales to educational institutions in 1968.

First prize in the contest was awarded to a seventeen-page research paper entitled "Hamlet and the Player" by a student at Vassar College. Echoing Grove's study guide, which notes that "the Player is the richest role in *R & G Are Dead*,"[87] the paper opens with the claim that "the player is just as much the hero as the title characters."[88] The paper's second paragraph effectively reveals how thoroughly the formal and philosophical challenges of experimental theater had been domesticated into standard literary critical tropes:

> Tom Stoppard has done what many college undergraduates now aspire to do in their papers; he has responded to a work of art not just critically but artistically as well. This, I think, is the highest compliment one can pay another artist. Stoppard has fashioned a play (whose central figure is the Artist, the player) based on a play (whose concern, in a great many respects, is Art). He has not just affirmed Shakespeare by choosing Shakespeare's characters to make a story, or by balancing the "existential" mentality with Renaissance melancholy or the heroic death of Hamlet with the silent offstage deaths of Rosencrantz and Guildenstern; he has affirmed Shakespeare simply by making a self-conscious play, one that has no other meaning than itself. *Rosencrantz and Guildenstern Are Dead* is finally "about" only *Rosencrantz and Guildenstern Are Dead*.[89]

What follows is a lengthy development of the revealing analogue between the undergraduate essay and the work of art that comfortably recuperates existential angst into glib irony.

The author dwells explicitly on the relation between text and performance in his analysis of the exchange between Guildenstern and the Player during the rehearsal scene when, in response to Guildenstern's question, "Who decides?," the Player responds, "*Decides?* It is written." As the author notes, "The word 'written' can have two meanings; first it is the 'written' text of the play which the players must follow . . . Secondly, 'written' suggests a fate which has been pre-determined." And he further elaborates that "the two meanings of 'written' can, of course, be one if we understand that the function of the dramatist, the artist, is to show fate operating in life, that is, to center his dramas and his art around the fact of death." This assimilation of death into art, which will predictably lead to a conclusion about the immortality of art, forms the familiar argument of this paper, but the author is refreshingly aware of the degree to which the urgency of existentialism's philosophical challenge gets lost when it is rendered as a problem for literary analysis. Thus, in commenting on Guildenstern's resistance to the Player's assertion, he claims, "He is not unlike many of us who write essays on the existential hero and Camus's words in *The Myth of Sisyphus* about 'the unyielding evidence of a life without consolation' and then go on to worry about getting an 'A.' We are still looking for the consolation."[90]

In its confident self-consciousness, this essay illustrates how completely the initial controversy over a play like *Waiting for Godot*, the paperback version of which had sold more than a quarter of a million copies by 1968, had been accommodated to the American classroom. The student is effortlessly comfortable with both the formal and philosophical difficulties of the avant-garde, even to the point of indicating the ironies of this easiness. In its emphasis on the *literariness* of these difficulties—the author ranges across the modern canon from Twain to Eliot to Hemingway to Yeats—the essay also reveals how essential the print versions of these plays were to this process. The author can console himself with the "immortality" of art only by assimilating the drama to its scripted form; performances, after all, are ephemeral.

Grove had chosen a topic, a comparison of Shakespeare and Stoppard, which in and of itself was calculated to subordinate performance to print. As Worthen affirms, the "New Bibliography," which determined the print format of Shakespeare's plays during this era (and Shakespeare was far and away the most-assigned English-language playwright across the educational spectrum), "tended to see the impact of theatre . . . as a distraction from, and corruption of, the proper transmission of the author's writing," thus envisioning "an author writing for posterity in print, producing an ideal and complete dramatic script that he knew could not be fully realized on stage."[91] By asking students to compare Stoppard (and, implicitly, Beckett) to the author whose work had effectively established the standard format for the play in print, Grove was affirming its remarkable success in marketing avant-garde theater as an explicitly literary genre whose authors were comparable to the most revered playwright in the canon.

3. The End of Obscenity

The reputation Grove established over the second half of the 1950s for publishing quality literature was crucial to its success in the battles over obscenity and freedom of expression that took up much of Rosset's time, energy, and money in the first half of the 1960s. Starting with *Grove v. Christenberry* (1959), the Post Office case over *Lady Chatterley's Lover* that inaugurated the rapid dismantling of the Comstock Act; reaching a frenzied peak with the multiple trials and tribulations of Henry Miller's *Tropic of Cancer* across the country; and concluding with the exoneration of William Burroughs's wildly explicit *Naked Lunch* in Massachusetts in 1966, Grove Press was central to the process that its lawyer Charles Rembar called the "end of obscenity" in his 1968 account of the trials. Rembar concludes his story with the lines, "So far as writers are concerned, there is no longer a law of obscenity," and indeed censorship of the printed word in the United States essentially ended in the 1960s.[1]

Rosset planned his decade-long battle against censorship with both deliberation and determination; in one unpublished autobiographical fragment, he calls it "a carefully planned campaign, much like a military campaign."[2] Throughout this campaign Rosset and his lawyers—in addition to Rembar he worked with Edward de Grazia, Elmer Gertz, Ephraim London, and many others—emphasized Grove's reputation as a publisher with literary credentials. In his affidavit for *Grove v. Christenberry*, Rosset affirmed that Grove publishes "works of a serious literary and artistic nature."[3] And for the many cases involving *Tropic of Cancer*, Rosset and his lawyers fashioned a boilerplate affidavit specifying that most of Grove's titles "are in what is called the 'quality paperback' field" and that many of them "are in use in colleges and universities throughout the country, having been specifically adopted in various courses by departments and by individual instructors and teachers."[4] In turn, Rosset and his lawyers solicited the expert testimony of these academics to attest to the literary value of the texts charged with obscenity.

As Frederick Schauer affirms in his study *The Law of Obscenity*, the use of expert testimony "took on new meaning" after the passage of *Roth v. US* in 1957, the first case in which the US Supreme Court directly addressed whether obscenity constitutes an exception to First Amendment protection for freedom of speech and the press. Before that landmark case, experts were generally (and not always successfully) deployed to attest to the literary merit of works deemed obscene; after its passage, lawyers and their expert witnesses were provided with what Schauer deems to be "a uniform standard definition of obscenity": "whether to the average person, applying contemporary community standards, the dominant theme of the material taken as a whole appeals to the prurient interest."[5] In the wake of the so-called constitutionalization of obscenity precipitated by *Roth*, experts found that, in addition to establishing the literary value of purportedly obscene texts, they were also being asked to help the court determine the nature of the "average person" and of the "community standards" that "average person" should apply.

The court ruled against Samuel Roth, the "booklegger" who had earlier attained notoriety for pirating *Ulysses*. But First Amendment lawyers realized that by defining obscenity as material "utterly without redeeming social importance," the court had provided them with an important weapon in the campaign against censorship. *Roth* represents the initial articulation of what Rosset's lawyer Edward de Grazia later called the "Brennan Doctrine," a developing definition of obscenity formulated by Supreme Court Justice William Brennan that would make it easier for "defense lawyers to demonstrate that the works of literature or art created by their clients were entitled to First Amendment Protection."[6] As De Grazia's far-ranging study, *Girls Lean Back Everywhere: The Law of Obscenity and the Assault on Genius*, affirms, "experts" such as literary critics, authors, journalists, publishers, and college professors were central to this legal demonstration. Indeed, according to de Grazia, "The only significant breakthrough to freedom that was made over the past century by authors and publishers ... was made when the courts were required by law ... to admit and give weight to the testimony of 'expert' authors and critics concerning a challenged work's values."[7]

The gold standard of literary value for all of these experts and the publishers who retained them was James Joyce's *Ulysses*, whose exoneration a generation earlier by Judge John Woolsey had become a landmark both in the battle for freedom of expression and in the academic canonization of modernism. Before the *Ulysses* case, the literary value of modernist texts had been difficult to legitimate because they had not stood the test of time. They had not become "classics" by the only standard widely recognized by the public at large: outliving their authors. The obscenity trial in this context functioned as a ritual of consecration whereby modernist texts could be affirmed as "classics" by experts on literary value. It enabled an alliance between publishers, lawyers, and literary critics that was crucial to providing mainstream acceptance for modernism by replacing the test of time with the patina of professionalism.

The US government itself acknowledged this emergent category when, in Section 305 of the Smoot-Hawley Tariff of 1930, it allowed a Customs exception for "so-called classics or books of recognized and established literary . . . merit . . . when imported for non-commercial purposes."[8] Bennett Cerf's lawyer Morris Ernst and his co-counsel Alexander Lindey leveraged Smoot-Hawley in their petition to the Treasury Department arguing that *Ulysses* is a "modern classic": "We have long ago repudiated the theory that a literary work must be hundreds or thousands of years old in order to be a classic. We have come to realize that there can be *modern* classics as well as ancient ones. If there is any book in any language today genuinely entitled to be called a 'modern classic' it is *Ulysses*."[9] Over the next few decades, it became the job of literary critics to affirm the category of the "modern classic," which Grove used both in its legal defense and in its commercial promotion of *Lady Chatterley's Lover*, *Tropic of Cancer*, and *Naked Lunch*.[10]

During this period, the legal and economic extensions of obscenity were closely linked, since the federal government did not provide copyright protection for works deemed obscene. The illegitimacy of obscenity as literature, in other words, was reinforced by its exemption from the category of intellectual property. Joyce and Lawrence had no legal recourse against piracy, since they could establish no American copyright for their texts. Cerf's decision to publish *Ulysses* promised to doubly affirm it as both a modern classic exempt from Customs confiscation and as legitimate intellectual property from which the author could profit.[11] In order to establish *Ulysses*'s classic status and discourage further censorship and copyright challenges, Cerf included in Random House's version of the text Woolsey's "monumental decision," a foreword by Ernst, and a letter from Joyce detailing his piracy woes, establishing a paratextual convention that Rosset followed closely in packaging Lawrence, Miller, and Burroughs.

Cerf used *The United States of America v. One Book Called "Ulysses"* to leverage Joyce's masterpiece into Random House's "first really important trade publication."[12] *Ulysses's* modernist credentials were affirmed by its entry into the middlebrow marketplace, a paradox sustained by the successful marketing of modernism and the canonization of the new criticism that mandated the moral "disinterest" of literary value. What Susan Stewart identifies as a "'properly' transgressive space" was established by an alliance between the expertise of academic critics and the marketing savvy of modern publishers; the "obscenity" of modernism was contained by its aesthetic consecration.[13] The *Ulysses* case provided legal sanction for this containment. The law had acknowledged the expertise of literary critics, which in turn transformed the subversive tendencies of modernism from a liability to an asset in the cultural field. More than any other postwar American publisher, Grove Press capitalized on this transformation.

The Professors versus the Postmaster

The idea to publish an unexpurgated edition of *Lady Chatterley's Lover* was originally suggested to Rosset by Mark Schorer, whom Rosset confirmed was "a major figure in the beginning." He became instrumental in defending, legitimating, and publicizing the text. A native midwesterner with a PhD in English from the University of Wisconsin, Madison, Schorer joined the English Department at UC Berkeley in 1945, where he served as chair from 1960 to 1965. A recipient of three Guggenheim Fellowships and a widely respected critic and novelist informally known as the "Lionel Trilling of the West Coast," Schorer became Rosset's academic point man for *Lady Chatterley's Lover*, negotiating (ultimately unsuccessfully) with Lawrence's widow for the rights, providing Rosset with a list of experts from whom to solicit testimony, and writing the introduction to the Grove Press edition, originally published in the inaugural issue of the *Evergreen Review*.[14]

In early 1954, Rosset wrote to Ephraim London, already well known for having exonerated Roberto Rossellini's film *The Miracle* of charges of obscenity, for legal advice on how to proceed with a defense of *Lady Chatterley's Lover*. London responded, "The Ulysses case suggests an approach,"[15] and Rosset in turn wrote to Schorer that "Ephraim feels that the best mode of procedure might be to more or less do what the ULYSSES people did."[16] Schorer provided Rosset with a list of potential experts, including Edmund Wilson, Jacques Barzun, Henry Steele Commager, and Archibald MacLeish. Rosset fashioned a boilerplate letter to be sent to these men, emphasizing that "in order to fight most effectively against such repressive and outmoded censorship, we shall need written opinions from responsible and eminent citizens to the effect that the book has literary value."[17] Barzun and Harvey Breit both provided testimonials that eventually appeared in the flyleaf of the Grove hardcover edition, and MacLeish wrote a preface to supplement Schorer's introduction. Lawrence's American biographer, Harry Moore, also supplied copy for the flyleaf, contending that "the time is overdue for an American publisher to make a fight for LADY CHATTERLEY'S LOVER such as the one made . . . in New York in 1933 and 1934 . . . for Joyce's ULYSSES."

Obscenity, however, was not the only problem. There was no US copyright registered to *Lady Chatterley's Lover*, precisely because it had been deemed obscene. Rosset wrote to Frieda Lawrence's British agent, Laurence Pollinger, and to Alfred Knopf concerning the copyright to the text. Although Ephraim London had reassured him that the unexpurgated version was in the public domain, and he had received encouragement from Frieda to publish it, Rosset also knew that Knopf had in 1932 published an expurgated version to which it owned the copyright. Writing to Pollinger in June 1954, Rosset claimed, "As you know, LADY CHATTERLEY'S LOVER is no longer in copyright; however, in the happy (if not too likely) event that we can overcome censorship and proceed with publication, we will, as a courtesy, pay a standard royalty to the Lawrence estate."[18] Ominously, Pollinger responded, "I am not, I am afraid, prepared to agree to your statement that this novel is no longer in copyright in America . . . Of one thing I am absolutely certain, and that is that LADY CHATTERLEY'S LOVER is copyright[ed] in all the countries that signed the Berne convention."[19] Later that summer, Rosset wrote to Knopf, summarizing the efforts he had made and asking for reassurance that, if he succeeded in exonerating the book, he would be free to profit from its publication. As he argued, "We think we should win, and we also think that if we undertake the work and win the case we should then be the publisher of the book and thus gain any profits which might occur."[20] Knopf deferred to Pollinger, whose position was strengthened after Frieda Lawrence died in 1956, leaving the British agent as the literary executor of the Lawrence estate. On the advice of Ephraim London, Rosset temporarily shelved the project.

Three years later, encouraged by the passage of *Roth* and by London's successful defense of the French film version, Rosset decided to proceed with publication, but then he ran into problems with London. According to Rosset, "We were in Boston with a bunch of Lawrence specialists, we were having lunch at Harvard, I disagreed with London on something . . . he said, 'When you're with me, do what I say.' And I said, 'You're fired.'"[21] The young man he hired to replace him, Norman Mailer's cousin Charles Rembar, had never argued a case in court. But Rembar was a quick study and recognized the importance of the Supreme Court's decision in *Roth*, which defined obscenity as material lacking "redeeming social importance." As Rembar meticulously documents in *The End of Obscenity*, this language was central not only in the *Lady Chatterley* case but also in the cases involving Miller's *Tropic of Cancer* and in the 1966 Supreme Court case exonerating *Memoirs of a Woman of Pleasure*. By 1968, the Supreme Court, partly through Rembar's influence, had altered the definition of obscenity to material "utterly lacking redeeming social value," effectively excluding print from prosecution.

Rosset had originally intended to precipitate a Customs case as Cerf had done with *Ulysses*, but the legal confrontation was ultimately with the US Post Office, meaning that it directly challenged the Comstock Act, which was almost a century old. The hardcover was impounded by the postmaster of New York in May 1959, the same month it made the *New York Times* bestseller list. A hearing was scheduled that included the Readers' Subscription as co-plaintiff. As Jay Topkis, the counsel for Readers' Subscription, affirmed in his opening testimony, "Our business depends completely on the use of mails. We operate through the mails exclusively. When we can't send mail, we are out of business."[22] Readers' Subscription president Arthur Rosenthal elaborated in his testimony later that day the extent to which book clubs helped publishers like Grove reach an academic market: "We do direct mail largely to what I call the university community: graduate students, assistant professors, professors."[23] Not only did Readers' Subscription market to academics but its selections were in turn determined by them, as Rosenthal further affirmed: "Readers' Subscription was founded in 1952 with three very prominent literary critics, W. H. Auden, poet, Jacques Barzun of Columbia, Lionel Trilling of Columbia, as people who were charged with the responsibility of selecting the books for this organization."[24] The presence of Readers' Subscription as co-plaintiff affirms the centrality of the burgeoning academic community as both audience and authority in the trials to come.

Rosset was the first witness called, and the Post Office lawyer promptly challenged his testimony's relevance, objecting that he "failed to see where we can gain anything by the testimony of the publisher of this book." Rembar, referencing Earl Warren's concurring statement in *Roth*, rebutted that "the conduct of the publisher is one of the elements that the courts have held relevant in a proceeding of this kind."[25] Then Topkis, citing Woolsey's contention that "the intent with which the book was written must first be determined," expanded the scope and relevance of Rosset's testimony by claiming, "Here, we don't have the author, we have the publisher."[26] Rosset further legitimated and distributed his implied expertise in divining Lawrence's intentions, testifying that he "engaged Professor Schorer as an expert on this book, to be certain of the fact that when we published, we would have the authentic edition." He then recounted his efforts to solicit expert opinions, after which Rembar and Topkis offered reviews of the book as evidence of its literary value. Over the objection of the prosecutor, the judicial officer, "relying on the decisions in the *Ulysses* case," accepted them into evidence.[27]

The competence and relevance of expert testimony were central issues in this initial hearing. Rembar and Rosset had retained Malcolm Cowley and Alfred Kazin, and the government persistently challenged the nature and scope of their expertise. Both men emphasized their academic credentials, with Cowley offering that he had "been visiting professor at many universities" and Kazin similarly claiming, "I have been a visiting professor in various universities both here and abroad, at Harvard, Smith, Amherst, Cambridge."[28] Both men described themselves as literary sociologists with expertise that encompassed both the interpretation and reception of literature. Cowley identified himself as "a literary critic and historian . . . I have made somewhat of a specialty of the folkways of readers and writers; that is, my last book . . . was more or less a book of literary sociology rather than criticism."[29] Kazin also identified his specialty as "the trends of literary taste, what the public has responded to, what it has bought."[30] Both men claimed that Lawrence's intention was to encourage sexual fulfillment in marriage and that the public, particularly on college campuses, was becoming increasingly tolerant of sexual explicitness, such that Lawrence's text was no longer as offensive to public taste as it was when originally written.

Arthur Summerfield, Eisenhower's postmaster general, was unconvinced and issued a departmental decision on June 11, 1959, concluding that "any literary merit the book may have is far outweighed by the pornographic and smutty passages and words, so that the book, taken as a whole, is an obscene and filthy work."[31] Rosset's response was two pronged. First, he appealed to the court of public opinion, compiling "A Digest of Press Opinions" on Summerfield's decision to be distributed "in the Public Interest." All of these opinions, from newspapers across the country, challenged Summerfield's competence to determine literary merit, many directly contrasting his authority with that of the critics whose evaluations he overruled. Thus, one opinion for the *San Francisco Examiner* of June 18, 1959, asserts: "Dear Mr. Summerfield . . . You say 'Lady Chatterley' is obscene. Are you as well qualified to judge a work of literature as Mark Schorer, Archibald MacLeish, Malcolm Cowley, Alfred Kazin and the host of other renowned scholars and critics who say it is not?"[32] In the same month, *Lady Chatterley's Lover* reached number 5 on the *New York Times* bestseller list.

Next, Rosset and Rembar decided, along with Readers' Subscription, to sue the postmaster general of New York, Robert Christenberry, in federal court for impounding the book. Judge Frederick van Pelt Bryan's decision for the US District Court, issued on July 21, 1959, and affirmed by the US Court of Appeals for the Second Circuit, finally overturned the Post Office ban. In his decision, which was published in full in the *Evergreen Review* and incorporated into the paperback edition of the text, Bryan affirmed that "Grove Press is a reputable publisher with a good list which includes a number of distinguished writers and serious works. Before publishing this edition Grove consulted recognized literary critics and authorities on English literature as to the advisability of publication. All were of the view that the work was of major literary importance and should be made available to the American public."[33]

Three days after Judge Bryan issued his decision, New American Library, which Knopf had licensed to publish an expurgated edition of *Lady Chatterley's Lover*, sent out a "Signet Gram" announcing publication of "the unexpurgated and complete edition of 'Lady Chatterley's Lover,' under their exclusive license for paperbound reprints of 'Lady Chatterley's Lover,' granted by contract authorized by the author's estate more than 10 years ago, still in full force and effect and just reconfirmed by the Lawrence estate and its literary executors."[34] No sooner had Rosset won the legal battle over obscenity than he found himself in a subsequent struggle over intellectual property. He brought suit against New American Library, not for copyright infringement, since it had been established that the book was in the public domain, but for "seeking to mislead and deceive the public" with its avowals that its edition was "complete" and "authorized."[35] As *Publishers Weekly* affirmed, this was less a legal issue than a matter of "the ethics of the publishing industry."[36] Most industry insiders believed that Rosset's assumption of the original risks of publishing the unexpurgated edition gave him the exclusive right to profit from it and also acknowledged that "Grove's performance in publishing its $6 hardbound edition of the book and in advertising and promoting it was in keeping with the book's high literary standing" and had indeed been responsible for its legal exoneration.[37] Grove settled with New American Library in the fall of 1959, with both companies agreeing to acknowledge the legitimacy of each other's versions.

The design and composition of both paperback editions deploy a series of paratextual conventions intended not only to legitimate the literary authenticity of the text but also to distinguish it from their more salacious rivals in the field, eschewing illustration entirely for descriptive and promotional blurbs (in an unpublished interview, Rosset called the cover "very carefully uninteresting").[38] Like the hardcover, Grove's paperback edition included Schorer's introduction and MacLeish's preface (framed as a letter to Rosset), now further supplemented by Bryan's decision. On the front cover, in red caps, is trumpeted "THIS IS THE GROVE PRESS EDITION, THE FIRST UNEXPURGATED VERSION EVER PUBLISHED IN AMERICA"; on the back cover it reiterates, again in red caps, "THIS AND ONLY THIS IS THE COMPLETE REPRINT OF THE FAMOUS GROVE PRESS $6.00 BEST SELLER." As if any question could remain, the front cover also includes, in yellow print against a red circular background, "This and only this is the uncensored edition making today's headlines!" (Figure 21).

The Signet edition also announces tautologically that it is the "complete unexpurgated authentic authorized edition" and includes a statement on the back cover from Pollinger testifying, "This Signet Edition is the only complete unexpurgated version of LADY CHATTERLEY'S LOVER authorized by the estate of Frieda Lawrence for U.S. publication" (Figure 22). The Signet edition also included an afterword by Harry Moore, whose endorsement had originally appeared on Grove's hardcover edition. Despite the competition from this and other paperback versions, the mass-market edition of *Lady Chatterley's Lover*, distributed by Dell, became Grove's first bestseller, with sales of almost 2 million copies by the end of 1960, and the legal battle provided a firm foundation for the reputation Grove continued to build over the course of the decade for challenging legal restrictions against freedom of expression.

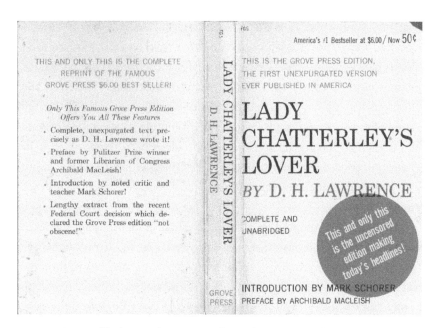

Figure 21. Front and back cover of Grove Press edition of *Lady Chatterley's Lover* (1959).

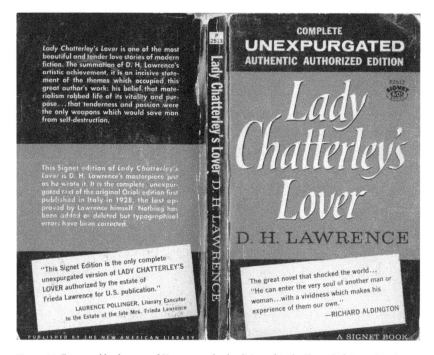

Figure 22. Front and back cover of Signet paperback edition of *Lady Chatterley's Lover* (1959).

Freedom to Read

Rosset had not really liked *Lady Chatterley's Lover*, but he thought that its ex-oneration would increase his chances of legally publishing Henry Miller, whose work he had admired since his undergraduate years. New Directions had published Miller's less explicit writing, but Jay Laughlin was unwilling to publish the *Tropics*, which remained banned in the United States and Britain. Rosset was determined to bring them out, but Miller initially turned down his generous advance. As Rosset recounted to me, "I had tried to get Miller and totally failed. I'd gone to California, to Big Sur . . . and he said no . . . he said he couldn't stand the idea. If I published it, it would be read by college students." But Rosset persisted, and with the help of Girodias, whose father had originally published both *Tropics*, and Miller's German publisher, Heinrich Ledig-Rowohlt, he finally managed to get Miller to agree to publication in the United States in 1961, with a substantial advance of fifty thousand dollars. Unlike the case of *Lady Chatterley's Lover*, which had been fairly easy and inexpensive to defend with the one Post Office case, *Tropic of Cancer* was suppressed and litigated in numerous venues across the country, while simultaneously enjoying many months on bestseller lists in those same venues. Henry Miller became both a cause célèbre and a succès de scandale, and the strategies of both his accusers and defenders illustrate how the elite aesthetics of modernism collapsed into a popular politics of sexuality in the 1960s.

Miller's work had never been easy to categorize or evaluate. His biography, particularly his expatriation in the 1930s, tended to align him, albeit somewhat belatedly, with the modernist Lost Generation, but his unseemly and unwavering focus on this biography tended to violate the evaluative protocols critics used to canonize the work of that generation. Edmund Wilson, reviewing the then unavailable *Tropic of Cancer* for the *New Republic* in 1938, called it "an epitaph for the whole generation of American artists and writers that migrated to Paris after the war" and "the lowest book of any literary merit that I ever remember to have read."[39] In both his bohemian lifestyle and his literary experimentation Miller seemed to fit, if somewhat awkwardly, into the Lost Generation category. As one biographer describes, his aspiration was to be "a working-class Proust, a Brooklyn Proust."[40]

However, as *Partisan Review* editor Philip Rahv affirmed, "With few exceptions the highbrow critics, bred almost to a man in Eliot's school of strict impersonal aesthetics, are bent on snubbing him."[41] According to Rahv, Miller is incapable of this strict impersonality: "So riled is his ego by external reality, so confused and helpless, that he can no longer afford the continual sacrifice of personality that the act of creation requires, he can no longer bear to express himself implicitly by means of the work of art as a whole but must simultaneously permeate and absorb each of its separate parts and details."[42] In other words, Miller can't afford, both literally and figuratively, to practice Eliot's "impersonal" act of creation, even though his own aesthetic is clearly a dialectical response to that act, with whose Proustian protocols Miller was deeply familiar. Miller's gargantuan personality, his maddening mix of garrulous charm and aggravating arrogance, emerges in ambivalent resistance to the figure of the modernist genius he can't quite be.

Miller was not only too personal to be considered high modernist; he was also too popular, despite the difficulty in obtaining his work. As Kenneth Rexroth, writing on the eve of Miller's American apotheosis, proclaimed, "Henry Miller is really a popular writer, a writer of and for real people, who, in other countries, is read, not just by highbrows, or just by the wider public which reads novels, but by common people, by the people who, in the United States, read comic books."[43] Much of Miller's initial popularity was enabled not by the scattering of critical accolades but by the widespread smuggling of his banned books into the United States by GIs returning from World War II. In sum, Miller posed a problem for midcentury arbiters of literary taste.

Nevertheless, Rosset armed himself with an enormous battery of critical endorsements, since he knew from his experience with *Lady Chatterley's Lover* that they could prove that a text had redeeming social value. He solicited written comments from an impressive roster of critics, writers, and publishers, including Jacques Barzun, Marianne Moore, Lawrence Durrell, Archibald MacLeish, W. H. Auden, T. S. Eliot, Arthur Miller, Thornton Wilder, Vladimir Nabokov, Alfred Kazin, and Malcolm Cowley. Rosset was wise to prepare, as he was almost immediately engulfed in a firestorm of controversy involving more than thirty court cases and more than fifty instances of extrajudicial suppression across the country. Since he had agreed to indemnify booksellers against any fines or court costs and to handle all legal cases arising from the sale of Miller's book, Rosset found himself battling for the financial survival of Grove Press.

Grove's challenge is neatly summed up in the epigraph to Miller's *Black Spring*, the lesser-known second volume in the trilogy that begins with *Tropic of Cancer* and ends with *Tropic of Capricorn*: "What is not in the open street is false, derived, that is to say, *literature*."[44] This dig at the very modernism with which Miller simultaneously endeavored to associate himself received an inverse ironic commentary in the trials of *Tropic of Cancer*, as experts in literature attempted to prove they had the street credentials to evaluate the book. The first trial, somewhat inevitably, was in Boston, for which Rosset rehired Ephraim London, who assembled an illustrious cast of experienced expert witnesses, including Mark Schorer, Harry Moore, and Harry Levin. However, the judge was not impressed by the credentials of these scholars, interrupting Schorer's testimony with the quip that "all that was necessary in this case was to offer the book in evidence and then leave it to me, who knows everything about how the ordinary man feels and what his reaction would be."[45]

Assistant Attorney General Leo Sontag agreed and attempted to establish that Schorer and the other witnesses for the defense were not in touch with the American public and therefore could not be expected to represent the book's effects on an ordinary reader. Sontag proclaimed, "It's said that a rarified atmosphere exists on the campus at the University of California at Berkeley." The judge then required clarification: "Do you feel he is in an 'Ivory Tower' and therefore has no contact with ordinary human beings?" Sontag affirmed, "That is correct, your honor. The Professor is on a shelf by himself with others." Schorer then quipped, "I'd like to tell you sometime the non-'Ivory Tower' aspects of my life." London attempted to come to the rescue by reminding the court that "the judge's life is, if anything, more of an 'Ivory Tower' existence than that of a college professor." And the judge crankily responded, "We are on the street just the same as and as much as any ordinary being."[46]

Who's in the Ivory Tower and who's on the street, and from which position is it most legitimate to judge a book like *Tropic of Cancer*? The courtroom would have to wait for Harry Levin's testimony for an ironic resolution, although this was not fully recognized in the trial itself. London introduced him with the claim that "Professor Levin's qualifications are so many that I would like to save a great deal of time by merely reading a few of them in the record and having the professor acknowledge that these are his accomplishments."[47] The judge was unimpressed until London concluded that Levin was the Irving Babbitt Professor of Comparative Literature at Harvard University. The judge and Levin then discovered that they both studied under Babbitt as undergraduates at Harvard. Although Judge Goldberg in the end disregarded the expert testimony and found the book obscene, this incidental exchange affirms the degree to which Rosset's eventual triumph depended on the professional-class solidarity of the judges, academics, and publishers who participated in these trials, a solidarity that, somewhat ironically, could not fully include the author over whom they were struggling.

The Boston trial was handled in rem, meaning that the case was against the book itself. In the Chicago trial, handled by Elmer Gertz, the demographic alignments of the adversaries were far clearer. *Tropic of Cancer* was being illegally suppressed and confiscated across suburban Illinois, and the case pitted Grove against an array of small-town police departments, including Arlington Heights, Skokie, Glencoe, Lincolnwood, Morton Grove, Niles, Des Plaines, Mount Prospect, Winnetka, and Evanston. Rosset grew up in Chicago, where his father had been president of the Metropolitan Trust Company. Gertz surely must have felt reassured when Judge Samuel Epstein opened the proceedings with the claim, "I doubt if any lawyer, who is old enough, hasn't had some sort of business relationship with Barney Rosset."[48] During the course of this widely publicized trial, Gertz also established an ongoing epistolary relationship with Miller himself, who was finally becoming wealthy as *Tropic of Cancer* rocketed up the bestseller lists. As Gertz advised Miller on various tax-evasion schemes, Miller sent him rare and signed editions of his books. A number of socioeconomic allegiances and alliances, then, contributed to Grove's success in this landmark case, which Rosset saw as a "peak moment" in his career.[49]

Judge Epstein's ruling, which affirmed that "as a corollary to the freedom of speech and the press, there is also a freedom to read," became the basis of a nationwide campaign.[50] Rosset printed and circulated thousands of copies of the decision and published a "Statement in Support of the Freedom to Read" on the front cover of the July–August 1962 issue of the *Evergreen Review*, which also included *Chicago Sun-Times* book reviewer Hoke Norris's account of the Chicago trial. The statement, which runs over from the front cover onto the flyleaf (Figure 23), is followed by a long alphabetical list of signatories, including James Baldwin, Ian Ballantine, Saul Bellow, Louise Bogan, Richard Ellmann, Arnold Gingrich, Hugh Hefner, Jack Kerouac, Carson McCullers, Marianne Moore, Lionel Trilling, and Robert Penn Warren. The statement shifts the terms of defense from elite endorsement to democratic access, affirming that "the issue is not whether *Tropic of Cancer* is a masterpiece of American literature" but rather "the right of a free people to decide for itself what it may or may not read."[51]

No. 25
$1.00

EVERGREEN REVIEW

STATEMENT IN SUPPORT OF THE FREEDOM TO READ

We, the undersigned, strongly en-
dorse Judge Samuel B. Epstein's
defense of the freedom to read in
his historic decision in the Tropic
of Cancer case in Chicago. Judge
Epstein, by stating that the "right
to free utterance becomes a useless
privilege when the freedom to read
is restricted or denied," has put
the issue of police censorship CONTINUED INSIDE

Figure 23. Irving Cowman's cover for *Evergreen Review* issued after Grove successfully defended its right to publish *Tropic of Cancer* (1962).

Grove was unable to appeal either *Attorney General v. Tropic of Cancer* or *Franklyn Haiman v. Robert Morris et al.* to the Supreme Court; thus, while Miller's book remained a bestseller across the country in 1963, it was also unavailable in many locations, and Grove's coffers continued to be drained by litigation. Yet another of Grove's lawyers, Edward de Grazia, decided to appeal the Florida case of *Grove Press v. Gerstein*, which had been decided against *Tropic*, using the argument that the court had not yet determined "whether the Constitutional guarantees of free expression are not violated by the application of local, rather than national, 'contemporary community standards' to the question of whether a literary work may be suppressed as 'obscene.'" Further on in his petition, De Grazia clarified that the issue of national standards concerns both "free artistic expression and freedom to read," revealing his desire to incorporate Epstein's formulation into the Supreme Court's interpretation of the First Amendment.[52]

On June 22, 1964, the Supreme Court overturned the *Gerstein* decision and, in the attached case of *Jacobellis v. Ohio*, affirmed that "the constitutional status of an allegedly obscene work must be determined on the basis of a national standard. It is, after all, a national Constitution we are expounding."[53] It had been three years almost to the day since Grove had first issued *Tropic of Cancer*, and over that brief period Rosset had not only revolutionized the publishing industry but had also mobilized a cadre of publishers, academics, and artists in a successful effort to transform the cultural field itself by incorporating the literary underground into the mainstream.

Although the copyright to *Tropic of Cancer* was, as Rosset testified in the Chicago trial, "clouded," and Grove had rushed out a Black Cat paperback version in late 1961 to compete with anticipated pirated editions, the version that rocketed to the top of the bestseller lists in the early 1960s, with a copyright granted to Grove Press, has remained remarkably stable across time, and Miller's books, enormously popular and critically acclaimed throughout the 1960s, remain reliable titles on Grove's backlist. Featuring a gushing introduction by Karl Shapiro celebrating Miller as "the greatest living author," a laudatory preface by Anaïs Nin (rumored to have been penned by Miller himself) promising that his book "might restore our appetite for the fundamental realities," and issued originally with a tastefully unadorned cover, Grove's version of *Tropic of Cancer* made it into the margins of the modernist canon and onto reading lists at colleges and universities across the country, as Miller had dismissively told Rosset it would. Although Grove chose not to incorporate any trial transcripts or legal decisions into the text itself, it was able to further capitalize on the controversy a few years later when it published E. R. Hutchison's study, *Tropic of Cancer on Trial: A Case History of Censorship*, which had started out as a dissertation at the University of Wisconsin, Madison.

The 1960s were Miller's decade, as Grove was finally able to publish both the *Tropics* and his Proustian magnum opus, *The Rosy Crucifixion*. And they sold well; in June 1965, Miller occupied the top four positions on the *New York Post*'s bestseller list, and he remained on bestseller lists across the country for the remainder of the decade. *Tropic of Cancer* alone eventually sold more than 2.5 million copies in Grove's mass-market edition. Furthermore, something of an academic industry emerged around his work, as professors and critics strove to legitimate and account for his popularity. One of the more influential of these, Ihab Hassan of Wesleyan University, in his 1967 study *The Literature of Silence: Henry Miller and Samuel Beckett*, proudly proclaims, "Henry Miller, who has survived both Faulkner and Hemingway, is finally honored in his country."[54] Hassan celebrates Miller as "the first author of anti-literature," and he explains Miller's use of obscenity in illuminating terms: "In his work, the physical body of men and women is anatomized only to be finally transcended; obscenity is a voice of celebration. Obscenity is also a mode of purification, a way of cleansing human sensibilities from the sludge of dogma, the dross of hypocrisy."[55] Hassan's section on Miller, "Prophecy and Obscenity," renders Miller's work in an apocalyptic frame, illustrating that, in the 1960s, the aesthetic transgressions of the avant-garde were increasingly understood in political terms. Indeed, Hassan opens his study, which significantly twins Miller and Beckett as "the two masters of the avant-garde today," with the proclamation that "criticism may have to become apocalyptic before it can compel our sense of relevance."[56] As a member of the cultural wing of the newly expanded and diversified professional managerial classes, Hassan can be seen as a spokesman for the cadre of critics and writers that canonized the cultural coordinates of the New Left's political agenda.

The Last Master Piece

As the litigation over *Tropic of Cancer* was proceeding across the country, thousands of copies of *Naked Lunch* were languishing in the Grove Press warehouse on Hudson Street. Though the perennially impecunious Girodias was pressuring him to distribute it, Rosset wanted to wait until the litigation over Miller died down. Anticipation over *Naked Lunch* in countercultural circles had been growing since the publication of portions in the *Chicago Review* in 1958 had earned the censure of the University of Chicago administration, prompting editor Irving Rosenthal to found the journal *Big Table* expressly to publish the offending excerpts. The Post Office impounded the first issue of *Big Table*, prompting a trial whose eventual success inspired Girodias to publish the novel in Paris. Rosset published excerpts in the *Evergreen Review* in 1961, and then, buoyed by Burroughs's critical coronation at the Edinburgh Writers' Conference organized by John Calder in August 1962, Grove brought out its hardcover edition. In early 1963, a Boston bookseller was arrested for selling the book, and Rosset retained the services of Edward de Grazia to defend him. As with the earlier cases, they closely followed the precedents from *Ulysses*, soliciting an impressive panel of experts, including John Ciardi, Norman Mailer, and Allen Ginsberg, to substantiate that Burroughs's book was a "modern classic." Although the case was originally in personam against the bookseller, De Grazia had it changed to in rem against the book, ensuring that the expert testimony would focus on the text itself.

As was not the case for *Lady Chatterley's Lover* and *Tropic of Cancer*, it proved challenging to find experts who could establish an authoritative version or interpretation of *Naked Lunch*. The prosecuting attorney, William Cowin, understandably doubted that it had a structure as coherent and intentional as that of *Ulysses*. Thus, he asked the first expert witness, John Ciardi, "When he put these notes or writings, however you would refer to the book, together, do you feel that he knew what he was doing; that he was conscious that he was actually writing this book called NAKED LUNCH?"[57] After all, the first Grove edition begins with "Deposition: Testimony concerning a Sickness," in which Burroughs claims, "I have no precise memory of writing the notes which have now been published under the title *Naked Lunch*."[58] As one early critic affirmed, the challenge of the defense in this trial was to "prove to the court's satisfaction that *Naked Lunch* is a book."[59]

As in the cases of *Lady Chatterley's Lover* and *Tropic of Cancer*, Grove solicited a revealing combination of literary and sociological experts for the trial of *Naked Lunch*. In addition to Ciardi, Mailer, and Ginsberg, De Grazia retained Paul Hollander, a newly hired assistant professor of sociology at Harvard specializing in deviance and delinquency. Hollander claimed to be the first professor to offer a sociology of literature course at Harvard. Thus, his defense of *Naked Lunch* was based on sociological rather than aesthetic value: "From the point of view of the sociology of literature specifically, I think the book has merit because it presents a social type or a segment of society or subculture . . . So, in so far as the sociology of literature seeks to understand society via or through novels, this book is informative." He then goes on to clarify: "The world he presents is an underworld, a subculture alienated from and contemptuous of the norms, values and standards of society at large. People who belong to this underworld consciously or unconsciously, deliberately and spontaneously, are engaged in flaunting these standards and norms."[60] Hollander's contention that literature that accurately reflects subcultural and countercultural experience has a sociological value independent of its literary merit became central to Grove's legitimation of many of its books in the later 1960s.

In the end, neither the aesthetic nor the sociological argument convinced the judge in the Boston trial, who found the text obscene, claiming that "the author first collected the foulest and vilest phrases describing unnatural sexual experiences and tossed them indiscriminately" into the book.[61] His ruling was overturned upon appeal, but only because the US Supreme Court had, in the intervening months, clarified that a text could be suppressed only if it was "utterly without redeeming social value." The Massachusetts Supreme Judicial Court was forced to concede that "it appears that a substantial and intelligent group in the community believes the book to be of some literary significance," and therefore it could not be deemed obscene.[62]

Rosset used these expert opinions, as well as the ultimate decision of the Massachusetts Supreme Court, to leverage sales of *Naked Lunch*, as he had done with *Lady Chatterley's Lover* and *Tropic of Cancer*. In a 1962 letter to booksellers he compares *Naked Lunch* to "other famous modern classics of American and English literature—including James Joyce's *Ulysses*, D. H. Lawrence's *Lady Chatterley's Lover*, and Henry Miller's *Tropics*"—and then quotes a series of critics and authors justifying the comparison.[63] Grove also published excerpts from the trial transcript in the June 1965 issue of *Evergreen Review* and included them, along with the Massachusetts Supreme Court decision, as front matter in the Black Cat mass-market edition issued in 1966, by which time the hardcover had sold more than fifty thousand copies. By November 1966, the mass-market edition had reached number 1 on the *New York Post*'s bestseller list.

The excerpts incorporated into this volume do not include the exchanges with the academic experts who testified at the trial. They focus instead on the testimony of Norman Mailer, who along with Mary McCarthy had been championing Burroughs ever since the Edinburgh Festival, and Allen Ginsberg, without whose editorial and promotional efforts Burroughs would probably never have been published. Mailer affirmed that *Naked Lunch* was "a deep work, a calculated work, a planned work" that drew him in "the way *Ulysses* did when I read that in college, as if there are mysteries to be uncovered when I read it."[64] And Grove recycled Mailer's laudatory claim that Burroughs is "the only American novelist living today who may conceivably be possessed by genius," originally quoted on the back of the hardcover edition, for the front of the paperback.

But Ginsberg's testimony indicated the transformation that had been wrought in American literary culture in the few years since the case of *Lady Chatterley*. By now the author of "Howl," which had been the first work of literature to be exonerated of charges of obscenity based upon the legal reasoning in *Roth*, was an international celebrity with credentials of his own, which he simply affirmed by noting, "I am a poet and have published."[65] The judge clearly thought that Ginsberg, in sandals and a three-piece suit, was the only person in the courtroom who might conceivably understand what *Naked Lunch* was about, and he plied him with questions about the political and sexual themes of the text, particularly as they are laid out in the section on the parties of Interzone. Ginsberg's expertise as a poet, not a scholar, was ratified when De Grazia asked him, "Didn't you once write a poem about *Naked Lunch*?" Ginsberg answered, "Yes, a long time ago." De Grazia asked Ginsberg if he had the poem with him, and Ginsberg answered that he did and that it appears in "a book of my own that is called *Reality Sandwiches*." The judge then asked where he might find the book, and Ginsberg answered, "Probably in Cambridge." Ginsberg concluded his testimony by reading aloud "On Burroughs' Work," a poem he had composed well before much of *Naked Lunch* had even been written, affirming that both his testimony and his poetry had achieved enough cultural legitimacy for De Grazia to solicit it and for Grove to republish it as part of the proliferation of paratexts that continued to grow around this novel.[66]

Mailer's and Ginsberg's presence as expert witnesses in the trial of *Naked Lunch* indicates the ascendancy of the generation that had been educated by the literary experts who had canonized modernism in the postwar American university. Mailer had studied with Robert Gorham Davis at Harvard; Ginsberg, with Lionel Trilling at Columbia. Both writers had modeled their iconoclasm on modernist innovators while simultaneously decrying their domestication by academic critics such as Davis and Trilling. Both men, in other words, wanted to translate the subversive energies of literary modernism into the political and sexual realm. The publication of *Naked Lunch*, a text that radically combined aesthetic innovation with sexual explicitness and political allegory, seemed to indicate the triumph of this vision.

Toward a Vulgar Modernism

Lawrence, Miller, and Burroughs all ended up on bestseller lists, and Grove's net sales for 1964 came to more than $1.8 million; but due to the extensive costs of litigation, the company was still operating at a loss. Nevertheless, Rosset decided to expand and moved to larger quarters at 80 University Place. Rosset and Jordan also decided to change the format of the *Evergreen Review* from a quarterly quarto to a bimonthly, and then monthly, folio-size magazine with glossy (and frequently racy) covers and a wider diversity of advertisers, emphasizing book,

record, tape, and poster clubs, as well as cars, cruises, clothes, and alcohol. According to Rosset, he and Jordan initiated the format change because they "felt
that there ought to be a larger audience for what we were doing. We'd reached
a plateau in circulation in the small size, about twenty thousand an issue, and
nothing we did managed to break through that ceiling." The quarto format was
helpful initially because "we were able to confuse the bookstores as to what we
were. We were treated both as a book and a magazine—we got the best of both
worlds. But it kept us within a certain circle. You didn't get into the world of big,
real magazines."[67] By 1964, the colophon was well established in bookstores and
college classrooms; it was time to move on to newsstands, to take it to the streets.

In his announcement of the change to subscribers, Jordan notes that the
magazine has been redesigned by Roy Kuhlman, "one of America's best-known
graphic artists," and will feature "drawings, collages, and many beautiful photographs (in color as well) to add to its new visual excitement." Indeed, *Evergreen Review* 32 featured a portfolio of erotic photographs by Emil Cadoo that
solicited the censorious wrath of the Nassau County district attorney, garnering additional publicity for the launch of the new format (Figure 24). Jordan
continues, "To inaugurate the new format, we have put together what is without a doubt the finest, most adventurous collection of modern writing to be
found anywhere between the covers of a magazine."[68] This issue did contain
an impressive roster of writers, most of whom were already closely associated
with the magazine, including Jean Genet, William Burroughs, Norman Mailer,
Michael McClure, Robert Musil, Jack Gelber, and Eugène Ionesco. It also featured a full-page ad for a new anthology edited by LeRoi Jones, *The Moderns:
An Anthology of New Writing in America*. Although not published by Grove,
the collection features a significant number of its authors, including Jones,
Kerouac, Burroughs, John Rechy (whose *City of Night* had rocketed to the top
of the bestseller lists in the preceding year), and Hubert Selby (whose *Last Exit
to Brooklyn* Grove had just released in hardcover). The ad copy announces
that "the significance of the literary upheaval that has been taking place in
the United States over the last decade is just beginning to be realized. A new
young group of writers has been at work creating an American fiction that is
completely separate from the fashionable literary world."[69] The magazine also
features full-page ads for Yale University Press's edition of Cleanth Brooks's
study of William Faulkner, for Grove's own publication of Beckett's *How It
Is*, for Riverside Records' LP of *Bentley on Brecht*, for Paul Goodman's novel

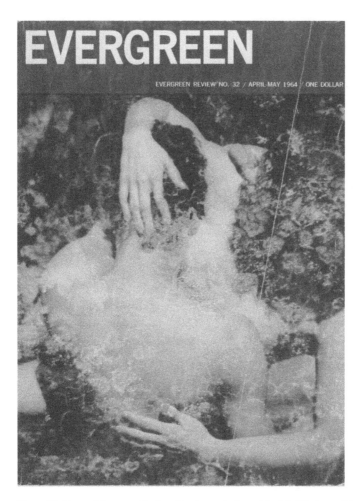

Figure 24. Cover of *Evergreen Review* after change in format (1964). (Photograph by Emil Cadoo)

Making Do, and for the *New York Review of Books*, the *Paris Review*, and the *Tulane Drama Review*, featuring a special supplement on the Living Theatre. As this ad copy indicates, by 1964 Grove had become central to the simultaneous popularization and institutionalization of modernism in the United States.

The modernism Grove promoted, as is so abundantly illustrated in the testimony at the obscenity trials of Lawrence, Miller, and Burroughs, solicited both elite and populist modes of legitimation. On the one hand, Grove relied heavily on the testimony of academic experts, depending on modernism's reputation for difficulty and complexity. On the other hand, Grove promoted the more populist proclamations of authors such as Miller and Burroughs, who were disdainful of academic expertise. The shift from freedom of expression to freedom to read, and the oscillation between literary and sociological testimony in these trials, reveals this tension, which was so central to the transitional location of modernism in the 1960s.[70] The cultural torque of this tension derived from the unprecedented sexual explicitness of these texts, which increasingly came to characterize avant-garde writing in this period. For this reason, I choose to call this developing canon of late modernism "vulgar modernism," both for its vernacular aspirations and for its erotic preoccupations. More than any other postwar publisher, Grove was responsible for putting vulgar modernism on the literary map.[71]

It was a modernism dominated by men. As the trajectory from Lawrence to Miller to Burroughs economically illustrates, Grove's battle against censorship began with a quintessentially high modernist preoccupation with adulterous women—inaugurated by *Madame Bovary* and *Ulysses*—and ended up with the highly homosocial and increasingly homosexual preoccupations of late modernist figures such as Burroughs and Jean Genet. When Grove began to publish Genet's homosexually explicit autobiographical novels, he had long been a hero to the Beats, and the popularity of his prose in the 1960s buttressed Grove's centrality to the realignment of postwar American masculinity. All of Genet's novels take place within homosocial institutions and networks—reform schools, prisons, the criminal underworld—and his overwrought stylization and spiritualization of these milieus helped provide a cultural consecration for the boy gang as dissident literary community in the United States.

Rosset had been interested in Genet since the early 1950s, but he cautiously began with the plays, waiting for a more permissive climate to bring out the far more homosexually explicit prose. Samuel Roth's publication of a pirated version of *Our Lady of the Flowers* forced Rosset's hand, and he had to proceed with publication earlier than he might have liked, beginning with an excerpt in the *Evergreen Review* in the spring of 1961. In the meantime, Bernard Frechtman had finished translating Sartre's massive study, *Saint Genet: Actor and Martyr*, for George Braziller, and Grove arranged to bring out at the same time, in hardcover, Frechtman's translation of *Our Lady of the Flowers*, with an ample excerpt from Sartre's study as an introduction. Rosset negotiated with Braziller for cooperative advertising and joint reviews, ensuring that Genet's novels would enter the United States in the existential embrace of postwar Europe's most respected and influential intellectual.

In essence, *Saint Genet* provided the "expert testimony" establishing that Genet's work had redeeming social value. And American reviewers were happy to have Sartre's philosophical help and cultural imprimatur in understanding these sexually explicit and formally difficult texts, which both celebrate and equate homosexuality and criminality as modes of aesthetic stylization and spiritual apotheosis. *Saint Genet* provided the philosophical vocabulary within which reviewers could situate its subject's literary output, framing both (male) homosexuals and criminals as "others" to mainstream middle-class culture. Genet's canonization in France, enabled by the patronage of Sartre and Cocteau, also helped reviewers situate him within a lineage of French *poètes maudites*, from Baudelaire to Rimbaud to Villon to Céline, providing further cultural cover for his sexually dissident identity. Grove continued to issue Genet's novels, initially in hardcover, over the course of the 1960s: *The Thief's Journal*, with a brief foreword by Sartre, in 1964, and then *Miracle of the Rose* in 1966. The book jacket for *Miracle of the Rose* features Genet's face framed by an iron grillwork that simultaneously suggests horns, a heart, and a headdress, an overdetermined image that distills the moral and political complexity of his canonization in the United States, where he was embraced by the counterculture and the political left (Figure 25).

Genet's novels considerably exaggerate his criminality, and it is worth remembering that the crime for which he almost spent his life in prison and for which he was pardoned by the French president in 1948, was stealing books from the quays along the Seine.[72] Many, if not most, of Genet's convictions were for book theft, which complements and complicates the circuits through which his own writing passed. *Our Lady of the Flowers* was, as Grove's flyleaf reminds us, originally written on the paper prisoners were given to make bags, and its characterizations were partly inspired by the pulp fiction Genet read as a boy. Until Gallimard published it in 1951, it was available only in limited, or pirated, editions and translations, its value inversely elevated by the criminal depths from which it emerged. In 1963, Grove's hardcover hit number 3 on the *New York Post*'s bestseller list; by 1967, it was in its fourth printing as a Bantam mass-market paperback; and by 1968, Bantam reissued it as a Bantam Modern Classic, marking Genet's successful, and indeed symptomatic, migration from the margins to the mainstream.

Grove's championing of authors such as Miller, Burroughs, Genet, Rechy, and Selby indicates the homosocial contexts in which most of the postwar

Figure 25. Kuhlman Associates' cover of *The Miracle of the Rose* (1966). (Photograph by Jerry Bauer)

struggles against censorship were initially negotiated. As Michael Davidson affirms, the literary communities that formed around the New York school, the San Francisco Renaissance, and the Beats exacted a "compulsory homosociality" that tended to exclude women but resolutely permitted, indeed required, acceptance of male homosexuality, rendering the traditionally rigid boundaries between heterosexual and homosexual orientation more fluid.[73] Davidson focuses on postwar poets, but the male-dominated author list and institutional organization of Grove Press reveal that this fraternal ordering of social relations characterized the countercultural publishing world as well. Grove embraced gay male writers and readers, publishing Spicer, O'Hara, Ginsberg, and many other openly gay authors in the *Evergreen Review*, and heavily promoted the work of John Rechy, whose semiautobiographical novels *City of Night* and *Numbers* chronicle the life of a male hustler with unprecedented explicitness. Grove's publication of these authors, and its active address to their audience during a time when homosexuality was still illegal across the United States, was a crucial component of its battle against literary censorship. Two novels,

Rechy's *City of Night* and Selby's *Last Exit to Brooklyn*, illustrate Grove's centrality to this realignment of US masculinity.

City of Night was a landmark in publishing, laying the groundwork for the emergence of gay literature as a lucrative market niche in the 1970s. Don Allen linked Rechy up with Grove in 1960 and provided crucial editorial assistance and emotional support to the young author in completing his first book. It became Grove's fastest-selling novel ever, enjoying six months on the *New York Times*'s bestseller list in 1963 and at one point selling more than one thousand copies per day. Grove aggressively pursued an international market, selling translation rights to publishers in France, Germany, Denmark, Portugal, Japan, Spain, the Netherlands, Norway, Sweden, Israel, and Poland.

Despite the novel's homosexual focus, Rechy rejected Kuhlman's suggestion that the cover feature a picture of a drag queen without title or author. As Rechy wrote to Seaver, "I want, very much, for this book of mine to be presented as a very serious work, shunning as far as possible any strong emphasis on it as a sensational exposé."[74] He further affirmed that he didn't want the jacket copy to categorize it as a "homosexual novel," writing later to Seaver, "My objection to the word 'homosexual' on the jacket is *merely* a reaction to it as much too clinical; and, really, much too explicit and restrictive regarding the book itself . . . Would 'sexual underworld' or 'sexual underground' or 'the world of subterranean sex' do just as well?"[75] Rechy's reservations situate his novel in the pre-Stonewall era, before the uprising that, among other things, made gay literature a mainstream marketing category, but they also illustrate the appeal of the underground as a cultural region in which such distinctions are less important, at least between men. Grove exploited these connotations of the term "underground" quite successfully in the later 1960s.

Rechy may not have wanted his novel to be promoted as "homosexual," but he couldn't prevent reviewers from perceiving it in those terms, nor is it surprising, given the book's focus, that they did. Peter Buitenhuis, in his review for the *New York Times*, opens by announcing, "This novel would surely not have been published as little as five years ago. Its issue by a reputable house marks how far the black hand of censorship has been lifted." But Buitenhuis sees no literary value in Rechy's narrative, calling him "an inept writer with a number of mannerisms that should have been suppressed by an editor." Rather, echoing Hollander's testimony in the trial of *Naked Lunch*, Buitenhuis recognizes the novel's sociological value, claiming it has "the unmistakable ring of candor and truth," and dubbing Rechy "the Kinsey of the homosexuals."[76] Rechy struggled against this pigeonholing, but Grove marketed him in the 1960s as a chronicler of the homosexual world. The cultural visibility of his books, and others published by Grove, provided an opening cultural wedge for the Stonewall riots of 1969, in which, as historian David Carter argues, "the most marginal groups of the gay community fought the hardest."[77]

A more aesthetically representative example of the vulgar modernism Grove helped establish in the 1960s was Hubert Selby, whose sensationally explicit *Last Exit to Brooklyn* Grove published in hardcover in 1964. Born and raised in Brooklyn and a close childhood friend of Gilbert Sorrentino (soon to become an assistant editor at Grove), Selby had little formal education but nevertheless developed a distinctive stream-of-consciousness style whose modernist antecedents were clear. Indeed, if Miller was the Brooklyn Proust, than Selby was its Joyce, and *Last Exit*, which vividly and clinically depicts the most marginal and desperate denizens of Manhattan's notorious neighbor, something of a latter-day *Dubliners*.

Explicit as it was, *Last Exit to Brooklyn* escaped censorship in the United States (though there was a landmark trial in Britain later in the decade); its unimpeded entry into the literary marketplace testifies to the remarkable transformation Grove had precipitated with the series of trials that preceded its publication. Furthermore, insofar as it positions the criminal underworld of Brooklyn against the sexual underground of Manhattan, it can be understood as an indigenous psycho-geographic map of Grove's vulgar modernist sensibilities. The reigning character in this landscape was the Queen, the central subject of Selby's second chapter, "The Queen Is Dead," which was also the lead story in *Evergreen Review* 33 in 1964. Edmund White credits Jean Genet with "the literary creation of the Queen, a creature who had existed only in folklore before Genet wrote his portrait of Divine" in *Our Lady of the Flowers*.[78] And Genet is specifically named by Selby's title character, Georgette, who "took a pride in being a homosexual by feeling intellectually and esthetically superior to those (especially women) who werent gay."[79] When Genet is mentioned, Georgette's love object, a Brooklyn ex-con named Vinnie, asks, "Whose this junay?" to which Georgette replies, "A French writer Vinnie. I am certain you would not know of such things."[80] "Such things" are precisely what made up the literary repertoire of the homosocial networks in which vulgar modernism circulated and that were in turn both chronicled and aestheticized by its principal avatars. The party that concludes "The Queen Is Dead" provides a set piece for this milieu, when Georgette recites Poe's "The Raven" to the accompaniment of a Charlie Parker record, at which point everyone at the party "knew she was THE QUEEN."[81]

The Queen's literary ascendance in the social circuits of vulgar modernism is further affirmed in the long story that forms the centerpiece of *Last Exit to Brooklyn*, "Strike," which chronicles the experiences of a Brooklyn lathe operator and shop steward named Harry during a strike at his factory. The story is less concerned with the strike itself than with the idleness the strike enables, allowing Harry to take up with a transvestite named Alberta. The contrast between the opening sex scene with his wife, with "Harry physically numb, feeling neither pain nor pleasure, but moving with the force and automation of a machine; unable now to even formulate a vague thought, the attempt at thought being jumbled by his anger and hatred," and the later sex scene with Alberta, where he experiences "the sudden overpowering sensation of pleasure, a pleasure he had never known, a pleasure that he, with its excitement and tenderness, had never experienced," reveals the utopian extensions of vulgar modernism's homosocial preoccupations.[82] These scenes, one in which a drag queen recites a poet canonized by Baudelaire to the tune of a bop saxophonist canonized by the Beats and the other in which a Brooklyn shop steward has his first experience of sexual fulfillment with a Manhattan transvestite, provide some of the contradictory cultural coordinates within which vulgar modernism briefly flourished.

And its time was brief. The principal authors Grove brought to the forefront in its battle against censorship—Lawrence, Miller, Burroughs, Genet, Rechy, Selby—received both critical and popular acclaim during the 1960s, but, with the notable exception of Burroughs, they are rarely taught or written about today. Rather, vulgar modernism emerged in the brief interregnum between high modernism and postmodernism, between the end of obscenity and the rise of pornography, as a transitional formation specific to the 1960s.

Up from Underground

In 1966, the US Supreme Court took up the case of Putnam's publication of John Cleland's eighteenth-century pornographic novel *Memoirs of a Woman of Pleasure*, which had been appealed along with *Mishkin v. State of New York* and *Ginzburg v. United States*. On March 21, Cleland's famous book was exonerated, but Ginzburg's and Mishkin's guilty verdicts were affirmed. The reasons for this split are informative. While *Memoirs of a Woman of Pleasure*, like *Ulysses* and *Lady Chatterley's Lover*, was being rescued from illicit underground circulation by a reputable publisher, Ralph Ginzburg and Edward Mishkin were pariah capitalists in the tradition of Samuel Roth, who had also been found guilty in the landmark case that bears his name. In affirming their guilty verdicts, the high court determined, in an argument similar to Earl Warren's reasoning in his *Roth* concurrence, that it "may include consideration of the setting in which the publications were presented as an aid to determining the question of obscenity."[83] The court decided, in other words, that a text's location in the cultural marketplace was relevant to determining whether or not it could be deemed obscene; if the publisher marketed it as obscene, the court would be more likely to agree. Although this "pandering" logic was maligned at the time, it was in essence an acknowledgment that the literary underground in which pirated masterpieces had circulated alongside pornographic pulp was coming to an end. Grove Press had successfully legitimated even the most explicit and graphic texts; men like Roth, Ginzburg, and Mishkin were no longer necessary.

The 1966 decision was an important step in the court's shift from an "absolute" to a "variable" definition of obscenity over the course of the 1960s, a shift that was particularly significant in the court's acceptance of a lower threshold when judging the legality of materials made available to minors. Following the logic elaborated by William Lockhart and Robert McClure in their influential article for the *Minnesota Law Review*, the court, realizing the difficulty of establishing a fixed definition of obscenity, was beginning to formulate a more flexible definition based on the audience to which the materials were directed. The most important consequence of this shift was the emergence of a relatively unrestricted "adult" market for sexually explicit materials, a market whose social and cultural legitimacy Grove helped establish.[84]

Thus, the split decision in 1966 put Mishkin and Ginzburg in jail, but it provided Rosset, whose reputation was at its peak, with the opportunity to move in on their turf, legally and profitably exhuming the entire literary underground of the modern era. Grove almost single-handedly transformed the term "underground" into a legitimate market niche for adults in the second half of the 1960s, starting with a campaign inviting readers to "Join the Underground" by subscribing to the *Evergreen Review* and by joining the Evergreen Club, which Rosset had started earlier that year as a conduit for distributing

Grove's rapidly expanding catalog of "adult" literature and film. By specifying its audience as "adult," by continuing to emphasize its literary credentials, and by concentrating its more explicit materials in the institution of a book club, Grove was able to turn the court's pandering logic to its advantage. Rosset dealt in the same wares as Ginzburg and Mishkin, but the combination of Grove's literary reputation and the restricted audience enabled by the club prevented him from suffering their fate.

In the opening months of 1966, "Join the Underground" appeared in full-page ads in *Esquire, Ramparts, New Republic, Playboy,* the *New York Times,* the *New York Review of Books,* and the *Village Voice* and on posters throughout the New York City subway system. Grove also distributed tens of thousands of free stickers to subscribers that began to appear on public benches and in public bathrooms across the country. The ad in the *Times* opens by provocatively specifying its target demographic: "If you're over 21; if you've grown up with the underground writers of the fifties and sixties who've reshaped the literary landscape; if you want to share in the new freedoms that book and magazine publishers are winning in the courts, then keep reading. You're one of us."[85] The ad chronicles how Grove spearheaded this transformation, from the court battles over Lawrence and Miller to its promotion and publication of the theater of the absurd and the French New Novel. In order to entice the audience expanded by its efforts to join the club and subscribe to the magazine, Grove offered a free copy of one of three titles: *Eros Denied* by Wayland Young, "which examines the awful mess the Western World has made of sex"; *Games People Play* by Eric Berne, the surprise bestseller that promises to "give people astonishing insights into parts of their lives they usually keep hidden"; and *Naked Lunch,* described as "an authentic literary masterpiece of the 20th century that has created more discussion, generated more controversy, and excited more censors than any other novel of recent times." The campaign was a big success, as Seaver reported to Harry Braverman: "The response by the Evergreen subscribers to the book club mailing has been overwhelming, and the full page advertisement in the *New York Times* last Sunday is going to produce at least 1500 members—an unheard of response."[86]

Buoyed by the success of the campaign—circulation for the *Evergreen Review* had nearly doubled from fifty-four thousand to ninety thousand in the first half of 1966—Jordan commissioned Marketing Data, Inc., that summer to distribute a survey to *Evergreen Review* subscribers. The survey established that, according to an article in *Advertising Age,* "the average member of the 'underground' is a 39-year-old male, married, two children, a college graduate who holds a managerial position in business or industry, and has a median family income of $12,875."[87] Jordan promptly mounted a follow-up campaign, boldly asking readers, "Do you have what it takes to join the Underground?" The ad prominently displays the survey results and then answers, "You have what it takes if you need what we've got: a collection of readers who are better educated than Time's; better off than Esquire's; and holding down better jobs than Newsweek's." It concludes, "All in all, the Underground magazine looks like it's going through the roof. Take a look at the charts above taken from our recently completed reader survey."[88] Although the promotional copy doesn't mention it, the first survey statistic reveals that *Evergreen*'s subscriber base was 90 percent male, affirming that the homosociality of Grove's literary and cultural network extended into its readership.

To these well-paid, well-educated, and predominantly male readers, adjacent to and interested in the countercultural communities that remained *Evergreen*'s core constituency, Grove channeled much of its catalog in the later 1960s, a catalog that was increasingly ballasted by pornography and erotica exhumed from the Edwardian and Victorian undergrounds. Rosset's sources for this material were many. He continued to plunder the Olympia backlist, including reissuing the Traveler's Companion series and an *Olympia Reader,* edited by Girodias, who had declared bankruptcy and moved to New York City in order, he hoped, to exploit the new freedom enabled by Grove. And Rosset bought out the entire stock of two antiquarian booksellers, the New York Bookstore in Manhattan and J. B. Rund in Brooklyn.

Rosset also purchased many titles from Phyllis and Eberhard Kronhausen, sex therapists and erotica collectors with whom he worked closely in the late 1960s (and who were affectionately known in the Grove offices as "Syphilis and Everhard"). The Kronhausens, who were prominently profiled by Sara Davidson in *Evergreen Review* 15, no. 91, published a variety of books with Grove, including *The Sexually Responsive Woman* (1964), *Walter, the English Casanova* (1967), and *Erotic Fantasies* (1969). They used their royalties from these and other books to collect erotic art from around the world, mounting a triumphant international exhibition at museums in Denmark, Sweden, and Germany in the summer of 1968. Grove published two lavishly illustrated volumes based on the exhibition.

In the late 1960s, Grove reissued in popular editions virtually every title whose publication had previously been forbidden by Comstock-era laws, thereby transforming the structure of the cultural field. In effect, Grove brought Francophone and Anglophone materials whose value had been based in their rarity into mainstream American print circulation, briefly achieving a considerable cash infusion for the company that would, in the end, only hasten its decline.[89]

Sade in America

Lauded by legendary literary luminaries Charles Baudelaire and Guillaume Apollinaire, the wildly explicit writings of Donatien-Alphonse-François de Sade had been understood as the secret subterranean source of the amorality of modernism since its inception. But Sade's work had been unavailable legally in both the Francophone and Anglophone literary marketplaces until the postwar era. Before then, Sade's unavailability buttressed his mystique: simply having read him could indicate membership in an exclusive club. As part of its effort to popularize modernism, it was inevitable that Grove would publish Sade.

Indeed, Rosset's interest in Sade went back to the beginnings of Grove, when he published a carefully sanitized selection of his writings, chosen and translated by Paul Dinnage as an "anthology-guidebook," prefaced by Simone de Beauvoir's now-classic essay from *Les temps modernes*, "Must We Burn Sade?" Published in hardcover in May 1953, Grove's selections followed Edmund Wilson's lengthy *New Yorker* article of 1952, "The Vogue of the Marquis de Sade," which deprecated the hagiographic bias of foundational Sade scholars Maurice Heine and M. Gilbert Lely (whose biography of Sade Grove later published) but praised Beauvoir's essay as "perhaps the very best thing that has yet been written on the subject."[90] Wilson declined to write an introduction for the volume but agreed to let Grove use his article in its promotional efforts. Although the more explicit sections were left in the original French, Grove nevertheless promoted the volume in its press release as "one of the first attempts to make available in English large selections of what the Marquis actually wrote."[91] Sporting an untranslated epigraph from Baudelaire's *Journaux intimes* exhorting the reader, "Il faut toujours revenir a de Sade, c'est-à-dire a l'homme naturel, pour éxpliquer le mal" (We must always go back to Sade, that is, to the natural man, to understand evil), and concluding with a chronology and bibliography compiled by Dinnage, this small volume anticipates the scholarly seriousness with which Grove published Sade in the 1960s.

In the same year that Grove issued this sanitized collection, Austryn Wainhouse, using the baroque pseudonym Pieralessanddro Casavini, published his unexpurgated translation of *Justine* with the Olympia Press. Over the next decade Wainhouse, a Harvard graduate on what became permanent leave from his doctoral studies at the University of Iowa, translated a large selection of Sade for Girodias under this pseudonym. These translations became the foundation for the massive three-volume, two thousand-plus-page edition of Sade's work that Wainhouse and Seaver, who had originally met as members of the Merlin collective, assembled for Grove in the mid- to late 1960s, after the risk of censorship had been eliminated by the successes with Lawrence, Miller, and Burroughs.

Girodias hounded Seaver for royalties on Grove's edition of Sade, prompting Wainhouse to clarify the informality of their arrangements in Paris: "I used to see Girodias almost daily, and never had need to write to him save when I was out of Paris . . . *Never* did I sign a *contract* with him. Nor did I ever sign anything that, in my opinion, would constitute a proper *agreement*."[92] Six months later, Seaver impatiently wrote to Girodias: "Til now I have refrained from commenting on your several snide and insulting allusions to my collaboration with Austryn on these two American editions of the works of Sade. But, very frankly, my patience with you and your paranoia is running thin. You have no claim to these Sade translations and you know it. If ever you had done business in a correct and ethical manner, you might have had a claim to many things; but it was your choice not to."[93] The contrast between the literary underground, in which work was frequently done for hire and copyright claims were at best clouded, and the publishing mainstream, in which intellectual property claims were codified, is well illustrated by Girodias's inability to capitalize on his early role in making Sade available to an English-speaking public.

Seaver had initially envisioned a one-volume edition, but Wainhouse convinced him to adopt the more ambitious three-volume plan. In the June 1965 issue of *Evergreen Review*, Seaver laid the groundwork for the imminent publication of the first volume with an essay entitled "An Anniversary Unnoticed," juxtaposing the much publicized 400-year anniversary of Shakespeare's birth with the unacknowledged 150-year anniversary of Sade's death. For Seaver, Sade was as important as Shakespeare, and the essay places him in the company of Baudelaire, Flaubert, Zola, Joyce, Lawrence, and Miller, as great writers whose books have outlived their initial condemnation to become literary classics and further reminds readers that "Swinburne, Baudelaire, Lamartine, Nietzsche, Dostoevsky, Lautreamont, and Kafka kept one or more of Sade's major works at hand, to read and contemplate."[94] His ultimate hope was that the work of Sade could be made available to more than these "fortunate few."

To realize this hope, Grove sent a promotional letter to selected customers offering the first volume of its collection at a discounted price with a free ten-day examination period and a money-back guarantee. The letter, signed by Alexander Rends but probably written at least partially by Seaver, calls Sade "the most talked-about, controversial, and infamous writer who ever lived" and places his work in the company of *Ulysses*, *Lady Chatterley's Lover*, and Miller's *Tropics*, as "famous classics of world literature" that have "been unavailable in their complete form to readers in this country."[95] Conceding that Sade is "one of the best known" but "also one of the least read authors of all time," Grove offers to rectify this asymmetry with the publication of its "Huge 'First American Edition.'" And, echoing Seaver's article quite closely, the letter proudly announces that it is time "to give American readers the first opportunity to make a fair assessment of this writer—the man who has been simultaneously condemned as a 'devil' and as the 'connoisseur of horror,' and hailed as 'the Divine Marquis' and 'the freest mind that ever existed.'" Possibly as a sop to Girodias, the letter offers to bundle the volume with *The Olympia Reader*, which is described as offering "scintillating excerpts from 40 books, most of which have never before been published in the United States . . . books that have had long subterranean careers and sold only 'under the counter' at exorbitant black market prices."

As this letter affirms in its detailed description of the volume's contents, Grove's edition of Sade is particularly noteworthy for its extensive paratextual apparatus. The first volume (published in hardcover in 1965 and then in mass-market paperback in 1966), which includes *Justine* and *Philosophy in the Bedroom* along with other minor works, features two scholarly introductions: one by Jean Paulhan, whose membership in l'Académie française is prominently noted on the front cover and who compares Sade's work to "the sacred books of the great religions";[96] and one by Maurice Blanchot, the French novelist and literary theorist, who makes a "discreet request, addressed to all Sade's publishers present and future: when dealing with Sade, at least respect the scandalous aspect."[97] These introductions are followed by a forty-eight-page chronology of Sade's life. The selections themselves are then followed by an extensive bibliography of primary and secondary work. The back cover quotes authors such as Baudelaire ("it is necessary to keep coming back to Sade, again and again"), Swinburne ("this Great Man to whom I am indebted"), and Apollinaire ("the freest spirit that has ever lived").

The second volume (released in hardcover in 1966 and in mass-market paperback in 1967)—most of which is taken up by what Seaver and Wainwright call Sade's "masterpiece," the wildly explicit and unfinished comprehensive catalog of sexual atrocities practiced by an incestuously constituted circle of libertine aristocrats upon a carefully selected harem of boys and girls at an isolated chateau, *The 120 Days of Sodom*—also includes two introductions. One is a revised translation of Beauvoir's "Must We Burn Sade?," which proclaims that Sade "deserves to be hailed as a great moralist";[98] and the other is Sade scholar Pierre Klossowski's "Nature as Destructive Principle," an excerpt from his seminal study *Sade mon prochain*, in which he notes that Sade's work resembles "the analysis of evil for evil's sake which we find in Saint Augustine's *Confessions*."[99] Its back cover quotes prominent American academics praising the publication of the first volume, including Wallace Fowlie ("a courageous publication"), Henri Peyre ("an event of importance in American publishing"), and Harry T. Moore ("it is highly important that we have this authentic and definitive edition"). As it did the first volume, Grove promoted the second aggressively, issuing a lengthy newsletter announcing its publication of what is called "Sade's Masterpiece—the Cornerstone of His Life Work." When Irving Kristol at the Mid-Century Book Club refused to offer it as a selection, Rosset bought the club and hired its president, Myron Shapiro, boosting the membership of the Evergreen Club to nearly one hundred thousand members. The third volume, published in both hardcover and paperback in 1968, features only the massive novel *Juliette*. All three specify on the back cover along the bottom border that "the sale of this book is limited to adults," and the hardcover editions were all offered through the Evergreen Book Club at discounted prices.

These extensive paratexts describe a migration from European to American protocols and centers of consecration. Sade begins as the dirty secret of Francophone modernism, lauded by such luminaries as Baudelaire, Apollinaire, Bataille, and Blanchot but generally unavailable to the common reader in French or English until after World War II, when Jean-Jacques Pauvert began to publish unexpurgated versions of his most notorious work. Then, with Olympia Press and the Merlin collective as a conduit from France to the United States, Grove in effect domesticated the Sadean aura, first through the herculean efforts of Seaver and

Wainhouse and then with the imprimatur of established American academics such as Fowlie and Peyre. Grove's Sade, in other words, is the inevitable culmination of the canonization of European modernism in the American academy.

He also represents the apotheosis of a belief in the subversive power of writing that was both activated and vitiated by the unopposed publication of his work. The biographical and critical material incorporated into the Grove Press volumes all emphasize that Sade did not truly begin to write until he was imprisoned and that, not unlike Genet, his obsessive writerly regime during his lengthy incarcerations can be understood as a vengeful and vindictive assault on the system that condemned him. Grove fetishizes this writing with facsimiles of his script on the endpapers of all three volumes (Figure 26). The first volume also includes facsimiles of his letters (from Seaver's private collection) as well as the order of the minister of the interior forbidding him access to "pencils, pens, ink, or paper."

This fetishization of writing correlates with a conviction about the effectivity of reading. In his account of translating Sade, published in the *Evergreen Review* in 1966, Wainhouse affirms, "Sometimes it happens that reading becomes

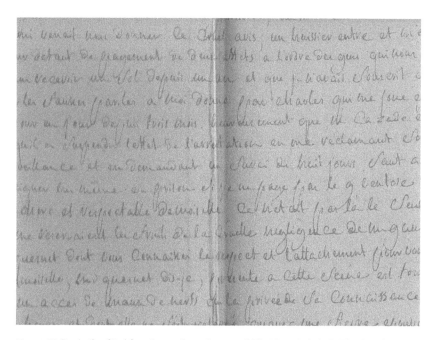

Figure 26. Facsimile of Sade's script on the endpapers of *The Marquis de Sade: The Complete Justine, Philosophy in the Bedroom, and Other Writings* (1965).

something else, something excessive and grave; it sometimes happens that a book reads its reader through."[100] In their translator's foreword to the first volume, Seaver and Wainhouse somewhat evasively elaborated: "Whether or not it is dangerous to read Sade is a question that easily becomes lost in a multitude of others and has never been settled except by those whose arguments are rooted in the conviction that reading leads to trouble. So it does; so it must, for reading leads to nowhere but to questions."[101]

In the postwar era, these questions tended to involve the metaphysical and historical extensions of the problem of evil. The publisher's preface, which follows the translator's foreword, confirms, "Now, twenty years after the end of the world's worst holocaust, after the burial of that master of applied evil, Adolph Hitler, we believe there is added reason to disinter Sade."[102] Wilson in his *New Yorker* piece had already noted that "the atrocities [Sade] loves to describe do not today seem as outrageous as they did at first,"[103] and Albert Fowler affirms that "it would be difficult to conjure up a holocaust more to the Marquis's liking than the bombing of Hiroshima or a threat more suited to his imagination than that of the hydrogen bomb."[104] Using the vocabulary elaborated by John Peters in *Courting the Abyss*, one can understand the postwar Sade as an "abyss-artist" whose entire philosophic and aesthetic program is based in moral negation, and Seaver and Wainhouse as "abyss-redeemers" who "recognize the peril of the fiery deluge but believe that (vicariously) fathoming hell's lessons justifies the risk of the descent and trust that enlightenment will follow their forays."[105] The constant coupling of liberty and evil in the proliferating metadiscourse about Sade in the 1960s situates Grove's publication of his work within the larger framework of the postwar crisis of liberalism, whose adherents had been forced by the Holocaust and the atomic bomb to face the nihilism that had always shadowed its individualist ethos and that was currently squandering what remained of its moral capital in the jungles of Vietnam.

Seaver succeeded in getting Sade's anniversary noticed in the terms he intended. One month after Seaver's article was published, Alex Szogyi reviewed the first volume of Grove's edition in the *New York Times* and opened with this paragraph: "One hundred and fifty years after his death in 1814, it is perhaps ample time for the Marquis de Sade to be welcomed into the public domain. For a world conscious of its own absurdity and the imminence of its possible destruction, the intransigent imaginings of the Marquis de Sade may perhaps be more salutary than shocking." Szogyi goes on to praise Grove's "generous, handsome, critical edition, beautifully printed with two major essays on the Marquis's work." He then concludes with the question, "May we not see his work as an immense plea for tolerance in a false and antiquated society?"[106] This oddly unselfconscious juxtaposition of an absolute evil analogous to Hitler or the atom bomb and an absolute liberty dedicated to the tolerance of any and all deviance and desire epitomizes the contradictory image of Sade that Grove propagated. Sade was simultaneously a symbol of the evil of which humanity had recently proven itself capable and the freedom toward which it purportedly aspired. Seaver perceived this paradox more acutely than Szogyi and significantly thought it could be resolved only through making the work widely available. As he notes in his *Evergreen Review* essay, "Which is he: devil or saint? Or perhaps both? Obviously, it is impossible to know until the doors are at last flung open and his works made available to more than the fortunate few."[107] This aspiration was also realized: by 1967, the Black Cat edition of the first volume had sold more than 240,000 copies.

As Elisabeth Ladenson notes in her wonderful study *Dirt for Art's Sake*, "The idea of Sade as the incarnation of liberty was to have a great deal of staying power."[108] Focusing on the popular cinematic renditions of Sade that followed the mainstream publication of his work, Ladenson concludes that Sade "has become a sort of libertine Dalai Lama, dispensing wisdom and preaching personal liberation through the shedding of sexual and social inhibition."[109] But this Sade could only emerge once he had been purged of the aura of evil that legitimated reading him in the first place. Sade entered the American literary marketplace in the 1960s as an avatar of evil, and his evil was frequently framed in explicitly religious terms. However, as Hannah Arendt's contemporaneous discourse on "the banality of evil" indicates, this religious framework was residual, and the successful integration of Sade's work into the American literary marketplace in the end diminished the satanic aura associated with it.

Open Secrets

After the work of Sade, the most notorious and voluminous example of underground literature published by Grove is the eleven-volume anonymous autobiography *My Secret Life*, which documents the sexual exploits of a Victorian gentleman whose identity has never been established with certainty. Grove had brought out Frank Harris's gargantuan *My Life and Loves* without any censorship troubles in 1963. Rosset knew that Stephen Marcus, associate professor of

English at Columbia University and associate editor of the *Partisan Review,* was devoting two full chapters of his groundbreaking study *The Other Victorians* (1966), based on his research in the Kinsey Institute Archives, to the extremely rare manuscript of *My Secret Life.* Grove eventually made extensive use of *The Other Victorians* in its packaging and promotion of *My Secret Life*—it was offered for free to Evergreen Club members who purchased the massive autobiography in the two-volume hardcover edition—and in legitimating its entire enterprise of unearthing the literary underground of the Victorian era.

As in its publication of Sade, Grove's approach to *My Secret Life* was assiduously scholarly. The publisher's preface quotes extensively from *The Other Victorians,* paying special attention to bibliographic description and detail and concluding that "in the interest of preserving the authenticity of a document of great importance, which until now has been available only to a very few scholars, it was deemed best to make as few changes as possible."[110] Grove commissioned former Kinsey Institute archivist Gershon Legman to write the introduction. One-time editor of the short-lived little magazine *Neurotica* and author of the Freudian anticensorship tract *Love and Death* (1949), Legman was prominently profiled by John Clellon Holmes in the *Evergreen Review* in December 1966 as an eccentric bibliophile, independent scholar, and stubborn adherent of the "last cause" of personal sexual liberation.[111]

Legman's introduction, which opens with the interesting claim that "bibliography is the poor man's book collecting," is forbiddingly fastidious, laying out at considerable length the little-known history of the surviving bibliographies of erotic literature and putting forth his theory that the author of *My Secret Life,* known in the text only as "Walter," was actually the erotic book collector and bibliographer Henry Spencer Ashbee, also known as "Pisanus Fraxi," whose bequest of his collection to the British Library formed the nucleus of its notorious "Private Case."[112] Grove's massive box-set, two-volume, hardcover edition runs to well over two thousand pages, supporting Legman's contention that *My Secret Life* "is not only the most erotic but also . . . the *largest* autobiography ever published."[113]

As with so many of the "underground" classics that Grove published in the 1960s, *My Secret Life* was in the public domain, and within a month of its initial release in December 1966, advertisements for another version began to appear in prominent periodicals. Rosset quickly requested an injunction against the company, Collector's Publications, whose version was a hastily assembled photographic reproduction of Grove's. Since that process spared Collector's Publications the considerable costs of assembling the text from its initial manuscript form, the court granted Rosset's injunction based on unfair competition. Grove also issued a press release announcing that it was searching for "Walter's" heirs in order to pay royalties. As in previous cases, the legitimacy of Grove's labors in producing a definitive edition trumped the tenuousness of its claims to copyright. Collector's Publications' plans to issue its own edition never came to fruition. Within three years, Grove's "abridged but unexpurgated" Black Cat edition, distributed by Dell, had sold nearly 750,000 copies.

If the publication of Sade was understood as the disinterment of the underground of Enlightenment rationalism, the publication of *My Secret Life* was understood, with Marcus's study providing authority, as the exhumation of the underworld of the Victorian novel. As the publisher's preface favorably recaps, "One of the most interesting aspects of *My Secret Life* is the way in which it relates, and adds a new dimension, to the Victorian novel." It then cites Marcus's contention that "it adds considerably to our understanding of the Victorian novel if we read it against such scenes as those represented in *My Secret Life*, if we understand that the Victorian novelists were aware of such scenes, and that their great project, taken as a whole, was directed dialectically against what such scenes meant."[114] The preface concludes by citing a review of Marcus's study affirming that *My Secret Life* "is the other side of the Victorian novel, what Dickens and Meredith and George Eliot and Thomas Hardy were obliged to leave out. And if only for this reason . . . it should be published as soon as possible."[115]

My Secret Life was widely reviewed in both popular and scholarly publications from *Time* and *Newsweek* to *Psychiatric Quarterly* and *Victorian Studies*. The *New York Times* review was written by Cambridge University professor J. H. Plumb, who confirms that Grove's publication "helps to adjust our vision of 19th-century England and Europe" but also warns that it is "only a fragment of evidence" and that Marcus "has only scratched the surface." He concludes that "in the 19th century, industrial society was creating new patterns of living, not only economic or social but also sexual. And we ought to give to the Victorians the close attention that we give to savage and primitive societies. The material abounds."[116] Over the next five years, Grove made sure that this material became available both to scholars and to the general public, bringing out an entire catalog of underground "classics" under a series of new imprints such as Venus Library, Zebra Books, and Black Circle. Between 1966 and 1971, Grove published such titles as *The Boudoir: A Victorian Magazine of Scandal,* whose back cover claims that "circulating from hand to hand, this daring assortment of exotica was at one time enjoyed only behind closed doors. Now, at last, it can be read by all"; *Forbidden Fruit,* whose jacket copy informs us that "the recent 'discovery' of an entire body of underground Victorian and Edwardian litera-ture ... has given us a new perspective on life in that luxuriant era"; *Green Girls,* which the jacket copy attributes to "the annals of the Victorian underground"; *Gynecocracy,* by Viscount Ladywood, celebrated as the "first American publi-cation of the long-suppressed Victorian classic"; *Harriet Marwood, Governess,* which the jacket copy describes as "redolent of the exquisite patchouli in the works of those unknown delineators of the strange and delicious *bizarreries* of the outwardly upright Victorians"; *The Lustful Turk,* billed as "a rare col-lector's item—a classic example of the Victorian Age's underground novel"; *A Man with a Maid,* extolled as "one of the most famous underground novels of Victorian England. An erotic classic suppressed for 75 years sheds new light on life in Victorian times"; *The Modern Eveline,* which "offers yet another fasci-nating description of life and love among the not-so-stuffy English aristocracy around the turn of the century"; *New Ladies' Tickler; or, The Adventures of Lady Lovesport and the Audacious Harry,* billed as "one of those extraordinary books from Victorian times in which the characters absolutely refuse to be unhappy"; *The Pearl,* a complete reissue of "the underground magazine of Victorian Eng-land" that "flourished on the subterranean market until December, 1880, when it vanished as mysteriously as it appeared"; and *Sadopaideia,* which "may well rival *My Secret Life* as an important literary discovery."

Most of these titles were offered at a discount in hardcover through the Evergreen Club, many were prominently reviewed, and a number of them be-came paperback bestsellers: for example, on June 29, 1968, *Man with a Maid* and *The Pearl* were numbers 2 and 3, respectively, on the *New York Post's* bestseller list. This popularity conveniently contrasted with their prior limited availabil-ity, and indeed collectibility, which Grove frequently emphasized on its jacket copy and in its promos for the book club. *The Memoirs of Count Alexis* is billed as an "extraordinary volume—limited to only 700 copies in its privately printed original edition"; *The Abduction of Edith Martin* is a "relentlessly faithful re-production of a privately published erotic classic, limited in the early 1930's to an edition of only 250 copies"; and *"Frank" and I,* one of the many flagellation novels Grove reissued, is billed as "originally published in 1902 in an edition of

350 copies for private subscribers." *My Secret Life*, of which only three known copies of the author's original printing of six were extant when Grove brought out its popular edition, epitomized this shift from private to public circuits of distribution, which transformed the publishing industry by eliminating the literary underground. Kuhlman, now successfully incorporated as Kuhlman Associates, designed the covers for most of these texts, frequently deploying illustrations from the eras of their initial publication (Figure 27).

By the late 1960s, the Evergreen Club had abandoned any pretention to literary value and became a source for anything sexually explicit that Rosset could acquire, including sex manuals, gay porn, stag films, and erotic art catalogs. Many titles were bundled, including the Olympia Five, originally penned by the Merlin collective as part of the Traveler's Companion series, as well as such imaginatively titled series as Wild Nymph Flesh (ten titles including *The Missionary's Daughter*, *Flesh on Fire*, and *The She-Slaves of Cinta Vincente*) and Strange Passionate Hungers (ten titles including *Lustmaster*, *Sorority of Submissive Girls*, and *A Hunger in Her Flesh*).

Figure 27. Kuhlman Associates' cover for *Two Novels from the Victorian Underground* (1969).

At this point, Grove was openly parodying the paratextual apparatus it had deployed in its earlier campaigns, quoting such pseudo-professionals as A. M. LeDeluge and G. Howard Guacamole, MD, who says of one title, "On the whole, I found this book instructive and entertaining. It is absolutely stuffed with redeeming social value and is a lot of laughs." The expert testimony Grove had solicited for its earlier battles had been so successful that it was no longer necessary; its form had become so conventional that it was susceptible to parody.

And Barney Rosset was now a celebrity. He was prominently profiled twice in 1969, first for the *Saturday Evening Post* in "How to Publish 'Dirty Books' for Fun and Profit" and then for *Life* magazine in "The Old Smut Peddler." Both pieces border on the hagiographic and reveal a certain paradox in Rosset's public image. If his reputation for impulsiveness and irrationality was becoming legendary, these profiles prove that he was in fact shaping his public biography—from the Francis Parker School to the Army Signal Corps to the trial of *Lady Chatterley*—with shrewd purposefulness. As Albert Goldman notes in the *Life* article, "Rosset wants to be famous and he knocks himself out to cooperate with the press," elaborating that "Rosset treats the intimate recesses of his private life as if they were public record."[117] In fact, both articles are remarkably reticent and respectful about Rosset's private life, representing him as settled and satisfied with his third wife, Christina, pictures of whom are prominently featured by both magazines.[118]

Rosset's private life meshed with his public image as a pornographer more directly than either of these profiles imply. He had a reputation as a womanizer, by all accounts he cheated on his wives, and his nighttime escapades at sales conferences and book fairs were legendary. Nat Sobel confided in me that when Christina was pregnant, Rosset got another woman pregnant at the same time, and "the two women met with their big bellies on the street and Christina knew that the child was Barney's." Herman Graf assumed that the two were swingers, stating with a big grin, "He had a great sex life" and adding that "hookers appealed to him." According to Sobel, "All the juicy stuff about Barney will never appear in print."

. . .

In his profoundly influential study *The History of Sexuality* (1978), Michel Foucault famously attacked the "repressive hypothesis," as exemplified for him by Freudian critics like Marcus, forcing scholars in the United States to rethink entirely the philosophical and political assumptions behind the struggle against censorship detailed in this chapter. Foucault almost single-handedly inverted our understanding of censorship, proclaiming that the Victorian era that we had previously seen as "repressed" in fact witnessed "a regulated and polymorphous incitement to discourse" about sex that his short study proceeds to document.[119] Yet Foucault's historical examples of this incitement are notoriously scanty and selective. Indeed, only two of them were available in English at the time his study was published: *The 120 Days of Sodom* and *My Secret Life*. Before Grove published them, it is fair to say that only a handful of readers would have had any access to these texts in any language. For Foucault, these two examples of "scandalous literature" are representative of the historical incitement to discourse, despite the fact that, as he himself admits, almost no one read them at the time they were written. *The 120 Days of Sodom* existed only in manuscript form until Maurice Heine brought out a three-volume limited edition in the 1930s, which was the basis for Grove's American translation. A mere six copies of *My Secret Life* had been privately printed by its author during his lifetime, only three of which were extant when Grove brought out its edition. These authors may have been motivated by an incitement to discourse, but their discourse had a profoundly restricted audience until after World War II. If we adjust our historical lens to understand these texts in terms of readership and access, instead of authorship and production, a somewhat different story emerges, a story less of liberation than of legitimacy. Grove moved the pornographic from the margins to the mainstream by making it legally accessible to "adult" consumers as well as professionally legitimate as an object of scholarly scrutiny. Ironically, Foucault's study was made possible by this very transformation, which, arguably, constitutes the "repressed" element of his revisionary history.

4 Reading Revolution

In 1961, Grove reprinted Edgar Snow's classic text *Red Star over China*, originally published to great acclaim by Random House in 1938, as the eighth title in its newly inaugurated Black Cat mass-market imprint. Snow's hagiographic, and ultimately prophetic, history of the struggles of the Chinese Communists had been a formative influence on Barney Rosset. When he was stationed with the Army Signal Corps in China during the war, Rosset had Snow's text with him and, based on his reading of it, felt himself to be the only American who knew that the Communists would prevail. The front matter for the Black Cat edition classifies *Red Star over China* as "one of the basic source books of modern Chinese history, as a satisfying and enlightening tale for the general reader, and even as a handbook of guerilla warfare during World War II for anti-Nazi partisan fighters in Europe and anti-Japanese guerillas in Southeast Asia." In his preface to the 1944 edition, Snow had commented on the global audience for his book, which offered English-speaking readers "an entirely new conception of Chinese character" while providing practical political guidance for resistance movements in India, Burma, and Russia. He further noted that the Chinese translation was widely pirated, with "many editions produced entirely in guerilla territory," a testimony to Mao's shrewdness in allowing Snow exclusive access to himself and the northwestern region of China held by the Communists after the legendary Long March.[1] *Red Star over China* is a rare example of a book that intervened in the historical process it chronicled, and in that sense it can be seen as a model for the "revolutionary handbooks" Grove published in the 1960s.

As civil rights gave way to Black Power, the Vietnam War radicalized the New Left, and independence movements and student uprisings swept the globe, Grove issued a variety of titles billed as "handbooks" for revolutionaries, including Frantz Fanon's *Wretched of the Earth*; Régis Debray's *Revolution in the Revolution?*; Che Guevara's *Reminiscences of the Cuban Revolutionary War*;

Robert Lindner's *The Revolutionist's Handbook*; David Suttler's *IV-F: A Guide to Draft Exemption*; Tuli Kupferberg and Robert Bashlow's *1001 Ways to Beat the Draft*; Students for a Democratic Society (SDS) radicals Kathy Boudin, Brian Glick, Eleanor Raskin, and Gustin Reichbach's *The Bust Book: What to Do until the Lawyer Comes*; Julius Lester's *Look Out, Whitey! Black Power's Gon' Get Your Mama!*; and *The Autobiography of Malcolm X*, as well as collections of speeches by Malcolm X, Che Guevara, and Fidel Castro. Like *Red Star over China*, these pocket-size paperbacks combined empirical evidence of with practical guidance for the attainment of revolutionary consciousness and the realization of revolutionary programs during a time when world revolution seemed imminent to many in the Movement.

Furthermore, in the second half of the 1960s, Grove expanded and enhanced both the investigative reporting and the radical rhetoric of the *Evergreen Review*, publishing double agent Kim Philby's revelations about British and American intelligence; Ho Chi Minh's prison poems; extensive reports on urban riots and ghetto activism; eyewitness accounts of the events of May 1968, the Democratic Convention in Chicago, and the trial of the "Chicago 8"; interviews with My Lai veterans and other exposés on the Vietnam War; and numerous articles by and about the New Left, Weather Underground, Black Panthers, and other revolutionary movements throughout the world. In these efforts, Grove sought to merge literary and political understandings of the term "avant-garde" in the belief that reading radical literature could instill both the practical knowledge and psychological transformation necessary to precipitate a revolution.

Black and White

Also in 1961, Richard Moore, chairman of the Committee to Present the Truth about the Name "Negro," issued a statement calling upon "intellectuals, writers, journalists, and leaders of important cultural and civic organizations of people of African descent to take decisive action on this question with full rather than 'deliberate speed.'"[2] Moore's call was precipitated by Grove's publication of the English translation of Janheinz Jahn's groundbreaking study *Muntu: The New African Culture*, which opens with the affirmation, "We speak in this book . . . not about 'savages,' 'primitives,' 'heathens,' or 'Negroes' but about Africans and Afro-Americans, who are neither angels nor devils but people."[3] *Muntu* had become a bestseller at Moore's Frederick Douglass Book Center in Chicago, and he hoped to speed this terminological reformation by capitalizing on its popularity among the burgeoning population of African American readers. As Donald Franklin Joyce affirms in his study of black-owned publishing houses in the United States, the era between 1960 and 1974 witnessed rapidly rising literacy rates and educational levels among African Americans, as well as increased government funding for public education and libraries in African American communities, expanding the economic viability and cultural autonomy of the black reading public.[4] Grove endeavored to provide "revolutionary" reading for these radicalizing readers alongside the principally white counterculture that made up its primary audience throughout the 1960s.

As discussed earlier, Jahn had leaned heavily on the authority of Frantz Fanon in his introduction to *Muntu*, going so far as to offer a quotation from *Black Skin, White Masks* (unavailable in English at the time) as "a motto at the head of this book." The quotation, appearing only a handful of pages after the excerpt cited by Moore, reads, "For us the man who worships the Negroes is just as 'sick' as the man who despises them. And conversely the black man who would like to bleach his skin is just as unhappy as the one who preaches hatred of the white man."[5] Although the English translation retains the term "Negro" for the French *nègre*, Jahn refers to Fanon himself as an "Afro-American" and offers *Black Skin, White Masks* as advocating the same cultural relativism that grounds his own analytical method. By the time Jahn finished *Neo-African Literature: A History of Black Writing* in 1966 (followed by Grove's English translation in 1968), Fanon had posthumously become an international icon of African revolution and Jahn felt the need to engage his work more critically. In the final pages of this highly ambitious scholarly study, Jahn, this time discussing *The Wretched of the Earth*, argues that "Fanon's analysis leaves no room for a free literature of independent writers." Sticking to his cosmopolitan guns, Jahn warns his readers that "all purely psychological, political, or sociological interpretations . . . must always remain inadequate, for they neglect the aspect which makes literature what it is."[6]

In 1970, S. E. Anderson reviewed Grove's edition of Jahn's study for the recently established journal *Black Scholar*. His opening paragraph illustrates the political and rhetorical transformations that marked the emergence of black studies in the United States: "Practically every brother and sister into a 'black thing' has read Jahn's first book: *Muntu*. Many of us without question take *Muntu* as the gospel truth on black culture. Many of us even think that Janheinz

Jahn is a brother!" Affirming that Jahn is indeed white, Anderson, a founding member of the Black Panther Party and the Black Arts movement and director of one of the first black studies programs in the nation, cautions that his scholarship, while constituting a useful resource, perpetuates "a dangerous dependency upon a white analysis of our existence."[7] Directly inverting Jahn's statement in defense of his method, Anderson affirms that "it is in the realm of social and political analysis, *not* the interpretation of Neo-African styles and patterns, where Jahn fails." Thus, he argues that "the conflict between Fanon and Jahn—and between the contemporary white critic and the revolutionary black writer—is that of understanding and dealing with the political and psychological components of black literature."[8] Anderson leaves no doubt where his allegiances lie, and while he concedes that Jahn's work should be read by African Americans, he makes it clear that Fanon should guide their political practice, as well as their evaluation and understanding of the newly renamed "black writing."

Grove published all of Fanon's major work, enhancing the company's reputation as a primary resource for revolutionary reading in the United States, and as with most of its international literature, Grove's acquisition of Fanon was routed through Paris. The English translation of *The Wretched of the Earth*, Fanon's second book but in 1965 the first to be published in the United States, was originally commissioned in 1963 by Présence Africaine, the enormously influential Pan-African journal and publishing house founded in the late 1940s by Alioune Diop, for distribution in Anglophone Africa. Like the Algerian revolution on which the book's conclusions are based, its publication was widely understood as a signal event in the proliferation of anticolonial wars and independence movements that were transforming the map of the world in the 1950s and 1960s.

The Wretched of the Earth features a preface from the ubiquitous Jean-Paul Sartre, whose imprimatur provided both cultural ballast and interpretive guidance for readers unfamiliar with Fanon's work. Sartre's famous preface, addressed specifically to "European" readers, affirms that the book is not addressed to white people and therefore must be read differently by them. In particular, Sartre exhorts his audience: "Have the courage to read this book, for in the first place it will make you ashamed, and shame, as Marx said, is a revolutionary sentiment." For Sartre, all Europeans, including those descendants who occupy that "super-European monstrosity, North America," are implicated in the colonial system that disqualifies them from membership in the intended audience of Fanon's book.[9] In its 1965 press release announcing the hardcover publication of *The Wretched of the Earth* in the United States, Grove emphasizes Sartre's advice with an affirmation from LeRoi Jones that "Fanon's book should be read by every black person in the world . . . Sartre's introduction should be read by every white person."[10]

The mainstream press took little notice when Grove brought out *The Wretched of the Earth*, with the *New York Times* restricting its coverage to a one-paragraph announcement headlined "Handbook for Revolutionaries."[11] Grove also placed ads in the *Times*, billing the book as "the handbook for a Negro Revolution that is changing the shape of the white world" and affirming that "its startling advocacy of violence as an instrument for historical change has influenced events everywhere from Angola to Algeria, from the Congo to Vietnam—and is finding a growing audience amongst America's civil rights workers."[12] But it was the iconic Black Cat mass-market paperback, issued in 1968 and eventually selling more than 250,000 copies, that came to typify this quintessentially Sixties genre. Its design both invokes and obscures Sartre's advice. The bottom half of Kuhlman's famous cover features an uncredited photograph of a riotous crowd, partially transformed into an abstract ink blot by its reduction to high-contrast orange and black. The title above is glaring white, with the author's name and the Black Cat colophon in green and the tagline "THE HANDBOOK FOR THE BLACK REVOLUTION THAT IS CHANGING THE SHAPE OF THE WORLD" in orange, linking it to the photo below (Figure 28). The back cover features Sartre's exhortation from the preface—"Have the courage to read this book"—without including the audience qualification that follows. The back cover also features a blurb Grove solicited from Alex Quaison-Sackey, the first black African to serve as president of the UN General Assembly, affirming that the book "must be read by all who wish to understand what it means to fight for freedom, equality and dignity." Grove's paratextual packaging, then, helped establish a generic category—the revolutionary handbook—that it exploited over the course of the late 1960s and early 1970s, but it also generated a contradictory discourse about the practical use of such handbooks, especially regarding the racial identities of their readerships.

For the white readers who made up the bulk of its constituency, Grove offed Fanon as a source of insight into subaltern psychology, a tactic that was particularly, and somewhat embarrassingly, evident in its marketing of *Black Skin, White Masks*, published in 1967. The front cover of the Black Cat edition, issued the following year, invokes the imagery promulgated by the popular New York run of Jean Genet's *The Blacks*: a photograph of an expressionless black

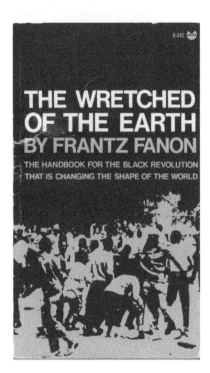

Figure 28. Roy Kuhlman's cover for the Black Cat edition of
The Wretched of the Earth (1968).

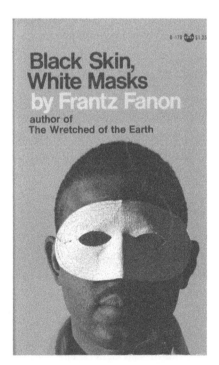

Figure 29. Roy Kuhlman's cover for the Black Cat edition of
Black Skin, White Masks (1968).

man wearing a white mask over the upper half of his face, his eyes exposed but not visible, with only the right side of his face illuminated, leaving the left side in deep shadow. The background is brown and the title black, with the author's name a lighter brown. Together, image and typography reflect the tension between abstract dualism and concrete multiplicity that tends to shadow discourses of skin-color-based identity (Figure 29). Grove used this cover imagery to imply that, for white readers, the book would expose the psychological mechanisms hidden behind the white mask. Indeed, the ad for *Black Skin, White Masks* on the back cover of the June 1967 *Evergreen Review* features a photograph of Fanon himself with a white mask, underneath which are the questions: "Why the white mask? What is he hiding? What does he fear?" The copy underneath then promises that "BLACK SKIN, WHITE MASKS by Frantz Fanon, available at last in English, gives the answers." However, this ad, as well as the back cover of the book itself, features a quote from Floyd McKissick, former national director of the Congress of Racial Equality, asserting, "This book should be read by every black man with a desire to understand himself and the forces that conspire against him." Even though the primary audience for Grove's books in the late 1960s was the predominantly white counterculture, Rosset and his colleagues were nevertheless aware of a growing African American market for revolutionary literature, and they strove to address this audience as well.

In this effort, Grove was part of a growing mainstream awareness of and interest in the relationship between reading and racial demographics that accompanied the rise of the Black Power movement. In April 1967, the *New York Times* article "What the Negro Reads" reported on a survey of the reading preferences of African Americans. It concluded that they were reading "books on civil rights, the Negro's place in history, works on the Muslim and Nationalist movements and, being practical, self-help books."[13] Two years later the *Times* featured an article more pointedly entitled "Black Is Marketable," asserting that "last year the greatest paperback sales upsurge in any given cultural category occurred with those books dealing with aspects of Afro-American experience." To support this claim, the article cites Morrie Goldfischer, Grove's director of publicity, avowing that "only those books with revolutionary themes have shown comparative increases."[14] Throughout the late 1960s and early 1970s, Grove endeavored to exploit this heightened interest, publishing, in addition to Fanon, Herbert Aptheker's *Nat Turner's Slave Rebellion*; Turner Brown Jr.'s

Black Is; Aimé Césaire's *A Season in the Congo*; Paul Carter Harrison's *The Drama of Nommo* and *Kuntu Drama*; plays, poetry, and fiction by LeRoi Jones/Amiri Baraka; and a variety of other titles promoted in full-page ads as "the black experience in Grove Press paperbacks."

Grove's most successful and significant title in this category was *The Auto-biography of Malcolm X*, which Doubleday was originally to have published. The book was already in galleys when he was assassinated, but the subsequent threats and violence gave Doubleday cold feet. Rosset was quick to step in, issuing the hardcover in an initial printing of ten thousand copies in the fall of 1965 and the Black Cat paperback in the fall of 1966. Grove put its full promotional efforts behind the book, which was widely reviewed, discussed, advertised, and read over the course of the late 1960s, despite Malcolm X's overwhelmingly negative image in the mainstream white press. Truman Nelson, writing for the *Nation*, hailed it as "a great book"; and Eliot Fremont-Smith, writing for the *New York Times*, called it "a brilliant, painful, important book." Both these phrases were prominently featured in Grove's advertisements, many of which were full page, in both the black and the white press, as well as on the book's back cover. Harry Braverman, along with Jules Geller and Grove's house counsel Dick Gallen, was instrumental in both the design and the aggressive marketing of this profoundly significant Sixties text.

In the 1993 article "Merchandising Malcolm X," Gail Baker Woods claims that "after his death, the media basically ignored Malcolm X," but Grove's campaign, and the remarkable success of the book itself, contradicts her.[15] According to Grove's sales records, the paperback had gone into a ninth printing for a total of 775,000 copies by August 1968. By 1970, Grove had sold more than one million copies, making Malcolm X's image and story familiar to millions of Americans, both white and black. It was an image and a story of revolutionary conversion, as the tagline that runs across the front cover, in white type against a black background, confirms: "He rose from hoodlum, thief, dope peddler, pimp . . . to become the most dynamic leader of the Black Revolution. He said he would be murdered before this book appeared." Below these lines, which were used in all advertising for the book, the title appears in red. The bottom third of the cover features the now-iconic UPI photograph of Malcolm X, his lower lip held tensely beneath his teeth, his forefinger pointing forward and up. The gesture's authoritative power is enhanced by the photo's position at the bottom of the cover, which makes it look as though he is pointing to the title, as well as the prophecy above it (Figure 30). In the same year, Grove brought out the Evergreen paperback edition of Fanon's *A Dying Colonialism*, and the two authors appeared alongside each other in much of Grove's promotion of the newly renamed genre of black writing in the late 1960s.

The Black Cat edition's back cover features a single quotation from the final chapter, in yellow type, which predicts, "I do not expect to live long enough to read my book." The poignancy of this prophecy is deepened by the fact that reading is so central to the autobiography itself, as Malcolm X famously begins his conversion in the Norfolk Prison Colony's library, and he remained a voracious and omnivorous reader over the rest of his short and highly eventful life. As reviewers and critics have noted ever since, this conversion through literacy placed the autobiography in a tradition of African American writing running back to the slave narratives of the eighteenth and nineteenth centuries (as well as in a longer tradition of religious-conversion narratives running back through Saint Augustine), while its heavy emphasis on education and discipline placed its subject in the lineage of American self-made men epitomized

Figure 30. Cover of Black Cat edition of *The Autobiography of Malcolm X* (1966). (Photograph by UPI)

by Ben Franklin. Thus, Grove could promote Malcolm X both as a radical revolutionary and as a more conventional proponent of self-reliance. His image fused the opposed strands of African American leadership most starkly represented in an earlier generation by W. E. B. Du Bois and Booker T. Washington; thus, his autobiography could be marketed both as a revolutionary handbook and a self-help guide.

The promotional power of this image is illustrated by the Los Angeles Public Library's pamphlet "The Bibliography of Malcolm X," a list of books Malcolm X read in prison.[16] The pamphlet sports the same photo as the Grove edition, over which is the quote, "I have often reflected upon the new vistas that reading opened to me. I knew right there in prison that reading had changed forever the course of my life." Inside is a selection of the titles he read in prison, including a dictionary, Will Durant's *Story of Civilization*, H. G. Wells's *Outline of History*, W. E. B. Du Bois's *Souls of Black Folk*, Harriet Beecher Stowe's *Uncle Tom's Cabin*, Gregor Mendel's *Findings in Genetics*, the Bible, Shakespeare, and *Paradise Lost*. It then emphasizes that "anyone who lives, works, or goes to school in Los Angeles has free access to library materials . . . some of which might change and improve *your* life. Let the power of books work for you!" The library's reliance on the Grove design for its "bibliography" confirms the degree to which Grove's marketing succeeded in representing Malcolm X's autobiography as a testimony to the power of the printed word.

During his lifetime, Malcolm X had been an enormously popular speaker on college campuses, and his autobiography's emphasis on education and self-determination enhanced its popularity in universities, colleges, and high schools across the country. Its educational sales were further boosted when it was adopted by the Scholastic Book Club. To capitalize on and enhance this popularity, Grove's education department, which under Jules Geller had recently established a separate black studies program, issued a discussion guide for the text "as an aid to a meaningful exploration of the reality of life in America."[17] Mirroring the combination of revolutionary philosophy and pragmatic self-discipline promulgated by the text itself, the guide ranges from questions about vocabulary and plot to far more radical challenges such as whether ghettoes can be eliminated "by legislation and/or revolution," or whether African Americans should appeal to the United Nations in order to "internationalize the struggle." The guide also includes a list of courses in which the book has been adopted, ranging from high school English and social studies to college courses in history, sociology, philosophy, American studies, and even business administration. It concludes with a list of recommended reading, including Grove Press titles *Malcolm X Speaks, Black Skin, White Masks, Wretched of the Earth,* and *Look Out Whitey! Black Power's Gon' Get Your Mama!* Brought out in the watershed year of 1968, when *The Autobiography of Malcolm X* was its most widely adopted book for course use, Grove's study guide confirms the degree to which it was in the vanguard of the curricular revisions that transformed American education in the coming decades.

Not only did Grove publish and promote many texts that were instrumental in the transition from civil rights to Black Power but it also tracked and encouraged this transition in the pages of the *Evergreen Review,* which became increasingly associated with the New Left and the radicalization of the Movement over the course of the late 1960s. Initially, the principal writer responsible for reporting on African American issues (and Movement politics more generally) was the prolific journalist Nat Hentoff, a regular contributor to the magazine. In November 1965, in his article "Uninventing the Negro," Hentoff reported on the three-day conference "The Negro Writer's Vision of America," held at the New School and cosponsored by the Harlem Writer's Guild, which featured James Baldwin as keynote speaker, along with panelists LeRoi Jones, Sterling Brown, Abbey Lincoln, and others. According to Hentoff, "The main, if tangled, theme of the conference [was] the need to discard the very word, 'Negro.'"[18] He organizes his article around the recurring discussion of the term, including an endorsement of its abandonment by Richard Moore of the Frederick Douglass Book Center and a summation speech by John Killens concluding that "Afro-American is a more exact and scientific description of the black American."[19]

In the following year, Hentoff contributed "A Speculative Essay," more practically entitled "Applying Black Power." Noting the need for the nascent Black Power movement to shift "from rhetoric to programmatic action," Hentoff details a variety of community programs, from neighborhood patrols to black para-unions to economic boycotts, which could effect this translation.[20] He particularly emphasizes the importance of "black students and intellectuals," reporting favorably on the formation in New York of the Afro-American Students for Community Improvement and Development. He concludes optimistically that, with effective organization, "men like Stokely Carmichael and Floyd McKissick have an opportunity to make black power so meaningful that the main question asked a decade or two from now will be why it took so long in coming."[21] Together, Hentoff's articles effectively illustrate the linked objectives of the revolutionary handbooks Grove published in the 1960s: the radical transformation of consciousness and the practical attainment of political power.

Not until 1969 did the *Evergreen Review* hire an African American as contributing editor, and for the next few years civil rights veteran Julius Lester was a regular contributor to the magazine during its final turbulent period, providing additional credibility to its reporting on African American issues. Lester was aware of the aura of tokenism that would accompany his association with a magazine owned and run by whites, and he addressed the issue in a 1970 article, "The Black Writer and the New Censorship." Opening with the sentence, "In the latter half of the sixties more books by black writers were published than in any other decade of American history, which isn't saying much," Lester affirms the degree to which the explosion of interest in books by and about African Americans was being managed and mediated by an industry dominated by whites whose identity and experience rendered them incapable of fully understanding or evaluating the literature they were publishing.[22] Without naming names, Lester proclaims that "white editors are not equipped, by education or psychology, to evaluate a manuscript by a black writer." Nevertheless, he also concedes Grove's vanguard efforts in this emergent market, noting that "the publication of Frantz Fanon's *The Wretched of the Earth* and *The Autobiography of Malcolm X* preceded the black power explosion and . . . ran interference for the books which were to come."[23]

Though most of the books Lester mentions were handled by white editors and publishers, many of them were sold in black-owned bookstores that, according to an August 20, 1969, article in the *New York Times*, were springing up all over the country in the late 1960s. Frequently modeled on Harlem's legendary National Memorial African Bookstore, where Malcolm X himself used to spend time, these stores, owned and operated by African Americans and located in African American communities, were the principal outlet in those communities for the titles discussed here. Thus, even if the publishing industry in the 1960s remained dominated by whites, the retail and reception end of the communications circuit for black writing was becoming more autonomous. Such bookstores stocked a wide variety of titles issued by both black and white publishers, but the article notes that "if one book stands out, it is 'The Autobiography of Malcolm X.' Every shop ranks it a best seller."[24] Other popular titles included Claude Brown's *Manchild in the Promised Land*, Harold Cruse's

Crisis of the Negro Intellectual, Eldridge Cleaver's *Soul on Ice*, H. Rap Brown's *Die, Nigger Die*, and Frantz Fanon's *The Wretched of the Earth*.

Lester's contribution to this emergent canon was the wonderfully titled *Look Out, Whitey! Black Power's Gon' Get Your Mama!*, issued as a Black Cat paperback in 1969. The front cover illustrates Kuhlman's creative use of typography in his design of Grove's revolutionary texts. Clearly derived from the layout of the hardcover dust jackets for Fanon, the cover of *Look Out, Whitey!* features simply title and author in crude block caps against a white background, with "Look Out, Whitey" and Lester's name in black, "Black Power's Gon' Get Your Mama" in gray, and both exclamation points in red. As on the cover of *Black Skin, White Masks*, the color scheme comments on the racially divided audience addressed by the text, with "Whitey" in black and "Black Power" in gray, simultaneously affirming and complicating the dualistic presumptions of "white" and "black" identity (Figure 31).

The back cover elaborates on the rhetorical complexities of this design, with promotional commentary by white writers in black type divided by red ruled lines with the writers' names in gray: Truman Nelson, reviewing the book for the *New York Times*, calls it "a magnificent example of the new black revolutionary writing"; Hentoff, reviewing it for the *Nation*, calls it "a book that ought to be the basis for a whole year's work in every high school in the country"; and *Publishers Weekly* recommends it as "part of the survival kit America needs to remain a viable society." In typographically playing on the rhetoric of racial identity, and in categorizing the text itself as a pedagogically structured "survival kit," these paratexts illustrate the degree to which Grove's publication of Fanon laid the groundwork for the marketing of Lester's text, which subsequently appeared alongside those of Fanon, Malcolm X, LeRoi Jones, and others in Grove's promotion of black writing. It eventually sold more than one hundred thousand copies.

A title that even more explicitly illustrates how Grove's intervention in the 1960s discourse of racial identity relied on typographical tropes is Turner Brown Jr.'s *Black Is*, with illustrations by Ann Weisman. By inverting the nigh-universal convention of black type on a white page, *Black Is* foregrounds the degree to which the opposition of black and white is implicated in the very materiality of the printed book. The cover of the Black Cat edition is, appropriately, black, with both title and colophon in white. Inside, all recto pages are black, with Brown's provocative epigrams on race relations in white type, and all verso pages are

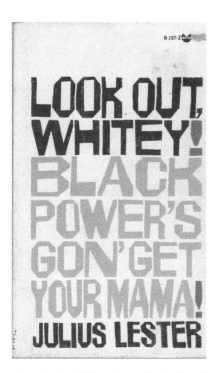

Figure 31. Roy Kuhlman's cover for the Black Cat edition of *Look Out, Whitey! Black Power's Gon' Get Your Mama!* (1969).

Figure 32. Cover for Black Cat edition of *Black Is* (1969).

white, with Weisman's illustrations in black ink. The first two pages oppose the publication information in black type against a white page with *Webster's* definition of the word *black* in white type against a black page. The definition is reproduced in full typographic detail, such that the word *black* appears in italics in all of the examples of usage. As both material object and text, *Black Is* illustrates the complex ways in which the design of the paperback book could, in and of itself, be part of the larger dialogue about racial identity (Figure 32).

Look Out, Whitey! is, by contrast, a relatively straightforward account of the historical antecedents to and causes of the transition from civil rights to Black Power in the 1960s, the central objective of which is to justify and explain its title's rhetorical structure. Thus, in the opening chapter Lester affirms, "No more did you hear black people talk about 'the white man' or 'Mr. Charlie.' It went from 'white man' to 'whitey'; from 'Mr. Charlie' to 'Chuck.' From there he was depersonalized and called 'the man,' until in 1967 he would be totally destroyed by one violent word, 'honky'!"[25] Later on, citing Ossie Davis's seminal *Ebony* eulogy for Malcolm X, which had achieved particularly wide circulation as an appendix to *The Autobiography of Malcolm X*, Lester affirms, "Blacks now realize that 'Negro' is an American invention which shut them off from those of the same color in Africa."[26] Lester predictably concludes by affirming the international alliances enabled by the terminological and political shift from civil rights to Black Power, noting that "Black Power is not an isolated phenomenon. It is only another manifestation of what is transpiring in Latin America, Asia, and Africa."[27] Citing Fanon as his authority, Lester prophesies that "the concept of the black man as a nation, which is only being talked about now, will become reality when violence comes."[28] The rhetoric of the title, then, is simply prelude to the revolution it presages.

North and South

The short-lived hope that this revolution might in fact happen was buttressed by the one that had already successfully occurred some one hundred miles off the coast of the United States only a decade earlier. Far more than the Algerian War, whose events and participants, Fanon notwithstanding, would have seemed relatively distant to many Americans, the Cuban revolution and its charismatic leaders inspired radical activists in the United States throughout the 1960s. Grove Press, in frequent collaboration with Monthly Review, became a central conduit for the dissemination of their words and images in the turbulent second half of that decade (as Rosset quips in an unpublished inter-view, "I loved the idea of Cuba. It was sex and politics, really connected!").[29] Visits to Cuba, forbidden by the State Department but frequently possible by way of Mexico or Spain, became de rigueur for committed activists and artists during the 1960s (including Richard Seaver and Barney Rosset, who, both left-handed, had to work a separate plot in the fields so as not to injure anyone with their machetes). *Evergreen Review* frequently published their accounts, starting with LeRoi Jones's "Cuba Libre" in the November–December 1960 issue, which also featured a "Declaration concerning the Right of Insubordination in the Algerian War," signed by a group of French intellectuals including Simone de Beauvoir, Jean-Paul Sartre, Marguerite Duras, Alain Robbe-Grillet, and Claude Simon. In late 1967, poet and photographer Margaret Randall reported on her "impressions, often at random" of her visit to Cuba to attend the "Encuentro con Rubén Darío" along with "some eighty other poets/critics/intellectuals from all over the world" for the *Evergreen Review*'s new section "Notes from the Underground." One of Randall's more noteworthy impressions is of "a book-store, enormous, called *La Moderna Poesia*" where she sees "books from all over the world, in quantity and quality to fill the demands of seven million people who know how to read and want to."[30] As Randall's report affirms, a central component of Cuba's revolutionary image involved both the democratization of literacy and the radicalization of the literary. Cuba modeled the conviction that reading and revolution are co-implicated.

After the revolution itself, the central event in the idealization of the Cuban model was the death of Che Guevara in Bolivia in 1967, which sparked an ex-tensive publishing campaign instrumental both in galvanizing Che's image as a romantic revolutionary and in affirming Grove's position as one of its key promulgators. As Michael Casey affirms in *Che's Afterlife*, the cover of the Feb-ruary 1968 *Evergreen Review*, which featured a painting by Paul Davis based on Korda's photograph, provided the now-famous image of Che with "its first widespread appearance in the United States."[31] Grove promoted the issue heav-ily, distributing posters throughout New York City and the rest of the country, announcing that "the Spirit of Che lives in the new *Evergreen*" (Figure 33).

This issue of *Evergreen Review* features Fidel Castro's eulogy for his fallen comrade, a reprint of journalist Michel Bosquet's report on Che's "last hours" for *Le nouvel observateur*, one of the opening chapters of Che's *Reminiscences of the Cuban Revolutionary War* (published in hardcover by Monthly Review and

then distributed as a Black Cat paperback by Grove), Che's 1965 farewell letter to
Castro (also included in *Reminiscences*), a "message" from Régis Debray along
with an account of his arrest in Bolivia, and a reprint of K. S. Karol's interview
with Fidel, also from *Le nouvel observateur*. The articles are set off as a separate
section introduced by a bright red title page featuring a reproduction of Korda's
photo above the phrase "The Spirit of Che." Below this title appears a quotation
from Bosquet's article reinforcing the self-consciously Christian iconography
of the portrait:

> If the Latin-American colonels and their Yankee advisers believe today, as *Time*
> magazine wrote a few weeks ago, that Che's disappearance deprives subversion of

Figure 33. Illustration of Che Guevara for the cover of *Evergreen Review* (February 1968).
(Illustration by Paul Davis)

much of its mystery and romanticism, they are doubtless committing the same error the Romans committed nineteen hundred and thirty years ago when they executed, together with two thieves, a Jewish agitator whose ideas eventually triumphed over the greatest empire in the history of the world.[32]

Prominently featuring the famous photo of Che's corpse surrounded by Bolivian military officials, this combination of eulogy, farewell, and reminiscence positions Che's martyrdom in explicit contrast to the dismissive reports promulgated by *Time*, here directly identified as the mouthpiece of the neocolonial forces responsible for his death. And the concluding lines of Fidel's eulogy, "El Che vive!," further affirm that "it will not be long before it will be proved that his death will, in the long run, be like a seed which will give rise to many men determined to imitate him, men determined to follow his example."[33] Grove hoped to fertilize the soil in which this seed could grow.

Toward this end, Grove published a Black Cat mass-market reprint of the Monthly Review's translation of *Reminiscences of the Cuban Revolutionary War*, Che's eyewitness account of the Cuban campaign from the landing of the *Granma* to the decisive battle of Santa Clara; and also in coordination with the Monthly Review, a Black Cat edition of his speeches, *Che Guevara Speaks*, edited by George Lavan and featuring the Davis portrait on the cover. Buttressing the rhetoric of redemption that was enhanced by his martyrdom, the concluding lines of *Reminiscences* affirm, "We are now in a situation in which we are much more than simple instruments of one nation; we constitute at this moment the hope of unredeemed America."[34] And the preface to *Che Guevara Speaks* announces that "the vanguard youth are . . . taking Che as their own: he will live for a long time to come in helping to shape the aspirations and goals of the new generation on whom the hope of the world rests."[35] Comparable to the paired marketing of *The Autobiography of Malcolm X* and *Malcolm X Speaks*, these books together promised to provide readers with both empirical evidence of and practical guidelines for the development of revolutionary consciousness. As Julius Lester affirmed in his October 16, 1967, editorial for the New York *Westside News*, reprinted the following year in the Black Cat edition of his *Revolutionary Notes* (billed on the back cover as "a book to carry to the barricades"), "Che Is Alive—on East 103rd Street."[36]

Che had kept a journal during the failed Bolivian campaign, and after his death rumors circulated widely that it was in the possession of the Bolivian military, sparking what *Publishers Weekly* called "The Che Guevara Sweepstakes," in which a variety of publishers, both mainstream and underground, scrambled to get their hands on all, or at least some, of what was briefly one of the hot literary properties of 1968.[37] As Fred Jordan recounted to me, "Everybody wanted to find the diaries, everybody. We wanted it, too." Working on a tip he received from connections he had at the Cuban mission to the United Nations, Rosset sent writer Joe Liss to Bolivia with eighty-five hundred dollars in small bills to see if he could acquire the sought-after journals. Liss was instructed to pose as a screenwriter (which he was) collecting material for a film on Che Guevara (which he wasn't). The screenwriting ruse was also the basis for the code Rosset and Liss established in order for Liss to report his progress without attracting suspicion. After a series of contretemps, Liss was able to hook up with Gustavo Sánchez Salazar and Luis Gonzales Sr., Bolivian journalists working on a book about Che's campaign, who initially suspected him a being a CIA agent. Liss was able to convince them otherwise, and they provided him with photographs of Che in Bolivia along with photostats of a small portion of the diary (which had, in fact, been scattered across Bolivia by various interested parties, making it impossible to obtain the entire document). Liss called Rosset, but they were unable to communicate effectively in the code they had established, so Jordan and Rosset flew to Bolivia to see for themselves. As Jordan further recounts, "We arrive in La Paz, and Barney disappears . . . I was furious." Eventually, Rosset and Jordan managed to negotiate for the photos and a larger portion of the journal and offered Salazar and Gonzalez an advance of twenty-seven thousand dollars on their book, which Grove published in translation the following year as *The Great Rebel: Che Guevara in Bolivia*.[38]

The risks involved in such a venture were confirmed on the night of July 26, 1968, when a fragmentation grenade was tossed through the window of Grove's University Place offices. Credit for the bombing was claimed by the Movimiento nacional de coalición cubano, which had timed the attack to coincide with the fifteenth anniversary of Fidel's famous raid on Batista's army in Santiago, but Rosset was convinced, although he was never able to prove, that the CIA was also involved. Grove continued to receive bomb threats in the ensuing months, and for a time fire engines mysteriously blared their sirens outside the offices on an almost daily basis, but Rosset, undeterred, published the excerpts in the August 1967 *Evergreen Review*. They were heavily illustrated, including a gruesome full-page photograph of Che's corpse, the tagline for which notes that "this and similar photographs are widely in demand by the Indian farmers of the area where Che was killed, to be framed and hung like ikons [*sic*] next to pictures of Christ."[39] The excerpts are supplemented by a two-page guide, "Who's Who in Che's Diary," providing names of the Cuban agents who accompanied him (which had been withheld from the official version of the journal issued by Cuba's Instituto nacional del libro), and illustrated with drawings by Carlos Bustos, the Argentinian artist arrested with Régis Debray.

Debray is an important figure in the network that produced and distributed the literature of revolution in the 1960s. His book, *Revolution in the Revolution?*, issued in hardcover by Monthly Review and as a Black Cat paperback in 1967, is an exemplary version of the so-called revolutionary handbook, and his itinerary illustrates some of the geopolitical realignments that occurred in that network over the course of the 1960s. Starting out as a student of philosophy at the École normale supérieure under Louis Althusser, Debray first visited Cuba in 1961, where he met with both Che and Castro; he traveled throughout Latin America in the early 1960s, after which he returned to France, where he wrote a number of influential articles in both French and Spanish on Cuban revolutionary strategy and the "Latin American way." In 1965, he returned to Cuba as a professor of philosophy at the University of Havana. In 1967, he went to Bolivia to join Che's campaign, where he was arrested shortly before Guevara himself was captured and killed. The Bolivian government sentenced Debray to thirty years in prison, and he became a cause célèbre around the world until his release in 1970.

Although Debray was arrested for aiding the insurgency, Grove claimed that his real crime was writing *Revolution in the Revolution?*, whose front cover bills it, citing *Newsweek*, as "a primer for Marxist insurrection in Latin America." The back cover specifies, in bold red type, "For having written this book, twenty-six-year-old Régis Debray is under arrest in Bolivia awaiting trial and a sentence that could be death before the firing squad." The front matter on the opening page elaborates that "whatever the Bolivian authorities may charge, Régis Debray's real crime is having written this book." The foreword goes on to quote none other than Jean-Paul Sartre (who had himself visited Cuba in 1960 and famously called Che "the most complete human being of our age") as affirming that "Régis Debray has been arrested by the Bolivian authorities, not for having participated in guerilla activities but for having written a book—*Révolution dans la révolution?*—which 'removes all the brakes from guerrilla activity.'"[40] Grove billed *Revolution in the Revolution?* as the ultimate crime of writing, a book that posed a threat not only to the First World powers striving to perpetuate neocolonial influence in Latin America but also to their Soviet and Chinese adversaries.

Revolution in the Revolution? partakes of the postwar realignment of anti-colonial struggle from an east-west to a north-south hemispheric axis, fore-grounding the very term "America" as subject and substance of revolutionary transformation. The book was originally written in Spanish and published in Havana, with an introduction by the Cuban author Roberto Fernández Retamar, as the inaugural volume in the Cuadernos series of the *Casa de las Americas* and with the explicit purpose of providing guidance for revolutionar-ies throughout Latin America. In their foreword, Monthly Review editors Leo Huberman and Paul Sweezy affirm that "Debray, though writing only in his ca-pacity as a private student of revolutionary theory and practice, has succeeded in presenting to the world an accurate and profound account of the thinking of the leaders of the Cuban Revolution." And they insist that, though the book was written with a Latin American audience in mind, it "represents a very real challenge to all revolutionaries everywhere."[41]

Revolution in the Revolution? was widely reviewed, and the framework within which the mainstream press presented it reveals that the idea of a "hand-book" for revolution had become an established generic category. The *New York Times* reviewed it as a "Guerilla Blueprint"; the *Nation* as a "Primer for Revo-lutionary Guerillas"; and, as we have seen, *Newsweek* called it "a primer for Marxist insurrection in Latin America." It ended up selling more than seventy thousand copies.

Even though Debray's ideas were met with varying degrees of skepticism, all reviewers agreed that the central conceptual and practical component of the book is the military "foco," the small group of guerrillas who in their very composition make up the seedbed of the revolution. The inaugural model of this utopian group formation is, of course, the eighty-two members of the 26th of July Movement who joined Fidel Castro and Che Guevara on the *Granma* for its famous voyage from Veracruz to Cuba, and the purpose of Debray's book is to prove that this model is appropriate to all Latin American countries under dictatorship. But the "foco," as Fredric Jameson has argued in "Periodizing the Sixties," is more than just a descriptive term; it is "in and of itself a *figure* for the transformed, revolutionary society to come," and, I would argue, it was in these utopian extensions that it would be so compelling to American readers during that brief interregnum in the late 1960s when world revolution, to both its adherents and its enemies, seemed historically possible.[42] While the empirical referent of the "foco" was geographically specific, its potential for replication and extension was vast and enabled any small group with enough radical fervor to consider itself in the vanguard of the revolution. As Debray himself confirms toward the end of his short book, "Fidel Castro says simply that there is no revolution without a vanguard; that this vanguard is not necessarily the Marxist-Leninist party; and that those who want to make the revolution have the right and the duty to constitute themselves a vanguard, independently of those parties."[43] *Revolution in the Revolution?* provided both ideological license and practical guidance for such self-constitution.

In a sense, Grove Press in the late 1960s was both experienced and perceived by members of the counterculture as something of a "foco," a small group of leftists committed to both modeling and fomenting a revolution. Not only did Grove have a revolutionary reputation that increasingly drew radical writers and readers into its orbit but its offices were a social nexus for Movement intellectuals, and every year idealistic young people migrated to New York City in the hopes of being able to work for Grove.

From Handbook to Reader

The author who most effectively modeled the radical possibilities of Grove's volatile nexus of aesthetic and political avant-garde sensibilities in the 1960s was Jean Genet, who became increasingly involved in revolutionary politics in the second half of the decade. Genet had, for all intents and purposes, stopped writing in 1961, and after the controversial 1966 Parisian production of his last play, *The Screens*, based on the Algerian War, he fell into a deep depression that lasted until the galvanizing events of 1968. After witnessing the suppression of the Paris uprising in May, Genet, partly funded by Grove, sneaked into the United States through Canada to attend the Democratic Convention in Chicago and report on it for *Esquire*, along with William Burroughs, Allen Ginsberg, and Terry Southern. Genet had agreed to write the article on the condition that *Esquire* also accept a second one condemning the Vietnam War. In the end, *Esquire* took the report on the convention but rejected the article on Vietnam, which was translated by Richard Seaver (who had accompanied Genet to Chicago) and published as "A Salute to 100,000 Stars" in the December 1968 issue of *Evergreen Review*.

Genet's "Salute" is structured as a poetic/erotic wake-up call to Americans mourning the soldiers killed in Vietnam. Opening with the question, "Americans, are you asleep?," Genet proceeds to evoke such a soldier's death—"brain exploded, members scattered, penis stupidly ripped off, butts in the sun"—contrasted with the family that "will hang a small star in the window of its house" in memoriam.[44] Contending that "your dead child is a pretense to decorate your house," Genet goes on to affirm that the causes of America's intervention in Vietnam are simultaneously political and aesthetic. Thus, he includes such parenthetical notes as "I think you are losing the war because you are ignorant of elegant syntax" and "You are losing this war because you do not listen to the singing of the hippies," and he concludes by encouraging Americans to remember "this line of Rilke: 'You must create chaos within yourselves so that new stars will be born.'"[45] Genet's "Salute" illustrates the persistence of modernist aesthetics in the political rhetoric of the counterculture. Even though both Sartre and Genet had condemned and abandoned "literature" as irredeemably bourgeois in the late 1960s, their political authority was still based in the cultural capital accruing to their literary reputations. Genet illustrates this persistence in his very person, as a "star" whose dissident charisma, based in the books and plays that were now popularly available throughout the country and the world, could enhance the visibility of groups participating in revolutionary struggle.

A few months later, *Evergreen* published an article that can be understood as a response to Genet's call for chaos: Jerry Rubin's "A Yippie Manifesto." Featuring a full-page photo of its author dressed as a Viet Cong soldier for his appearance at the House Un-American Activities Committee hearing to which he had been summoned, Rubin's famous manifesto affirms that "revolution only comes through personal transformation."[46] Invoking the spirit if not the letter of Debray's theory of the "foco," Rubin announces that "within our community we have the seeds of a new society. We have our own communications network, the underground press. We have the beginnings of a new family structure in communes. We have our own stimulants."[47] The Yippies' unique combination of absurdist humor and activist brio fused the political and aesthetic meanings of the avant-garde, and Grove was a central node in the communications network that distributed their irreverent calls to transformative action. In addition to featuring Rubin's manifesto in *Evergreen*, Grove published Ed Sanders's Yippie novel *Shards of God* (1970), distributed Abbie Hoffman's celebrated *Steal*

This Book (1971), and issued a set of satirical handbooks on avoiding work, making love, and beating the draft by Tuli Kupferberg.

Originally published as a stapled pamphlet by Oliver Layton Press in 1966 and then as a Black Cat paperback in 1967, *1001 Ways to Beat the Draft*, assembled by Kupferberg and Robert Bashlow, is a list of satirical suggestions for draft evasion (number 1 is "Grope J. Edgar Hoover in the silent halls of congress"; number 2 is "Get thee to a nunnery").[48] The list is interspersed with newspaper clippings, photos, cartoons, and other printed matter, both contemporary and historical, meant to communicate the absurdity and brutality of war in general, and of the Vietnam War in particular. The front cover features a World War I–era illustration of a soldier with his head being blown off by his own rifle; the back cover features a reproduction of an induction order addressed to Lyndon Johnson and signed by Nguyen Cao Ky (Figures 34 and 35). As a countercultural collage, *1001 Ways to Beat the Draft*, along with its companion volumes *1001 Ways to Make Love* (1969) and *1001 Ways to Live without Working* (1967), uses a combination of aesthetic and political tactics in an attempt to revolutionize the very structure and purpose of the paperback book.

In 1971, Grove agreed to distribute Abbie Hoffman's *Steal This Book*, a "handbook of survival and warfare for the citizens of Woodstock nation" that, according to Hoffman, had been rejected by more than thirty publishers, including Random House, Macmillan, McGraw-Hill, Harper and Row, and Ballantine. Organized into three sections—"Survive!," "Fight!," and "Liberate!"—*Steal This Book* is a surprisingly practical guide to revolutionary action, providing precise instructions for obtaining free food, clothing, and housing; setting up guerrilla broadcasting networks and organizing demonstrations; and getting first aid and legal advice, among other things. Extensively illustrated with photos of activists, panels from underground comics, and images culled from old newspapers and magazines, *Steal This Book* enacts the do-it-yourself aesthetic that it encourages its readers to replicate across the country. In its explicit address to a revolutionary subculture, it embodies the logic of the "foco" that had provided the political justification for Grove's investment in this Sixties genre.

Hoffman wrote the introduction to *Steal This Book* in jail, which he calls a "graduate school of survival."[49] It is something of an irony of history that Grove's canon of texts, including its revolutionary handbooks, ended up on the curriculum of graduate schools across the nation. In 1969, Grove issued a Black Cat paperback that anticipates this development. *The New Left Reader*,

Figure 34. Front cover of the Black Cat edition of *1001 Ways to Beat the Draft* (1967).

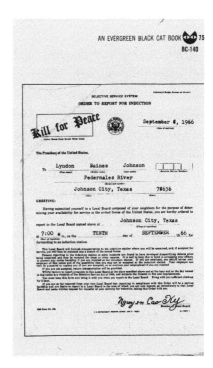

Figure 35. Back cover of the Black Cat edition of *1001 Ways to Beat the Draft* (1967).

Figure 36. Cover for Black Cat edition of *The New Left Reader* (1969).

edited by former SDS president and Movement "heavy" Carl Oglesby, features a marquee list of radical intellectuals, including C. Wright Mills, Herbert Marcuse, Frantz Fanon, Malcolm X, Fidel Castro, and Leslie Kolakowski, almost all of whom had been published by Grove in one form or another over the past decade. With the title in white, selected contributors' names in orange, and editor's name in red, against a black background within a red frame, the design of *The New Left Reader* uneasily integrates the various typographical tropes illustrated by Grove's revolutionary handbooks (Figure 36). Yet it is highly significant that this book, billed on the back cover as "for anyone who wishes to understand the complex thought behind the actions that are affecting the entire world," is called a "reader" and not a "handbook," and that, in offering the "philosophical and political roots" of the New Left, it also anticipates the turn to theory and the retreat into the university that quickly ensued.

Oglesby's organization of the anthology reflects its transitional position. Part 1, "Understanding Leviathan," includes pieces by C. Wright Mills, Herbert Marcuse, and Louis Althusser, along with excerpts from Stuart Hall, Raymond

Williams, and E. P. Thompson's *May Day Manifesto* of 1967. Part 2, "The Revolutionary Frontier," features work by Frantz Fanon, Fidel Castro, Malcolm X, and Huey Newton. Part 3, "A New Revolution?," features essays by student leaders Rudi Dutschke, Daniel and Gabriel Cohn-Bendit, Tom Fawthrop, Tom Nairn, David Treisman, and Mark Rudd, all commenting on the events of 1968, in whose immediate aftermath this anthology was assembled.

The year 1968 is, of course, a watershed in all histories of the 1960s, and it is notable that most of the figures from parts 1 and 2 of Oglesby's reader have since become canonical, but the new student leaders who contributed the materials for part 3 have, for the most part, vanished into history, providing a negative answer to the question asked by Ogleby's section title. But if Ogleby's desire to situate these student activists in the political vanguard remained unrealized, his knowledge that they represent a "new class," a class for whom figures like Althusser and Fanon are foundational, has come to fruition.[50] What *The New Left Reader* reveals in retrospect is the cultural significance of Grove's catalog for this new class. Once the possibilities of political action promised by its revolutionary handbooks were foreclosed, the political theories that informed them became required reading.

5 Booking Film

Barney Rosset had been interested in the cinema since he was a young man. After dropping out of Swarthmore College and returning to Chicago, he transferred to UCLA with the intention of studying film, only to find out that it did not yet have a film program. When his studies were interrupted by the US entry into World War II, his father managed to get him into the Army Signal Corps in China, where he became a photographic unit commander and motion picture cameraman. Upon his return, again with the help of his father, Rosset started a film production company, Target Films, through which he produced a single feature-length documentary, *Strange Victory*, on racial discrimination in the United States after World War II. Released in 1949, the film was well received critically and was shown at the Marienbad film festival in 1950, but Rosset had struggled with director Leo Hurwitz for creative control, and the film failed to recoup the $150,000 Rosset had invested in it.

In the 1950s, Rosset focused on establishing and expanding Grove's identity as a book publisher, but he remained interested in film. Starting with Amos Vogel's detailed report on the International Experimental Film Festival held in conjunction with the World's Fair in Brussels in the spring of 1958, he and Jordan ensured that developments in avant-garde cinema were closely followed in the pages of the *Evergreen Review*. In addition to regular contributions from Vogel, the review included frequent articles by Parker Tyler, whose classic study *Underground Film: A Critical History* Grove published in 1969. *Evergreen Review* also featured frequent interviews with prominent filmmakers ranging from Jean-Luc Godard to Roman Polanski to John Cassavetes. And Grove published a number of important monographs on experimental and international film, including V. I. Pudovkin's *Film Technique and Film Acting* (1960), Marie Seton's biographical study of Sergei Eisenstein (1960), Joseph Anderson and Donald Richie's study *The Japanese Film* (1960, with an introduction by

Akira Kurosawa), as well as two anthologies of film criticism edited by Robert Hughes, a professor of film studies at Hunter College and one-time president of the American Federation of Film Societies. Throughout the 1960s, Grove maintained close ties with the international cinematic avant-garde, from the *Cahiers du cinéma* in France to the indigenous underground scene in New York City, reflecting Rosset's sustained interest in the medium.

In 1963, Rosset established Evergreen Theater, Inc., to produce film scripts solicited from postwar authors. In the end, the company produced a single film, Samuel Beckett's *Film* (1964). Directed by Alan Schneider and starring an elderly Buster Keaton, *Film* was never widely released in the United States, though it did garner attention on the festival circuit. Then, in November 1966, Rosset purchased Vogel's legendary Cinema 16 library for forty-nine thousand dollars and in the next year established a separate film division for distribution, bought a theater on East 11th Street for exhibition, and hired Kent Carroll from *Variety* to oversee Grove's growing cinematic interests (Vogel also worked briefly for Rosset as film editor for the *Evergreen Review*). Also in 1967, Rosset acquired the only film on which Grove made a profit, Vilgot Sjoman's *I Am Curious, Yellow*, which became both a succès de scandale and a cause célèbre when it was confiscated by US Customs for obscenity in a case that made it all the way to the Supreme Court.[1] Energized by the film's success and flush with the cash flow it precipitated, Rosset began investing heavily in avant-garde, experimental, and documentary film from around the world, attempting to distribute titles as rentals for home viewing through the Evergreen Club and to exhibit them through film festivals in New York City and on college campuses across the country. While a number of the titles Grove distributed, including Jean-Luc Godard's *Weekend*, Alain Robbe-Grillet's *Man Who Lies*, Nico Papatakis's *Thanos and Despina*, and Nagisa Oshima's *Boy*, have since been canonized as classics of avant-garde and international cinema, Grove's film division became an economic drag on the company, as Rosset was unable to replicate the success of *I Am Curious, Yellow*. His indiscriminate investment in various cinematic ventures in the late 1960s was one of the multiple converging causes for Grove's financial collapse in the early 1970s.

Grove's film division was established in the interregnum between Old and New Hollywood, between the decline of the Production Code and the establishment of the ratings system, between the waning of the art-house scene and the innovation of the videocassette; its eclectic catalog, as well as the controversy over *I Am Curious, Yellow*, can be understood in terms of the instability of the American film industry during this transitional period. Generic and audience categorizations were in flux, as were the economic and technological mechanisms of exhibition and distribution. Grove's film division anticipated both the stabilization of the "adult" film market and the capitalization of home movie viewing before the distribution networks and technologies were fully in place for exploitation of either.

With the help of Robert Hughes, Grove also innovated the genre of the film book, producing a number of lavishly illustrated and annotated paperback screenplays for such landmark films as Alain Resnais's *Hiroshima mon amour* and *Last Year at Marienbad*, Akira Kurosawa's *Rashomon*, Francois Truffaut's *The 400 Blows*, Jean-Luc Godard's *Masculin Féminin*, and Michelangelo Antonioni's *L'avventura*, as well as Beckett's *Film* and Sjoman's *I Am Curious, Yellow*. As Richard Seaver affirms, these books were specifically conceived in response to the rising profile of cinema studies in the American university, and Grove sent them "to every film department in the country."[2] Cinema scholar Mark Betz confirms that Grove was a pioneer in this underappreciated genre, and Grove's efforts to popularize experimental cinema through the paperback book—both quality and mass market—represent its most important contribution to American film culture. The series was popular on university campuses, anticipating in a variety of ways the modes of reception and analysis that would establish these films as cornerstones of an emergent academic canon.[3]

New Novel / New Wave

The first two films for which Grove published screenplays were landmark collaborations between French writers already noted for their innovations of the New Novel and a director who became recognized, based on these two films, as a signal avatar of French New Wave cinema. *Hiroshima mon amour*, written by Marguerite Duras, and *Last Year at Marienbad*, written by Alain Robbe-Grillet, were both directed by Alain Resnais, previously known for his documentary shorts. *Hiroshima mon amour*, Resnais's first feature-length film, won the French Syndicate of Cinema Critics Award and the New York Film Critics Circle Award and was nominated for the Palmes d'or at Cannes. Duras received an Academy Award nomination for best screenplay. *Last Year at Marienbad* also won the French Syndicate of Cinema Critics award, as well as the Golden Lion at the Venice Film Festival. Robbe-Grillet was also nominated for an Academy

Award for his screenplay. Together these films foregrounded the relationship between the thematic and formal innovations of postwar French cinema and the French New Novel. Grove's print editions made these relationships accessible to examination and analysis in a manner and to a degree not possible when viewing the films, particularly in an era before the videocassette and DVD. Both titles sold more than twenty-five thousand copies over the course of the 1960s.

In the round-table discussion of *Hiroshima mon amour* that appeared in *Cahiers du cinéma* in 1959, conveniently translated and excerpted in the Criterion Collection booklet, these relationships were of central concern. In response to Eric Rohmer's opening gambit that "*Hiroshima* is a film about which you can say everything," Jean-Luc Godard responded, "Let's start by saying that it's literature," to which Rohmer added, "And a kind of literature that is a little dubious."[4] However, over the course of the discussion this "dubiousness" of the literary was qualified and, ultimately, disclaimed. Pierre Kast averred, "It's indisputable that *Hiroshima* is a literary film. Now, the epithet 'literary' is the supreme insult in the everyday vocabulary of the cinema. What is so shattering about *Hiroshima* is its negation of this connotation of the word."[5] And Godard agreed, conceding, "I think Resnais has filmed the novel that the young French novelists are all trying to write, people like Butor, Robbe-Grillet, Bastide, and of course Marguerite Duras." Ultimately, Rohmer concluded, "To sum up, it is no longer a reproach to say that this film is literary, since it happens that *Hiroshima* moves not in the wake of literature but well in advance of it," effectively placing cinematic technique in the avant-garde of literary innovation.[6]

Grove's Evergreen paperback version of the screenplay, translated from the French by Richard Seaver, confirms this film's role in changing the connotations of the term "literary" as a descriptor for the postwar cinematic aesthetic (as well as affirming the term "cinematic" as a descriptor for the New Novel). Like the Gallimard version from which it is derived, it achieves this reevaluation partly in its very publication, which, by including Duras's script as well as a preface, synopsis, and a set of appendices all written by her, presumes that the textual materials antecedent to the film's production are also important to its reception. However, the Evergreen version goes further than the Gallimard version by including seventy illustrations, selected by Robert Hughes, which foreground the collaborative dynamic between writer and director in ways that are unique to this genre. Unlike either the script or the film alone, Grove's *Hiroshima mon amour* allows the reader to examine in detail the relations between the two.

These relations are illustrated through the innovative design and layout of these paperback books. In her synopsis, Duras emphasizes that the purpose of the film's famous opening sequence juxtaposing images of the two lovers with images of the Hiroshima museum and parade is to show how "every gesture, every word, takes an aura of meaning that transcends its literal meaning," and this accretion of metaphorical meaning, achieved in the film through montage, is spatially reduplicated and, in essence, disarticulated, in the filmscript through the creative juxtaposition of image and text.[7] The images, in particular, are distributed in such a way that the page, instead of functioning to delimit or restrict, becomes a space to explore and exploit. Many of the images are unframed and off center, running flush with the edge of the page, and their positions relative to each other and the text vary from page to page, encouraging the reader to stop and contemplate the variety of meanings enabled by these juxtapositions. For example, in an early scene we see the images from the hospital and the museum, flush with the left margin of the verso page, sandwiching the image of the lovers embrace, flush with the right margin of the verso page. This visual framing of the embrace is in turn juxtaposed with the corresponding section of Duras's screenplay on the recto page:

> *(The hospital, hallways, stairs, patients, the camera coldly objective . . . Then we come*
> *back to the hand gripping—and not letting go of—the darker shoulder.)*
> HE: You did not see the hospital in Hiroshima. You saw nothing in Hiroshima.
> *(Then the woman's voice becomes more . . . more impersonal. Shots of the museum . . .)*[8]

The typographical interplay between the descriptions of the shots, rendered parenthetically in italics, and the dialogue, set off by uppercase speech prefixes, is mirrored in the juxtaposition of the images on the facing page (Figure 37). This series of juxtapositions encourages the reader to understand the literary text as antecedent to the film, to see Duras's words, which unfold with a certain poetic informality, as a set of instructions for the organization of Resnais's shots. They also allow the reader to appreciate books as supplemental to films. This supplementation became a crucial component in the emerging academic study of film, which presumes that reading film criticism and theory in book form is necessary for a full appreciation of cinematic form and meaning.

Similar possibilities are presented by the film script for *Last Year at Marienbad*, this time with more direct implications for the relation between the New Novel's predilection for description over narration and the New Wave's pre-

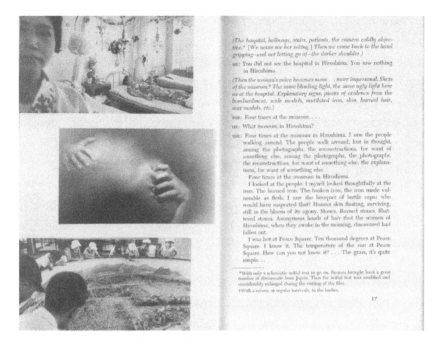

Figure 37. Layout of text and images in *Hiroshima mon amour* (1961, pp. 16–17).

occupation with tracking shots and depth of field. Roland Barthes had already established, in a foundational essay originally published in *Critique* in 1954, that "Robbe-Grillet requires only one mode of perception: the sense of sight."[9] Grove's Evergreen Original version of *Last Year at Marienbad* provides a privileged venue through which the reader can evaluate such a claim. Translated by Richard Howard from the version published by Éditions de Minuit, *Last Year at Marienbad* features more than 140 illustrations, again selected by Hughes. The very first image, a photograph of Robbe-Grillet gazing through an open set of venetian blinds, was also used for the cover of the Black Cat repackaging of the two novels (Figures 38 and 39).

These initial images of screenwriter and director confirm the degree to which *Last Year at Marienbad* was almost instantly canonized as a classic of collaboration. In the juxtaposition of Robbe-Grillet's vaguely menacing gaze, directed outward toward the reader through the blinds that divide his face, and Resnais's more relaxed pose, looking off to the left, we also see some of the tensions inherent in this collaboration, tensions Robbe-Grillet's claim obscures in the introduction that follows these images: "Alain Resnais and I were able to collaborate

Figure 38. Images of Alain Robbe-Grillet and Alain Resnais in the
Evergreen Original edition of *Last Year at Marienbad* (1962, p. 6).

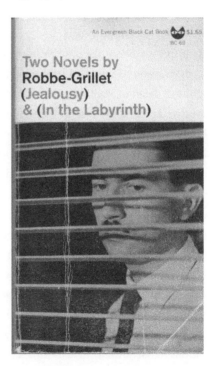

Figure 39. Roy Kuhlman's cover for the Black Cat edition
of *Two Novels by Robbe-Grillet* (1965).

only because we saw the film in the same way from the start."[10] As François Thomas affirms in his contribution to the Criterion Collection's booklet, this introductory essay perpetuated a myth of "perfect harmony" that is belied by Resnais's contemporaneous claim that, as Thomas notes, "Robbe-Grillet's writing was so precise that a robot could have directed the film by itself."[11] Grove's screenplay allows the reader to see how obsessively detailed Robbe-Grillet's writing was and how this descriptive detail, a hallmark of Robbe-Grillet's novelistic method as well, translates so effectively into the long tracking shots that characterize the film.

As with *Hiroshima mon amour*, the illustrations Hughes selected for *Last Year at Marienbad* are creatively positioned within the space of the pages, provoking a fruitful engagement between image and text that is possible only in this hybrid form. Thus, in its rendering of the long opening shot of the immense chateau's interior, we see Robbe-Grillet's precise instructions for camera movement and shot length, interspersed with X's lengthy description of the "silent deserted corridors overloaded with a dim, cold ornamentation of woodwork, stucco, moldings, marble, black mirrors, dark paintings, columns, heavy hangings," in turn framed by images correlated to this descriptive detail running along the bottom of both pages and in the upper third of the recto page, flush with the edges of each page.[12] The arrangement of the images encourages an analogy between the interior of the chateau as rendered by the camera and its description as rendered by the text. The degree to which the obsessive descriptive detail of Robbe-Grillet's novels can be correlated to the camera's perspective as thematized in the formal innovations of postwar cinema, to which Robbe-Grillet was increasingly drawn in the 1960s, becomes abundantly evident in this book, which provides a rare opportunity to perceive the two in direct juxtaposition (Figure 40). This correlation is reduplicated and reinforced by the degree to which X's opening narration, and indeed most of his dialogue, is itself obsessively descriptive and reads like instructions for the motion of the camera. Both Resnais and Robbe-Grillet claimed, in response to the many perplexed queries they received in the wake of the film's release, that the meaning of the film requires audience participation; but the book confirms that the film's form was almost tyrannically determined by Robbe-Grillet's meticulously detailed script. By making Robbe-Grillet's extensive instructions available to the reader, the Evergreen Original version of *Last Year at Marienbad* reveals how his innovations in narrative form achieve a certain apotheosis when they are translated

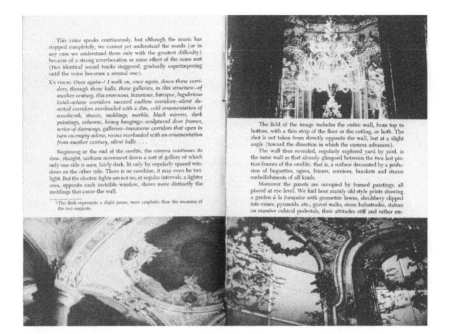

Figure 40. Layout of text and images in the Evergreen Original edition of *Last Year at Marienbad* (1962, pp. 18–19).

into a cinematic language, but it also serves to remind the reader of the written text as, paradoxically, a verbal description that precedes the existence of the image it details.

Film

Though they were able to obtain scripts from Duras and Robbe-Grillet, as well as Pinter and Ionesco, in the end Evergreen Theater, Rosset's second foray into film production, made a single film: Samuel Beckett's short *Film*, for which the author made his only visit to the United States in the summer of 1964. While generally considered a minor work in the Beckett canon, *Film* was well received on the festival circuit, garnering the Film Critics Prize at the 1965 Venice Film Festival, the Special Jury Prize at the 1966 Tours Festival, and the Special Prize at the 1966 Oberhausen Festival.

Although *Film* lacks any dialogue—it features the silent film star Buster Keaton in his last role—the Evergreen Original, issued in 1969, nevertheless capitalizes on Beckett's by-then uncontested stature as a literary auteur and provides a behind-the-scenes account of the film's production that further builds on the concept of the necessary supplement developed in Grove's earlier filmscripts. Beckett's authorship and authority are emphatically emphasized by the design of the text. Kuhlman's front cover features a pink-tinted photograph of Beckett gazing up through a strip of film (Figure 41), and the first illustration, opposite the copyright page, is of him sitting in the tiny room in which most of the film's action takes place. The text includes his complete script, which is not as detailed as Robbe-Grillet's for *Last Year at Marienbad* but is meticulous in its technical details (despite Beckett's lack of experience in filmmaking) and includes instructions for portions of the film omitted from the final cut. The lavishly illustrated script, which, like *Hiroshima mon amour* and *Last Year at Marienbad*, creatively exploits the space of the page to juxtapose word and image, is followed by Beckett's production notes, featuring a variety of technical diagrams specifying lines of sight, camera angles, and the disposition of figures within the room. These extensive technical details both emphasize Beckett as the auteur behind *Film* and establish his instructions as necessary for an understanding of its meaning. In particular, his specification of an "angle of immunity" beyond which the camera cannot move until the final scene provides a technical clue to the film's meaning, which can only be inferred from watching it.[13]

Beckett's notes are followed by an essay by Alan Schneider—already Beckett's go-to director in the United States—"On Directing *Film*," specifying his objective of achieving a "faithful translation of [Beckett's] intention," explaining why the initial exterior shots had to be omitted, and providing a detailed behind-the-scenes account of the film's production.[14] Schneider's essay, which consistently refers to Beckett as "Sam," is also illustrated with production shots that show Schneider, Beckett, and Keaton, as well as Rosset and Seaver, on the set. The final shot is of Keaton and Beckett standing side by side in the austere room, gazing at each other somewhat skeptically, Keaton with cigar in hand (Figure 42). These behind-the-scenes shots, along with the essay, illustrate the collaborative nature of filmmaking while simultaneously rendering it as secondary to the solitary act of writing. Placed as they are after Beckett's scenario and notes, and grounded in Schneider's stated philosophy of fidelity to Beckett's intentions (according to Rosset, Schneider "was obsessed by trying to do precisely what Beckett wanted him to do"[15]), these images render the making of *Film* as a story in itself, one that illustrates the subordination of collective endeavor to singular intention. If, in the many festival screenings of *Film*, Keaton

Figure 41. Roy Kuhlman's cover for the Evergreen Original edition of *Film* (1969). (Photograph by Steve Schapiro)

Keaton and Beckett in room set.

Figure 42. Behind-the-scenes shot of Buster Keaton and Samuel Beckett in the room set in *Film* (1969, p. 92). (Photograph by Frank Serjack)

frequently displaced Beckett as the center of attention, the book of *Film* corrects this misperception, firmly establishing Beckett as the literary auteur behind the cinematic product.

From Seeing to Studying

In the same year that Grove published the filmscript for *Film*, Robert Hughes became general editor of a short-lived Black Cat series of film books. Each edition features a prefatory "note" that Hughes adapted to the specific film, and each note is preceded by an epigraph from Jean-Luc Godard: "The most fantastic thing you could film is people reading. I don't see why no one's done it . . . The movie you'd make would be a lot more interesting than most of them are."[16] While the quote recommends filming people as they read, the book promotes people reading film, with Godard providing the cultural imprimatur legitimating the intellectual seriousness of the endeavor.

Hughes's groundbreaking series not only provided books about films but also revealed the degree to which the academic study of film would be predicated on a preference for the term "reading" over "viewing." His note opens by clarifying how the historically specific need for the hybrid genre he's producing illuminates this shift: "Making books from movies (apart from novelizations) is a relatively recent enterprise. But until everyone has inexpensive access to prints of his favorite movies and can 'read' them whenever he likes, this is one means toward understanding a particular film."[17] Not only does Hughes affirm that one cannot fully understand an avant-garde film through a single viewing at a theater but he further indicates that the form of attention required for such an understanding is analogous to reading a book.

However, these books are significantly different from the Evergreen Originals for *Hiroshima mon amour* and *Last Year at Marienbad*, which had fairly coherent and detailed scripts written by established novelists. For these books, "the principal text consists of a meticulous description of the significant action and a translation of the actual dialogue of the completed film rather than that of the 'final' (or original) shooting script, which often varies greatly from the final version of the film."[18] Furthermore, though Duras, Robbe-Grillet, and Beckett were all cinematic amateurs with little knowledge of the vocabulary of filmmaking, by 1969 the directors of these films were internationally recognized as masters and innovators of cinematic form, and Hughes in these books introduces a set of technical terms for camera position and movement, as well as specifies shot length in seconds. Finally, for each of these books Hughes hired a consulting editor—David Denby for *The 400 Blows*; Donald Richie for *Rashomon*; Pierre Billard for *Masculin Féminin*; and Georg Amberg for *L'avventura*—who figure as "experts" on the specific film. These consulting editors, most of whom worked in the emergent American field of cinema studies, selected the numerous frame enlargements and extensive supplemental materials that they saw as necessary to a full understanding and appreciation of each film.

The materials appended to *The 400 Blows* provide a scholarly introduction to the *Cahiers du cinéma* that was not only central to the genesis of this film and the career of its director but also to the methods and vocabulary of American film studies in its formative period. The script is followed by "A Collage from *Cahiers du cinéma*," the first item of which is the journal's obituary to André Bazin, followed by contributions from (and an interview with) Truffaut, Godard, Jacques Rivette, and Jacques Doniol-Valcroze, interspersed with reproductions of the journal's covers from the late 1950s. This section is followed by two additional interviews with Truffaut and a selection of American criticism. Both the order and the substance of the essays indicate the degree to which the American critics writing for *Sight and Sound* and *Film Quarterly* were taking their cues from *Cahiers du cinéma*, translations from which the *Evergreen Review* had exclusive rights during this period.

The form and content of these film books also illuminate how the auteurism associated with these directors altered literary models of creation and reception. The script for *Masculin Féminin* is followed by the two Maupassant short stories that Godard had been commissioned to adapt, but these stories are included only to affirm the degree to which Godard deviated from them, as illustrated by the selection of documents that follow: the first a contract between Argos Films and Robert Esmenard of the National Literary Fund, which owned the rights to Maupassant's stories, specifying that "the name of the author must always be projected on the screen and incorporated in the publicity in normal and visible lettering"; and the last a letter from Esmenard conceding that the film differs from the two stories to the extent that "no allusion to Maupassant should be made in the screen credits for *Masculin Féminin*."[19] This passing of the proprietary torch is followed by selections from Godard's "Script" (the scare quotes are in the text), the "working text" that he keeps in "a large sketch book with a blue cover."[20] This meticulous attention to Godard's written guidelines is further elaborated in the following accounts of Godard's directing methods, which specify that "the only thing the rest of the crew has as a guide, as a sort of work plan, is a thin note-book of a dozen pages or so, divided into what they call 'work sequences' . . . but when the real shooting starts, Jean-Luc Godard gets out his big sketchbook (an 8" × 12" spiral notebook with a blue cover)."[21]

The last section, "Criticism: France, England, and the United States," opens with a review by Georges Sadoul placing the film in its "proper literary category": "It is not theater, it is not a novel . . . ; like Diderot's work, it is much less a 'satirical' tale than an essay";[22] and it closes with Pauline Kael's review for the *New Republic*, which comments on the degree to which the characters in the film are Americanized in a way that makes them part of "an international society; they have the beauty of youth which can endow Pop with poetry."[23] There are thus two narrative arcs that structure the paratextual materials following the script of *Masculin Féminin*: one running from its literary antecedents to its cinematic results, and one running from its French to American critical reception. The two arcs form a larger story of what one might call, borrowing from Pascale Casanova, the *littérisation* of avant-garde cinema, which was a necessary precondition to its academic canonization. This Parisian *littérisation* is both illustrated and exemplified by these film books, a hybrid and transitional genre that provides a unique insight into the process whereby films were presented as texts that needed to be read both closely and repeatedly and whose difficulty requires reading other supplemental materials to be fully understood.

Though sales were modest, the series was nevertheless influential. *Film Quarterly* called the texts "the best recreations of films yet to be achieved in book form" (an accolade that Grove prominently displayed in its promotion of the series), adding that they "will probably be surpassed only when 8mm or EVR copies of films are available for home use and study." Until then, the review concludes, they "should prove extremely useful in film classes and for scholars working on close studies of film style."[24] For many scholars and students at the time, particularly those who didn't live in major metropolitan centers, these books would have been their first contact with these films. As critic and film scholar Adrian Martin notes in his essay for the Criterion Collection booklet on *Masculin Féminin*, the film initially "existed entirely in my head—as a perfectly imaginary object, a little like the ideal movie that Paul (Léaud) himself 'secretly wanted to live'—thanks to the fact that my only access to it at the time was through a gorgeous fetish object published by America's Grove Press, in 1969, a transcription of the film accompanied by many luminous frame reproductions."[25] Martin's essay is followed by an excerpt from Philippe Labro's "One Evening in a Small Café," an account of Godard's direction that also forms part of the Black Cat edition. Thus, the Black Cat film series anticipates both the form and function of the Criterion Collection DVDs with their special features and accompanying booklets. Indeed, the technology of the DVD itself, which enables the viewer to freeze individual frames and to move in and out of the film at any point and for any length of time, digitally realizes the form of "reading" to which Grove's series aspires.

Mark Betz affirms that these books, and others like them, were "instrumental in shaping academic film studies as it was forming in North America and later on in Britain," but he is mainly interested in how they "provided the mortar for film course organization" and less in how their physical design solicited ways of reading and reception that in effect Americanized the Parisian *littérisation* of avant-garde film during the heyday of auteurism.[26] Grove's pioneering series provided a curriculum for film studies courses during this foundational period; it also helped establish the cinematic text as a legitimate object of close reading modeled on the formal analysis of literary texts. This literary legitimacy was crucial to the cultural consecration of these cinematic texts, as illustrated by their inclusion in the Criterion Collection canon, whose design clearly derives from the series that anticipated them. Though this literary legitimacy was initially established in Paris, it was mass-produced and made academically operational by Grove's short-lived book series.

For Rosset, Grove's film books were part of a larger plan to exploit and promote academic interest in contemporary cinema through rental and festival programs. Grove's 1968 college catalog includes many films, and the suggested courses feature "imaginative combinations of books and films along interdisciplinary lines."[27] Thus, the catalog suggests using William Klein's *Mr. Freedom* and Kenneth Anger's *Scorpio Rising* in a course called "The Absurd as Reality"; Ousmane Sembene's *Mandabi* and Lionel Rogosin's *Come Back Africa* in "Africa—Culture and Myths"; Klein's *Float like a Butterfly, Sting like a Bee* and Agnes Varda's *Black Panthers: A Report* in "To Be Black in America"; and Yukio Mishima's *Rite of Love and Death* and Nagisa Oshima's *Boy* in "The New Japan." To facilitate this interdisciplinary and multimedia vision, Grove offered discounted rental rates to educational institutions.

Grove also promoted campus film festivals as a way to get its rapidly expanding catalog screened outside New York City. In a prominent full-page ad in the December 1969 *Evergreen Review* featuring college students sporting a sign asking, "Why wait for Godard? We want him *Now!*," readers are invited to "Bring Grove's Film Festival to Antioch or Ann Arbor, Oberlin, you name it!" The copy continues, "Now you can have your own film festival, right on your own campus. With films like Jean-Luc Godard's *Weekend*, Susan Sontag's *Duet for Cannibals*, Jaromil Jires' *The Joke*, Glauber Rocha's *Antonio das Mortes*, William Klein's *Mr. Freedom*, Ousmane Sembene's *Mandabe*. Films that have won awards in Cannes, Venice, and Berlin, and have brought audiences to their feet at the New York and San Francisco Film Festivals."[28] Rosset hoped to achieve with the cinematic avant-garde what he had already accomplished with the literary avant-garde: disseminate it from the exclusive culture capitals of Europe and the United States into university towns across the country. But the logistics of film distribution were expensive, and they did not align with the circuits Grove had established for books; the film division ended up being both a distraction for Rosset and a significant drain on the company's capital. As Kent Carroll affirms, the film division "was like a giant sponge soaking up everything, and detracting from the publishing side of the business."[29]

For Adults Only

In the end, Grove made money on a single film: Vilgot Sjoman's *I Am Curious, Yellow*. Rosset had read about the film by the Ingmar Bergman protégé in the *Manchester Guardian* during his annual trip to the Frankfurt Book Fair in 1967. Intrigued by its purported combination of sexual frankness and political critique, Rosset asked the president of the Swedish publisher Bonnier to put him in touch with the film's producer. He then asked Phyllis and Eberhard Kronhausen, who were in Europe collecting materials for their International Exhibition of Erotic Art, to view it. After receiving a positive report from the Kronhausens, he went to see the film himself, liked it, and promptly purchased the rights to distribute it in the United States.[30] Sjoman had already released two controversial films in the United States: *My Sister, My Love*, a story of sibling incest promoted "for those who love and those who make love!"; and *491*, based on Lars Gorling's novel (published, of course, by Grove Press) about seven delinquent boys who agree, as part of a psychological experiment, to live alone in a condemned building. The film *491* was charged with and then exonerated of obscenity in 1966. *I Am Curious, Yellow* was seized by US Customs in January 1968, and Grove had to arrange for critics, including Bosley Crowther for the *Times*, Stanley Kauffman and Richard Gilman for the *New Republic*, Andrew Sarris for the *Voice*, and Amos Vogel for Lincoln Center, to view it at the United States Appraisers Stores in New York City under an agreement that they would not "publicize the contents." These same critics, along with Norman Mailer, sociology professors Charles Winick and Ned Polsky, and Sjoman himself, were witnesses at the subsequent trial in May. A jury of seven men and five women found the film to be obscene, and while waiting for the case to be reviewed by the court of appeals, Grove issued a Black Cat paperback filmscript with more than 250 illustrations and extensive excerpts from the trial testimony. In February 1969, by which time the court of appeals had overturned the lower court's decision, the *Times* listed the filmscript as having sold 160,000 copies in the prior year, indicating that it was an integral component of the campaign that precipitated the phenomenal popularity of the film, which for the rest of the year was shown to packed houses by reservation only at the Evergreen Theater on East 11th Street and generated lines around the block for its continuous showing (seven times a day) at the Cinema Rendezvous on 57th Street. The film was widely reviewed and discussed, and Rosset aggressively pursued screenings across the country, retaining De Grazia to supervise the numerous legal challenges, and at one point going so far as to purchase an entire theater in Minneapolis when he couldn't find an exhibitor willing to show it. By September 1969, the film had made more than $5 million across the country, with Grove remunerating local civil liberties lawyers who defended against the numerous obscenity charges with a percentage of the box office receipts. In November 1969, it became the first foreign-language film to top *Variety*'s list of the top-grossing films. It ultimately earned more than $14 million.

Updating and interrogating the thematic tradition running back through Emma Bovary and Constance Chatterley, *I Am Curious, Yellow* focuses on the sexual experiences of a young woman, Lena Nyman, through the eyes of her older male creator, in this case the director Vilgot Sjoman. Both director and actress play themselves, providing the film with the self-reflexivity and ironic auto-commentary so common to avant-garde cinema and drama of the 1960s. Though tame by today's standards, even for mainstream R-rated film, the movie's sexual scenes, which included male full-frontal nudity, an extremely brief and fleeting kiss of a limp penis, and a number of simulated acts of intercourse in public places, including in front of Stockholm's Royal Palace, generated extensive controversy. The film also attempts, in ways that were central to its defense at trial, to thematically and formally relate sexual to political revolution, interweaving Lena's sexual experimentation with her political agitation against the Swedish class system and the war in Vietnam. In providing extensive testimony from the trial, Grove's Black Cat version is clearly designed to establish that the political themes of the film provide the redeeming social value justifying the sex scenes at a time when the film itself was still working its way through the appeals process.

The sale of the book, as well as admission to the film, which had been rated "X" by Jack Valenti's recently established Motion Picture Association of America, was limited to adults. *I Am Curious, Yellow* came out during, and in many ways was symptomatic of, the interregnum between the decline of the Production Code and the codification of the ratings system, an interregnum that also enabled the overlap between avant-garde and pornographic cinema exemplified by Grove's catalog as a whole. As Jon Lewis establishes in *Hollywood v. Hard Core*, during the first years of the ratings system there was extensive debate about which films should be designated with an "X" rating, which in that same year was given to, or independently chosen for, such films as Lindsay Anderson's *If*, Dennis Hopper's *Easy Rider*, and John Schlesinger's *Midnight Cowboy* (which won Academy Awards for Best Picture, Best Director, and Best Screenplay in 1970).[31] Eventually, Valenti's decision not to copyright the "X" designation resulted in its appropriation by the emerging hard-core industry, eliminating the inchoate cultural zone these films occupied at the time.

Rosset anticipated, though he did not in the end profit from, this transition. As Albert Goldman reveals in his *Life* magazine profile of August 29, 1969, "The Old Smut Peddler," Rosset foresaw the privatization of film viewing that would enable the pornographic market to consolidate legally:

> It's time to scale the movies down to human proportions. The moving picture camera today is just a very expensive typewriter. A Hollywood director can go home, like the young writer used to go home from the ad agency, and knock out a very good movie for $50,000. It's possible to take that movie and squeeze it into a cassette videotape the size of a book. And then one evening, when the kids are in bed, you can slip that cassette into your TV set and, without getting dressed or driving the car, you can watch *Tropic of Cancer* or *The Story of O* right in your own living room—where the censor can't go.[32]

First anticipating and then capitalizing on the Supreme Court rulings in *Stanley v. Georgia* (1969), which had made it legal to view hard-core pornography in the privacy of one's home, and in *Ginsberg v. New York* (1968), which had affirmed a lower legal threshold for determining obscenity with materials made available to minors, Rosset attempted to realize this vision through the now-notorious Evergreen Club. As with his forays into print pornography, Rosset cast a wide net, acquiring any and all erotic films he could find and offering them for sale and rental through the club. One promotional brochure trumpets, "Now you can have a nostalgic 'blue film' festival right in the privacy of your own den or living room!" Claiming to have "picked these films from the largest private collection of its kind," Rosset offers in the brochure such titles as *Broadway through a Keyhole, Sultan and Slaves,* and *Flaming Youth,* claiming they can provide "a unique look at the customs and morals of a never to be forgotten time."[33] Another letter promoting a film called *L* announces, "In the secret collections of Europe's Millionaire Connoisseurs of Erotica, there are films so provocative, so incredibly earthy, the average collector can't even begin to imagine what they are like."[34] Yet another boasts that "the most famous actress of our time will 'go all the way' for you—in your own room!"[35] Grove deployed the same populist rhetoric with film as it did with print, advertising that materials previously reserved for wealthy elites were now being made available through legitimate mainstream channels.

These promotions anticipate with uncanny accuracy the direction the mainstream porn industry would take in the 1970s and 1980s, as videocassettes, DVDs, and then the Internet drove down the costs of production and enabled a privatization of consumption that made pornography into a legitimate industry leveraging the "X" rating to market its materials to an adult, and mostly male, audience. Indeed, Rosset's forays into pornography—particularly cinematic pornography—generated a political backlash against Grove that helps account for how and why this industry autonomized in the 1970s, leaving Grove as a relic of a former era before the consolidation of a separate "adult" marketplace.

6 Takeover

By the second half of the 1960s, Grove had become profitable, partly through its well-established connections to the booming academic market and the burgeoning counterculture, but mostly through its highly successful campaigns to legitimate and popularize sexually explicit writing and film. To expand on and exploit this profitability, Rosset decided in 1967 to take the company public with an initial public offering (IPO) of 240,000 shares at seven dollars each. The prospectus circulated for the IPO, issued by Van Alstyne, Noel, and Co. on July 25, 1967, provides a fairly complete profile of the company on the eve of its cultural and economic apotheosis. By that time, Grove Press had published more than one thousand titles, and the prospectus affirms that many of these titles "have been adopted as text and supplemental course materials at college, university, and high school levels," accounting for "approximately 35% of net sales."[1] As "other operations" of the company, the prospectus lists the Evergreen Book Club (which, supplemented by the membership of the recently purchased Mid-Century Book Club, claimed fifty-two thousand members in 1966), the *Evergreen Review* (claiming a circulation of seventy-five thousand copies per issue in 1966, the first year in which it posted a profit), and the recently purchased Cinema 16 library. The prospectus lists as property and equipment eighty-five thousand square feet of office space at 80 University Place, thirty thousand square feet of warehouse space at 315 Hudson Street, and a 162-seat theater to be used as "a showcase for Cinema 16." The prospectus specifies that "as of May 1, 1967, the Company employed a total of 85 persons. Of this number 9 were editors, 6 were salesmen and sales consultants, 9 were departmental heads and the balance were general office, warehouse and accounting employees. The Company has never had a work stoppage or strike and considers its relations with its employees excellent."[2]

Going public put a strain on these relations, resulting in unionization efforts and culminating in a feminist takeover of the press in 1970. But the term
"takeover" is also meant to suggest the ways in which Grove's revolutionary aspirations were both realized and revised by the rise of women's liberation. Like
those of the New Left more generally, Grove's politics and policies both encouraged and inhibited the women's movement; many of the books it published
provided both philosophical and practical insight into revolutionary thought
and action, but many of the attitudes held by its writers and editors were pa-
tently, even virulently, misogynist. In leveraging the former against the latter,
the feminist attack on Grove represents both a dialectical reversal and a final
rehearsal of the cultural revolution Grove inaugurated.

Going public was a fateful decision and a transformative moment in Grove's
history. Over the next few years, the company expanded exponentially as Rosset
rapidly spent the profits made on *I Am Curious, Yellow* on a variety of reckless ventures that brought the company to the edge of bankruptcy. In addition
to indiscriminately investing in foreign, avant-garde, and pornographic film,
Rosset in 1969 bought a massive, seven-story, forty-thousand-square-foot office building on the corner of Mercer and Bleecker and embarked on an ambitious series of architectural renovations, including an arched entranceway in
the shape of the letter *G* and a private elevator for himself and the other senior
editors; the renovations ultimately cost more than $2 million. The value of the
building was declining even as it was being renovated, due to a collapse in the
New York real estate market at the time.

Grove was no longer a company; it was a corporation, albeit a countercultural one. To maintain this countercultural reputation, Grove issued its first
annual report "in the guise of an *Evergreen Review* special issue," ambitiously
announcing that its objective was to become "a new kind of communications
center for the sixties."[3] The annual report proudly trumpets the company's
growth and expansion, profiling its new education department, book club division, and film division; citing the effusive critical praise for recently published
titles by Borges, Fanon, Burroughs, Pinter, and Beckett; and featuring a portfolio of sample advertisements, including the full-page "Join the Underground"
ad that appeared in the *New York Times*.

As the number of its employees rose, Rosset's relations to them became
both more distant and more strained. In an effort to maintain the charismatic
community at the company's core, he had special hotlines installed in the of-

fices of his senior staff that went directly to him. As Nat Sobel told me, "We had what Barney called the hotline. This was in the late sixties when Barney didn't want to talk to anyone. Barney had already built an elevator so he could go to the office without seeing anybody. Only Fred and Dick were on that same floor." As the company grew, the original tight-knit cadre of Rosset, Seaver, Jordan, Sobel, and Goldfischer began to disintegrate (Braverman had already left for the *Monthly Review*). In particular, Sobel and Rosset fought frequently over Rosset's reckless investment in film, which Sobel felt was distracting from the core mission of selling books. As he related to me, "The place was in chaos, and I'd been particularly vocal about the way the film division had been taking all of Fred and Dick's time."

Grove's preference for hiring radical youth contributed to a highly undisciplined atmosphere, particularly at the book club, where Myron Shapiro's burgeoning staff was frequently stoned and rarely showed up to work on time. According to Seaver, "Book club employees worked for sums ranging from seventy-five to eight-five dollars a week in jam-packed cubicles, breeding resentment and discontent."[4] Some of Grove's more politically engaged workers perceived Rosset's decision to go public in terms of the wider incorporation of the publishing industry and felt that Grove's employees should respond by unionizing. Finally, some Grove employees, both female and male, were beginning to question the sexual politics of the press, both in what Rosset chose to publish and in how he dealt with his staff.

"The times were insane," Fred Jordan told me, and indeed all the political energies of the radical downtown scene were coming to a head. The Stonewall riots of 1969 had inaugurated the Gay Rights movement, and radical feminist groups such as WITCH and New York Radical Women were beginning to challenge the male-dominated ethos of the New Left. Valerie Solanis could frequently be seen standing outside the Grove offices with an ice pick. "She actually really tried to kill Dad," Ken Jordan told me. "Yeah, she was after me," his father answered. "She was outside with an ice pick . . . She wanted to kill Barney."

It all came to a head on April 13, 1970, when a group of women led by activist Robin Morgan occupied the executive offices of the Mercer Street building, demanding union recognition and asserting that Rosset had "earned millions off the basic theme of humiliating, degrading, and dehumanizing women through sado-masochistic literature, pornographic films, and oppressive and exploitative practices against its own female employees."[5] Morgan had been instrumental in the seizure of *Rat,* one of New York City's signature "underground" newspapers, four months earlier, in which she had published "Goodbye to All That," her radical valedictory to the sexual politics of the New Left; her landmark anthology, *Sisterhood Is Powerful,* was already in production with Random House when she staged the Grove takeover. As the premier publisher of "underground" literature in New York City, Grove was a logical follow-up to the *Rat* action, particularly after Morgan was fired along with eight other employees for what an arbitrator later affirmed to be unionization activities.[6]

Grove undeniably had a blind spot in regard to gender politics. Though it had published a handful of significant titles by women, including a selection of novels and plays by Marguerite Duras, the company's catalog was heavily tilted toward male authors, and most of the handful of books by women that it did publish were erotic confessions, diaries, and autobiographies—frequently anonymous or pseudonymous—such as Sandrine Forge's *Lily: The Diary of a French Girl in New York,* Edith Cadivec's *Eros: The Meaning of My Life,* and Katmoubah Pasha's *Memoirs of a Russian Princess.* Furthermore, *Evergreen* in the later 1960s had gained a reputation as being the *Playboy* of the counterculture, featuring racy covers, nude photo spreads, and "adult" comics such as *Barbarella* and *Phoebe Zeitgeist.* Finally, even though Grove employed many women, some of whom had been with the company since its beginnings, its upper management and senior editorial staff were all male, and Rosset's reputation as a womanizer and swinger aggravated the company's image as a bastion of male chauvinism and a purveyor of pulp pornography.

Nevertheless, Grove's popularization of pornography was a necessary antecedent to its political critique. As Richard Ellis affirms, invoking Walter Benjamin's foundational theory of the "aura," "Decensorship transfers the erotic/pornographic from the realm of ritual to the realm of politics."[7] By democratizing access to previously forbidden texts, Grove "debracketed" the aura that had been generated around obscenity in the modern era, making the category more directly accessible to political, rather than moral or aesthetic, critique. The "end of obscenity," in other words, precipitated the politics of pornography, casting a crucial historical sidelight on Catharine MacKinnon's polemical claim that "obscenity law is concerned with morality, specifically morals from the male point of view . . . The feminist critique of pornography is a politics, specifically politics from women's point of view . . . Morality here means good and evil; politics means power and powerlessness."[8] The story of Grove's rise and fall reveals how the moral discourse of good and evil that proliferated around pornography in the 1960s generated the conditions of possibility for a political discourse of power and powerlessness in the 1970s.

The Story of O, the first selection for the Evergreen Book Club after the initial "Join the Underground" promotion, conveniently crystallizes, both in its content and in its publishing history, the volatile passage from erotic ritual to pornographic politics that culminated in Grove's downfall. The pseudonymously authored third-person narrative of a woman subjected to sadistic sexual slavery by her lover and his aristocratic associate, *Histoire d'O* had originally been published in Paris in 1954 by Jean-Jacques Pauvert, the brash postwar upstart already notorious for issuing unexpurgated editions of the Marquis de Sade. Pauvert had encouraged Grove to publish a translation early on, writing to Seaver in 1960, "Now that you have succeeded in modifying American law a bit with *Lady Chatterley's Lover*, why don't you do a translation of Pauline Réage's lovely book *The Story of 'O'*, to which I have the exclusive rights?"[9] Seaver and Rosset were interested, but they proceeded with caution. In 1964, after three copies of the French edition had been held up at Customs, Seaver wrote to Pauvert: "This book shouldn't be published in America, at least in our opinion, until the terrain has been carefully prepared by the publication of many books such as Miller's Tropics, books by John Rechy and Burroughs and, more recently, Genet and Frank Harris."[10] Later that year, William Kristol declined to offer it through Readers' Subscription, writing that "the people who have read it believe that our members—most of them good family men and women—would be outraged at receiving it as an automatic selection."[11] Kristol's refusal was yet another spur to Rosset's decision to start a book club of his own in the following year.

Speculation about the author's true identity had been rampant upon the book's original publication in France and was reignited when Grove brought out its translation in the United States; many thought that it must have been written by a man. Not until 1994 was it publicly revealed that the author was Dominique Aury, a pseudonym for Anne Desclos, editorial assistant to and sometime lover of literary lion and influential editor of the *Nouvelle revue française* Jean Paulhan (who had himself been suspected of being the author), for whom it had originally been written, partly to woo him back to her and partly to prove to him that a woman could write like Sade, whom he greatly admired.[12] Desclos, a member of the French Resistance, an avid reader of

English, American, and French literature, and a formidable critic and translator in her own right, was the only woman in Gallimard's inner circle of editors and authors in the immediate postwar era, and her authorship of the *Story of O* should be understood in terms of this anomalous position within the homosocial literary milieu of the time, in which Sade was a particularly potent model of literary creation. In terms of the sexual politics of modernist publishing, *The Story of O* can be understood as something of a feminist Trojan horse; while its content seems to confirm all the worst stereotypes of feminine masochism and submission, it also marked the beginning of a series of demographic and discursive transformations that precipitated the rapid disintegration of the male-dominated world it so coolly anatomizes.

When Grove brought out *The Story of O*, speculation about the real identity of the translator, Sabine d'Estrée, was less common, though this, too, was assumed to be a pseudonym. Payment records in the Grove Press archives establish that Richard Seaver translated the book, a fact confirmed by his widow upon his death in 2009.[13] Seaver's pseudonymous identity ironically illuminates the claim in the translator's preface, originally published in the *Evergreen Review* in 1963, that "*Story of O*, written by a woman, demands a woman translator, one who will humble herself before the work and be satisfied simply to render it, as faithfully as possible, without interpretation as such."[14] Seen in the light of Seaver's authorship, this claim takes on considerable, and complex, significance. In the figure of Sabine d'Estrée, we see the translator as transvestite, as a male reader taking the opportunity to "assume" the role of the female masochist as opposed to the male sadists of the narrative. The many embedded secret identities behind the production of this text indicate that these positions map onto the more "literary" roles of writer and reader, author and translator, and, most literally, editor and editorial assistant. Indeed, shortly after the landmark publication of *The Story of O* Robin Morgan Pitchford, at the time an aspiring poet and Movement activist, joined Grove's editorial staff under Seaver, a position from which she was fired some years later for attempting to organize a union.

The story of *The Story of O*, then, is very much a story about literature. In "A Girl in Love," Réage's introduction to the sequel, *Return to the Chateau*, published by Grove in 1971, the author describes the genesis of the text in the experience of two secret lovers for whom books held

> the most important place. Books were their only complete freedom, their common country, their true travels. Together they dwelt in the books they loved as

others in their family home; in books they had their compatriots and their brothers; poets had written for them, the letters of lovers of time past came down to them through the obscurity of ancient languages, of modes and mores long since come and gone—all of which was read in a toneless voice in an unknown room, the sordid and miraculous dungeon against which the crowd outside, for a few short hours, beat in vain.[15]

The "girl" has already told her lover that she could write the kinds of stories he enjoys reading, and *The Story of O* then emerges when she, "instead of taking a book to read . . . began to write the story she had promised." The story she writes is self-consciously Sadean, a narrative of serial enslavement and torture meant to prove, again according to Réage, that "prison itself can open the gates to freedom."

Like the slave narratives that are in some sense its generic antecedent, *The Story of O* relies on extensive paratextual legitimation. Preceding the text itself are three introductions: Seaver/d'Estrée's "Translator's Note," André Pieyre de Mandiargues's "A Note on *Story of O*," and Paulhan's "Happiness in Slavery."[16] For Paulhan, the desire for slavery is inherently feminine, but he sees Réage's ability to write the fantasy with such purity as betraying a masculine nature. Thus, he writes, "Woman you may be, but descended from a knight, or a crusader. As though yours were a dual personality, or the person for whom your letter was intended was so constantly present that you borrowed his taste, and his voice."[17] That Paulhan was himself the person for whom the letter was intended compounds the ironies here.

Not surprisingly, Grove made much of the novel's Parisian antecedents in marketing it to an American readership. Seaver's translator's preface, which also fronts the Evergreen Club newsletter promoting *Story of O*, opens anecdotally, announcing that "in July of 1954, one of the most curious—and most mysterious—novels of recent times appeared under the imprint of a young French publisher, Jean-Jacques Pauvert: *Histoire d'O* [*Story of O*]. Its author was Pauline Réage, a name completely unknown in French literary circles, where everyone knows everyone. The work was greeted with considerable respect by the critics, who none the less clearly did not know what to make of this latter-day, female Sade."[18] The fact that Seaver is the author of these lines stitches the *Story of O* more tightly into the larger story of Grove's transatlantic network, as the preface places the novel in the postwar Parisian milieu in which he and Rosset first established their literary connections and from which they would acquire so much of the literature that made Grove famous. *The Story of O*'s reception in the United States must be understood in terms of this shift from an exclusive European modernist milieu in which the text could be interpreted as a species of sexual ritual to a mainstream American milieu in which the emergence of New Social Movements was precipitating a postmodern politics of sexuality that would condemn the text as a premier example of patriarchal sexism.

The Story of O was reviewed twice in the *New York Times*, and both reviews are reproduced in full in the *Evergreen Club News*. Claiming that "what it resembles most is a legend—the spiritual history of a saint and martyr," Albert Goldman warns that "Pauline Réage is a more dangerous writer than the Marquis de Sade."[19] This danger, for Goldman, consists in the threat of identification on the part of the male reader, as the book makes "real to the reader those dark and repulsive practices and emotions that his better self rejects as improbable or evil." Goldman concludes that, for the book's male readership, which includes himself, "our situation is rather embarrassing: for men pick up pornographic books, as they do prostitutes, intending to take their pleasure and then repudiate the instruments that have provided it. But this moral stratagem will not work with Réage."[20]

Eliot Fremont-Smith also sees the text as groundbreaking, arguing that its publication "marks the end of any coherent restrictive application of the concept of pornography to books."[21] He concludes that this challenge to the very category of pornography also threatens the "distinctions pornography helps to maintain—between men and women (or ladies), between generations, and so on—all of them somewhat false, all of them partial devices for not seeing ourselves in candid relation to each other."[22] Both of these reviews acknowledge that *The Story of O* presents a particular challenge to the reader's sexuality and gender identity, a challenge specific to the time and place of its publication.

Both reviewers are also acutely aware of the contrast between the novel's American apotheosis and its original appearance a decade earlier in France, which places it in a Francophone lineage extending back to "that old workhorse of libertinage, the Marquis de Sade."[23] Ultimately, this gradual democratization and demystification of Sade and his heirs helped expose the raw politics of power that tended to be obscured by the various moral and religious frameworks within which his work had conventionally been framed. It is crucial to note, in this regard, that sexual positions do not necessarily map onto sexual identities in the Sadean universe. Women can be, and frequently are, as sadistic as men, a fact that tends to reduce everyone to positions of power and power-lessness ultimately determined by status more than sex. It is the aristocratic "fortunate few" who exploit everyone below them, whether male or female. The unfettered publication of what we might call the Sadean canon, including *The Story of O*, the mass-market edition of which had sold more than 450,000 copies by the end of 1969, buttressed the feminist contention that pornography is, ultimately, about power.[24]

. . .

In her most recent autobiography, Robin Morgan, who in fact helped Seaver with his magisterial Sade project, claims, "As a woman I need no country. As a New Yorker, my city is the world."[25] Morgan's pithy synecdoche conveniently illustrates the geopolitical specificity of the Grove takeover. It was both a reso-lutely local intervention in the cultural politics of Greenwich Village and a sym-bolic action whose significance resonated into the national and international networks of which New York City had become the nexus. As a crucial node in this nexus, Grove was a strategic target.

Morgan was the only ex-Grove employee among the nine women who par-ticipated in the occupation, though she was advised by Grove's former house counsel, Emily Jane Goodman, whom Rosset, ironically, had recently hired in order to increase the number of women in powerful positions at Grove (in a clear sign of the deterioration of Rosset's relations with his employees, Good-man called him "a one-man dictatorial operation who lives off the money peo-ple pay for dirty books").[26] The manifesto issued by the women echoes both the rhetoric and the politics of "Goodbye to All That," identifying Rosset not only with the sexism of the New Left but also with the capitalism of the culture industries. With "no more" replacing "goodbye" as the anaphoric invocation of a series of negative proclamations, the manifesto chants, "No more using of women's bodies to rip off enormous profits for a few wealthy capitalist dirty old straight white men, such as Barney Rosset!"; "no more mansions on Long Island for boss-man Rosset and his executive yes-men flunkies, segregated mansions built with extortionist profits from selling *The Autobiography of Mal-colm X*"; and "no more Latin American executive junkets for the rich men who sell the books of Che, Bosch, Debray to get rich while the Latin cities they visit are choked with hungry babies!"[27]

Rosset and Jordan were in Copenhagen, which had recently legalized pornography and become a key source of erotic films for Grove, when the occupation occurred; they were taken completely by surprise. According to Rosset,

> I called Grove from Denmark, and I got my secretary and I said, "Hi, how's every-
> thing?" And she says, "Fine." "Everything going ok?" I ask. "Well there is something
> special today; I'm on the 6th floor." Our office was on the 7th floor. "Well why?" said
> I. "Well," she says, "some other people are in your office." "WHAT?" In my office I
> had all my personal letters and records. And they had barricaded themselves into
> my office. I said, "Get 'em out!" And she said, "No, they won't come out." I said, "Go
> in and throw them out." "No, nobody wants to do that." . . . So I said, "Let me speak
> to somebody else." So I spoke to Dick Seaver and a guy named Myron Shapiro.
> And nobody really wanted to get them out. I mean I'm going crazy. What are they
> doing while they're in there? They did smash up the furniture but they didn't steal
> the documents, which is utterly amazing! But they sure smashed the place up, and
> hung flags out the window like they'd taken over Grove Press. And here I am sitting
> in Denmark—rather cleverly planned, wouldn't you say? Well, I said, "If none of
> you have enough guts to get them out, call the police." So they called the police. But
> the girls inside the office, the ones barricaded inside, said, No, they only wanted to
> be arrested by women cops. So they went out and looked for women cops, but they
> couldn't find any. So finally the men cops had to go in and carry them out.[28]

The spectacle of handcuffed women being removed from the Grove Press offices by the New York City police permanently damaged the company's radical
reputation and divided its constituency. Julius Lester supported Morgan, writing to Rosset that "for Grove, revolution is a matter of profit, not of life-style,
behavior or attitude toward others" and that "if the charges against the women
aren't dropped and the demands [not] met, I am left with little choice but to
see that no future books of mine are published by Grove Press, that no further
articles of mine appear in the *Evergreen Review* and that my name no longer be
listed in *Evergreen* as a contributing editor."[29] Carl Oglesby publicly resigned in
a letter to the editor addressed to Fred Jordan in the July 1970 *Evergreen Review*.
He was followed in the next issue by journalist and activist Jack Newfield. Overnight Grove went from being a platform for the New Left to being a symbol of
its disintegration.

Oglesby's lengthy letter, copied to Robin Morgan at *Rat*, is also a valedictory, a testimony to what Grove had achieved over the previous fifteen years.

Hearkening back to 1955, when he'd "picked up a paperback book called *Molloy* by a man named Beckett," Oglesby reminisces that, in the late 1950s and early 1960s, "Grove's name was almost the same as an author's. No Grove book would be a waste of time. A Grove book would know what the problem was and would probably move the discussion along to a broader, better understanding of it."[30] However, if "the problem" had been, with Grove's help, better understood, it had by no means been solved, and Oglesby affirms that "we are still not able to fix the importance of the literary movement that Grove was so crucial to, and the reason for this is that we do not see this movement as having completed itself."[31] For Oglesby, the figure who offers to solve this problem and complete this movement is Robin Morgan:

> Robin Morgan really is what you—your magazine, your house—have merely pretended to be. She really is that very real wolf which, at their best moments, the fiction and the social criticism one will have sometimes found in Grove had been all along demanding. No? Was it not explained to you that it was for such self-possessed and revolutionary people that you published this heretic, that outcast, claiming to find the way of redemption in the sin of Genet and the way of responsibility in the crime of Guevara? Isn't it terrible how it ends now? The New Man you've been trying to summon with an incantation jointly authored by some of the best writers of our period at last materializes in the magic circle, right there behind the sixth-floor barricades—and good God, it's a woman. Nine women, in fact. So what does the sorcerer do, his spells and charms at last having worked? He calls the fucking police, he calls the fucking police, he calls the fucking police, he calls the fucking police.[32]

Jordan responded by reminding Oglesby that, with the exception of Morgan, none of the occupiers worked at Grove, and he attempted to redirect the terms of the debate, asserting that the core issue was censorship, aligning Morgan with Gerald Ford, the Republican congressman who had recently railed against the *Evergreen Review* on the floor of the House of Representatives, as "strange bedfellows," and asserting that "the cops were called in opposition to Robin Morgan's fascist demand for mindless book burning."[33]

As this heated exchange indicates, the struggle over unionization at Grove was at its heart a struggle over what sort of collectivity was most appropriate to the achievement of its revolutionary vision. If Rosset had begun as a "sorcerer" whose powers commanded the allegiance of a small group of loyal followers, he was now a corporate CEO with a massive countercultural constituency increasingly riven by its own internal contradictions. The company contained multitudes; it had become too large to run as an informal group of cultural insurgents. As Fred Jordan related to me, once he didn't know the names of the people he met in the elevator, he had to concede that the company could no longer function as it had in the past.

In the lead-up to the union vote, the Organizing Committee issued a series of election bulletins foregrounding the support they had received for their efforts to affiliate with the Fur, Leather, and Machine Workers Joint Board of the Amalgamated Meat Cutter and Butcher Workers (FLM) branch of the AFL-CIO ("They didn't have a legitimate beef," Graf told me he used to say). These supporters included literary critic Maxwell Geismar, who writes that "if a truly democratic union of people in publishing is to be formed they are lucky to have the furriers as advocates";[34] writer Edgar Snow, who affirms that "a union for all publishing people is required"; and Harry Braverman, who claims that "there is no question in my mind that every group of employees is entitled to self-protection against unilateral decisions, and to be consulted as a body on matters affecting their welfare. I see no reason why publishing should be an exception to this."[35]

In response to the unionization effort, a competing Committee for the Survival of Grove was formed, which issued its own collective statement entitled "What It's Really All About." Resolutely positioning Grove as an exception to the corporate rule in publishing, and in the American economy more generally, the statement begins by affirming that "Grove is forced to operate as a capitalist company in an essentially hostile capitalist world" and noting that "bankers don't see much point in giving money to the publisher of Frantz Fanon, Fidel Castro, Malcolm X, Régis Debray, etc." The committee goes on to note the wave of corporate mergers sweeping over the publishing industry and insists that, insofar as they "have been virtually alone in resisting this trend," they should also be exempted from the unionization efforts that were a response to it. The statement then eloquently describes the ethos at Grove:

> The people who worked for Grove identified wholly with the company's aims; the battle lines were never drawn between Grove management and Grove employees, but between Grove and the enemy outside. While Grove was still small, the spirit of battle pervaded every single department, and staff members could communicate freely with each other to keep informed of the crucial issues besetting the company. There was a genuine communal spirit without artificial class divisions.[36]

The statement concedes that "as, in the last two years, more and more people have joined us, it became more difficult to maintain the kind of personal communication between members of the staff that had prevailed in earlier days," but the committee still concludes that "the drive for outside unionization threatens to artificially divide Grove Press people along class lines . . . The enemy is no longer the hostile environment threatening the survival of Grove, but instead the opposing groups in the battle for outside unionization."[37]

As both sides in this battle affirm, Grove had become too large to be run as a small and loosely structured community united by its allegiance to Rosset and his vision. The "outside" environment against which Grove had struggled was itself undergoing transformation, partly as a result of Grove's success in bringing the margins into the mainstream. The question, then, wasn't only how Grove should be structured as a company but how it should position itself relative to the changed economic and cultural circumstances it had helped bring into being.

In the end, the employees decided, by a vote of 86 to 34, not to be represented by the FLM. Many Grove employees, not surprisingly, did not feel any strong class affiliation with this particular union. As one organizer remembered, "They didn't know what snobs we were. We were afraid of dropping down a class and associating with workers." Indeed, most Grove employees didn't feel like "workers" in the classic Marxian sense because, as this same organizer notes, "the main problem was that the union did not realize that we weren't workers in one important respect: we were not alienated from our work."[38]

As Claudia Menza, who joined Grove in 1969 and continued to work closely with Rosset in the ensuing decade, told me, "Most of us loved working at Grove, and why would we want to change that?" She continued, "I was making a really good salary at Grove, astoundingly good. We had health benefits. Some of us had bonuses at Christmas. Why do you want to change that? You are being treated well. You're not being exploited. So you had the dedication to this company you loved." She concluded, "We were sitting there thinking. I don't know, we're well paid, we love the work that we do, we love working with these people, and now you want to unionize us with the meatpackers? It doesn't make any sense."[39]

Meanwhile, Rosset's ongoing battle with Sobel was coming to a head. As Sobel told me in the backyard of his house on East 19th Street, which doubles as the offices of his literary agency,

> A couple of months before I got fired, we had a showdown, Barney and I, in front
> of the entire staff . . . We'd been having a Monday lunch, which originally gener-

ated out of Barney's office, and his secretary would bring in Chinese food and Fred and myself and Morrie and Dick would have lunch in Barney's office and bring a guest . . . As the company got bigger . . . it became too big for us to have and we had it at a restaurant . . . It was wonderful, and it was his idea. At these lunches, toward the late sixties, Barney kept coming after me . . . and expressing his displeasure about the sales of *Evergreen* magazine and talking to me in a way that he never talked to me personally; and at this particular lunch . . . Barney sat at one end of the table and I sat at the other . . . and Barney started in on me about the magazine, and I just got fed up . . . and so finally . . . I said, "Barney I don't come to this lunch every Monday to have you get on my case about the sale of the *Evergreen Review* at this newsstand on 8th Street and Sixth Avenue; can't we talk about something else, for Christ's sake?" And Barney said, "I'm the publisher, and if you don't like what I want to talk about, you don't have to sit here." And then there was deathly silence, deathly silence. Nobody said anything . . . It was the beginning of the end. That was the last lunch. Barney never had another lunch.[40]

By this point in our interview there were tears in Sobel's eyes. He concluded somberly, "When he decided to fire me, he asked Fred to fire me and Fred wouldn't do it. He asked Dick to fire me and Dick wouldn't do it. There was nobody else senior to me that he could ask to fire me, so he had do to it himself, which was something he'd never done before." By the end of the year, Seaver and Goldfischer would be gone as well. Sobel added a coda to his story: "On the other hand, he kept me on the payroll for a year, and that's how I started my own agency. So when he gave me a great break in hiring me, he gave me an even bigger break in firing me." He concluded, "My only regret is when I left Grove Press after being fired, I didn't cut the red phone and take it with me so I would have it on my desk for all eternity, knowing that phone will never ring again."[41] He and Rosset made up a few years later.

The company never recovered from the widely publicized takeover. Already overextended by overinvestment in film and the purchase and renovation of the Mercer Street building, Grove went into a financial tailspin. In 1970, the company lost more than $2 million. In the months following the takeover, Rosset fired seventy employees and vacated the Mercer Street offices, which he was forced to sell for only one hundred thousand dollars above its mortgage debt two years later. He had to end publication of the *Evergreen Review* in December 1971. In that same month, according to S. E. Gontarski, "Grove Press's liabilities exceeded its assets by nearly $5 million."[42] In 1972, Standard and Poor's index refused to issue further reports on the company; the next year the stock was essentially worthless. By 1974, Rosset was working out of a tiny office on 11th Street with a staff of fourteen.

When asked about the unionization drive, Rosset answered,

> The FBI was responsible. I knew it was them . . . They destroyed us . . . That takeover really was the end of Grove Press. We had like 300 and something employees when it started and we had like 20 when it was finished . . . The head of the union confessed to me he was an opportunist, and that he felt I was correct, it was an FBI instigated thing, and that he fell for it. The union was having a lot of trouble. The Furriers—it was a dying union. A left wing union that had been red baited almost out of existence during the McCarthy era. It had in its Constitution that you could not be a member of the union if you believed in violence or overthrowing the government. That was in their Constitution and it was forced on them by the McCarthy people . . . So we counter attacked—Do you want to be a member of a fucking union you can't even be a Black Panther? We didn't even say that, we just handed out the Constitution to everybody that worked at Grove.[43]

Until the Grove takeover, there had been, according to historian John Tebbel, only one strike of editorial employees in the entire history of American publishing. Traditionally a genteel "family" business fostering an image of collegial informality, publishing had been, as Tebbel affirms, "the lowest-paying part of the communications industry."[44] But the meagerness of its remuneration was supposed to be compensated for by the "psychic wages" accrued through working with and for literature, a commitment to which was assumed to be the motivation of anyone willing to enter into such an unprofitable and unorganized industry. And many who entered were young, college-educated women, most of whom were forced to begin their careers as editorial assistants at salaries well below subsistence level for New York City. Under these conditions, Grove's treatment of its employees, which included health benefits and a profit-sharing plan, was better than that of most of its Midtown brethren. Its hiring of women in positions of authority, it should be noted, also compared favorably with other publishers. Menza assured me that "Barney hired a lot of women, and depended upon a lot of women's opinions and worked closely with all of us," and Seaver, in his memoirs, affirms, "Women employees at Grove in key positions of editorial, production, and marketing were legion, and our work hours (thirty-per week), medical benefits, vacations, and holidays were well above industry average."[45] Nevertheless, the executive editors and upper management remained exclusively male.

By 1970, the "genteel" image legitimating, if not justifying, these conditions no longer obtained. Over the course of the prior decade, the American publishing industry had undergone a widely publicized series of mergers and acquisitions, permanently transforming its cultural and economic structure. In 1960, Random House had purchased Knopf; in 1965, RCA purchased Random House. The Times-Mirror Company purchased New American Library in 1963, and CBS purchased Holt, Rinehart and Winston in 1967. Companies that were not purchased by larger corporations went public. The consequent demand for economic accountability and fiscal responsibility made it increasingly difficult to run a company as recklessly as Rosset had. As Menza affirmed to me, "If you have a corporation, a large corporation, you have a lot more people to pay, and if you have a lot more people to pay, you can't afford to make mistakes, and if you can't afford to make mistakes, you can't take any chances."[46]

Furthermore, such developments increasingly integrated publishing into the larger culture and communications industries, undermining the claim that literature somehow existed outside the rationalized system of commodity exchange and labor relations. Rather, book publishing was now one of the biggest, and one of the few nonunionized, industries in a city that had become the cultural and economic engine of the emergent postmodern world system. The Grove occupation, in fact, was part of a larger effort by employees in the publishing industry to organize in response to these developments. The organizers had been in close communication with members of Harper and Row's house union, and, according to *Publishers Weekly*, the organizing meetings in the lead-up to the occupation were attended by "approximately 80 people from 12 publishing firms."[47]

Many of the lower-level employees in the publishing industry were women with college educations, literary aspirations, and heightened expectations who, like Robin Morgan, came to work for Grove in hopes that these aspirations and expectations could be met. As the Committee for the Survival of Grove specified in its statement, "We searched for the radical young as part of a deliberate hiring policy," and the radical young in turn "came to us looking for a place to work compatible with their point of view and their life-style."[48]

Most of these countercultural youth had first become familiar with Grove in college, where its colophon was by the second half of the 1960s associated with a veritable countercanon of "modern classics." Menza, for example, knew about Grove as a classics major at Oberlin; as she told me, "I'd heard of Grove because . . . when I was in school, we had used Grove Press; I mean, everybody had Grove Press books. You were either reading them on your own, or if you studied any drama, of course, you had Grove Press books." These books were becoming the subject of the scholarly articles and books produced by the burgeoning population of young people pursuing advanced degrees in literature.[49]

One of these books quickly became a classic in its own right and can be understood as a sort of literary analogue to Morgan's takeover. In May 1969, a letter from Ellen Krieber at Doubleday informed Grove that "we are planning to publish, early next year, a trade book entitled *Sexual Politics* by Kate Millett . . . In our book, we are quoting from several of your books . . . May we have permission to use these quotes in our book?"[50] Grove promptly sent a copy of the letter to Henry Miller, explaining that "enclosed is a letter from Doubleday and the material to which they refer. The author, Kate Millett, is quoting rather extensively from SEXUS and BLACK SPRING. We would normally give such permission for inclusion of quotes in a critical work. However, since this is not 'exactly' literary criticism, I would like to know whether or not you agree to quotations."[51] Miller sent the letter back, with his response scrawled across it: "I refuse to give permission to quote from my books."

Then, in June, Grove received a review copy of "Sexual Politics: Miller, Mailer, and Genet," a version of the book's introduction, which was to appear as the opening essay in the upcoming *New American Review*, Theodore Solotaroff's resuscitation of the New American Library's groundbreaking journal *New World Writing*. In his cover letter, Solotaroff notes that "Miss Millett's essay has been adapted from a Ph.D. dissertation which she is doing at Columbia. This might seem to be an unlikely source for writing that is as candid, partisan, and witty as Miss Millett's attack on the sexual attitudes of Henry Miller and Norman Mailer, and her defense of Jean Genet's. Considering, however, the outspokenness emanating from the campuses, Miss Millett's scholarly but devastating analysis of the cult of masculinity in two of our supposedly liberated writers is perhaps not so unexpected after all."[52]

Emily Jane Goodman, at the time Grove's recently hired house counsel, warned that Miller's refusal was on shaky legal ground: "Doubleday takes the position that Miss Millett's book is a critical work and that their excerpts from our authors would be within fair usage. We would have a very difficult time disputing this."[53] *Sexual Politics*, with extensive quotations from Miller and Genet, was published in 1970, the same year of the feminist takeover of the company. Its very title illustrates the shift from moral to political evaluative frameworks, and its methodological reliance on extensive quotation attests to the degree to which Grove's determination to make these texts legally available and democratically accessible was a condition of possibility for the political critique that followed.

Although it has been eclipsed by the more theoretically sophisticated feminist theory of the 1980s, *Sexual Politics* opens with what could arguably be a methodological and political credo for the next generation of cultural critics:

> It has been my conviction that the adventure of literary criticism is not restricted to a dutiful round of adulation, but is capable of seizing upon the larger insights which literature affords into the life it describes, or interprets, or even distorts. This essay, composed of equal parts of literary and cultural criticism, is something of an anomaly, a hybrid, possibly a new mutation altogether. I have operated on the premise that there is room for a criticism which takes into account the larger cultural context in which literature is conceived and produced. Criticism which originates from literary history is too limited in scope to do this; criticism which originates in aesthetic considerations, "New Criticism," never wished to do so.[54]

What Lionel Trilling famously called the "dark and bloody crossroads where literature and politics meet" had, of course, been a perennial subject for his generation of intellectuals, who had been central to legitimating the study of the figures Millet herself engages, but sexual politics, as opposed to sexuality, had been a blind spot for the predominantly male, and predominantly Freudian, coterie of critics who presided over the canonization of modernism.[55] Trilling's "liberal" imagination was no longer ascendant in the Columbia University English department where Millet was a graduate student. As George Stade, at the time an assistant professor on Millet's dissertation committee, proclaimed, "Reading the book is like sitting with your testicles in a nutcracker."[56]

Like the takeover of Grove Press, Millet's methodology can be understood at least partially in terms of the penetration of women into the homosocial spaces that were central to the circuits and sacred to the culture of late modernism. Millet affirms that Miller's "strenuous heterosexuality depends, to a considerable degree, on a homosexual sharing" and that his "sexual humor is the humor of the men's house, more specifically, the men's room."[57] Her generous quotation from Miller, which would have been legally impossible without

Grove's efforts to publish him in the first place, inverts the morally redemptive agency of Miller's earlier male critics. Thus, she opens by overturning Lawrence Durrell and Karl Shapiro's celebration of Miller as sexually liberating, arguing instead that "Miller is a compendium of American sexual neuroses, and his value lies not in freeing us from such afflictions, but in having had the honesty to express and dramatize them." And, deprecating Ihab Hassan's contention that this compendium is actually a (modernist) parody, Millett insists that "the major flaw in his oeuvre—too close an identification with the persona, 'Henry Miller'—always operates insidiously against the likelihood of persuading us that Miller the man is any wiser than Miller the character."[58]

If Henry Miller (both author and character) is the villain in Millet's study, Jean Genet, with whom she concludes both her introduction and the book itself, is its hero. For Millett, Genet "is the only living writer of first-class literary gifts to have transcended the myths of our era."[59] And Millet analyzes this transcendence in terms that anticipate the antiessentialist orthodoxies of later feminist and gender theory. In her introduction, she argues that Genet's homosexual characters "have unerringly penetrated to the essence of what heterosexual society imagines to be the character of 'masculine' and 'feminine,' and which it mistakes for the nature of male and female, thereby preserving the traditional relation of the sexes."[60] In her final chapter, she affirms that, in his homosexual parodies of heterosexual hierarchies, "Genet has demonstrated the utterly arbitrary and invidious nature of sex role. Divorced from their usual justification in an assumed biological incongruity, 'masculine' and 'feminine' stand out as terms of praise and blame, authority and servitude, high and low, master and slave."[61] Millet mobilizes the authority of Sartre's "brilliant psychoanalytic biography of Genet" to buttress her argument.

However, she also notes that *Saint Genet* was composed before Genet wrote his last three plays and that it therefore "leaves its subject still a rebel, failing to report his final metamorphosis into revolutionary."[62] Millet offers her own concluding analysis of Genet's final transformation as a dialectical resolution to Sartre's uncompleted existentialist argument. According to Millett,

> Alone of our contemporary writers, Genet has taken thought of women as an oppressed group and revolutionary force, and chosen to identify with them . . . Each of his last plays incorporates the sexual into the political situations: in *The Balcony* it is power and sex, in *The Blacks*, race and sex, in *The Screens*, sexual rank and the colonial mentality. Lawrence, Miller, and Mailer identify women as an annoy-

ing minority force to be put down and are concerned with a social order in which the female would be perfectly controlled. Genet, however, has integrated her into a vision of drastic social upheaval where her ancient subordination can produce explosive force.[63]

For Millett, sex is the last essentialist outpost in a discursive struggle that had maintained it as an exception that proved the rule for the solitary male rebel. Once Genet lays siege to this outpost, an authentic revolution becomes possible. In a dramatic dialectical reversal, Mailer's "White Negro" is replaced by Genet's Queen, the hipster-rebel by the sex radical.

On August 31, 1970, *Time* magazine featured Kate Millett on the cover and dubbed her "the Mao Tse-tung of Women's Liberation."[64] By then, *Sexual Politics* was in its fourth printing and had already sold more than fifteen thousand copies in hardcover. In September, it was prominently advertised in the *Evergreen Review* with the tagline, "The biggest power struggle of all has begun. And Kate Millet has written its call to arms." The same issue also featured Julius Lester's article "Woman—the Male Fantasy," in which Lester, still listed as a contributing editor, concedes that "*Evergreen Review* gratifies the ego of the sexually inadequate male."[65] Also appearing in this issue was Leo Skir's account of the Gay Liberation march celebrating the first anniversary of the Stonewall riots, and it is worth affirming that, unlike many of the other "underground" magazines, *Evergreen Review* had been consistently supportive of the uprisings, which permanently transformed the cultural geography of Greenwich Village, and that Grove Press published many of the books that provided cultural recognition and political legitimation for the sexual "underworld" whose energies fueled the Gay Liberation movement.

Finally, the September 1970 issue of *Evergreen Review* featured a reprint, translated by Richard Seaver, of an interview with Jean Genet from the *Nouvel observateur*, recounting his recent visit to the United States in support of the Black Panther Party. While Genet's books were by this time legally and popularly available, he himself had been denied a visa and had to sneak into the country, with Rosset's help, through Canada. As Genet recounts, he "went from city to city, university to university, working for the Black Panther Party, speaking on its behalf, and in behalf of Bobby Seale. To popularize the movement and to collect money. I went to MIT, Yale, Columbia, UCLA, etc. In this way, the most important American universities opened their doors to the Black Panther Party."[66] Genet refused to discuss his writing, claiming that it had no relevance for his political radicalism, but this itinerary belies his claim. What Genet was able to contribute to the Panthers was countercultural capital. By 1970, students across the country were familiar with his writing and its galvanizing inspiration for iconic figures such as Ginsberg and Burroughs. And all of that writing had been published by Grove Press.

In its few remaining issues, *Evergreen* did try both to incorporate and to respond to feminist criticism of the counterculture and the New Left. It published two essays from the foundational 1971 anthology of feminist criticism, *Women in Sexist Society: Studies in Power and Powerlessness*: Vivian Gornick's "Woman as Outsider" and Alix Shulman's "Organs and Orgasms." It also featured interviews by Claudia Dreifus with activists Bernadette Devlin and Germaine Greer, as well as an article by Dreifus, "Women in Revolutionary China."

But Grove had already laid the groundwork for its own demise. By funneling the pornographic margins into the cultural mainstream, it dissolved the aura that had previously shielded the personal, especially the sexual, from being understood as political. Grove's success also demystified the personal charisma whereby Rosset had commanded the loyalty of the men and women who were dedicated to his company. The campaign against censorship that he had spearheaded, in the end, left him behind. He had gone from avant-garde to arrière-garde, from hero to villain. But the decline in his personal fortunes must be understood in terms of the success of the collective project he was so instrumental in enabling. He had, almost single-handedly, precipitated the end of obscenity, but the result was a battle over the politics of pornography that he was ill-equipped to engage.

. . .

Rosset did manage to survive the 1970s, but he was never able to revive Grove's financial solvency or its cultural relevance. Even with the ruthless downsizing that followed the occupation, Grove still had cash-flow problems, and Rosset had to turn to his colleague Jason Epstein, at that point an executive at Random House, to prop up the company. Epstein convinced an aging Bennett Cerf that it would be tragic to let Grove go under, so for much of the 1970s Random House distributed Grove's titles, in return for which it received a portion of the profits. While not terribly favorable to Grove financially—Rosset had to cede the rights to a number of valuable backlist titles, including *The Autobiography of Malcolm X*—the deal enabled the company to continue its operations, but on a considerably reduced level of only a handful of titles per year.

Between 1970 and 1985, Grove continued to work the niches it had established for itself in the 1950s and 1960s. The company sustained its position in the vanguard of contemporary drama, publishing new work by Beckett, Pinter, and Stoppard and adding others, such as David Mamet, to its stable of playwrights. Grove also published a number of important anthologies of dramatic work, including the complete plays of Joe Orton, a multivolume Black Cat edition of Pinter's work, and Paul Carter Harrison's *Kuntu Drama: Plays of the African Continuum*. It continued to publish sexually explicit materials, frequently in association with the newly legitimate pornographic film industry, bringing out *Emmanuelle* and *Emmanuelle II* and an illustrated anthology of critical responses to *Last Tango in Paris*. The company also discovered or developed a number of important writers who would enter the postmodern canon, including Robert Coover and John Kennedy Toole, whose *Confederacy of Dunces* was its last bestseller under Rosset's leadership. Nevertheless, as Kent Carroll, who worked with Rosset throughout the decade, affirms, "During the '70s Grove lived on the income generated by its marvelous backlist."[67]

. . .

In 1982, Rosset made his last significant acquisition for Grove: Kathy Acker, whose work the company continued to publish after his departure. As a self-confessed female avatar of Grove authors such as the Marquis de Sade, William Burroughs, and Jean Genet, Acker represents the ambiguous legacy of Grove's signal achievement: the mainstreaming of the avant-garde. She exemplifies the radical feminist appropriation of sexual idioms and attitudes previously reserved for male modernist authors, revealing the degree to which this appropriation was a crucial component of the shift from modern to postmodern aesthetic and cultural sensibilities in the 1970s and 1980s. Acker herself is quite literal about this process in the last section of *Blood and Guts in High School*, when her protagonist Janey meets Jean Genet in Tangier. In the panoply of poetry, prose, and dramatic dialogue that follows, Acker enacts a series of plagiarisms and pastiches of Genet's work, including direct quotes from *Journal de voleur*, a stint in an Egyptian prison "for stealing two copies of *Funeral Rites*," a "terrible plagiarism of *The Screens*," and a concluding scene in an Alexandrian desert where "all Janey and Genet see are mirages or mirrors, pictures of themselves, images of the world which came out of themselves."[68]

In her appropriation of Genet, Acker incarnates Millet's vision of an anti-essentialist world in which sex roles are no longer linked to biological sex but are performed as a mode of political critique. But the limits and liabilities of this critique under a new postmodern dispensation must be conceded. Indeed, these limits are part and parcel of the literary legitimacy that Acker enjoys. Though her underground and avant-garde credentials are impeccable, they are also thoroughly integrated into the cultural field as a legitimate market niche and object of academic study. The legitimation of this niche, ballasted by the academic respectability of radical aesthetic and political practices, is the signal legacy of the cultural revolution Grove helped to effect, a revolution that vastly expanded the range of voices that can be heard without radically challenging the larger socioeconomic order in which they are speaking.

There is no editorial file on Kathy Acker in the Grove Press Archives. The only indication of her affiliation with the Rosset era is the manuscript of *Blood and Guts in High School* that Fred Jordan found on Rosset's desk upon his return to the company in the early 1980s. But, in a sense, the entire Grove Press backlist is Acker's archive, her fundamental point of reference and the source of whatever cultural power her work exerts. Indeed, the Grove Press backlist is a renewable resource of dissidence and dissent that continues to energize new generations of radical artists and activists.

. . .

In 1985, Barney Rosset, personally in debt and still struggling to keep the company afloat in the new environment of corporate conglomerates, sold Grove to Ann Getty and George Weidenfeld for $2 million. One year later, Getty fired Rosset as editor-in-chief. Though he continued to pursue a variety of publishing projects, his role as a significant force in the field he had radically transformed was over.

In my first interview with Fred Jordan I asked him what he thought was responsible for the decline of Grove's fortunes in the 1970s, and he answered without hesitating: "Barney!" We laughed. The next morning he called me in my room at the Chelsea Hotel to clarify: "The times had changed," he said, and it was no longer possible for Rosset to run the company as he had. When I put the phone down, I realized that both answers were correct. The story of Grove reveals how one man managed to set in motion historical forces that, in the end, passed him by.

Notes

Introduction

1. Barney Rosset, interview with author, 5 October 2009. Though no book has been written about Grove, S. E. Gontarski's published lecture, *Modernism, Censorship, and the Politics of Publishing: The Grove Press Legacy* (Chapel Hill, NC: Hanes Foundation, 2000), provides an excellent, if abbreviated, account that gives due credit to Rosset's background. A somewhat different, if equally informative, version can be found in his introduction to *The Grove Press Reader: 1951–2000* (New York: Grove Press, 2001). Gontarski also coedited and wrote the introduction for the fall 1990 edition of the *Review of Contemporary Fiction* devoted to Grove, which includes interviews with Rosset as well as a selection of editors and authors who worked with him ("Dionysus in Publishing: Barney Rosset, Grove Press, and the Making of a Countercanon," *Review of Contemporary Fiction* 10, no. 3 [Fall 1990]: 7–18). A number of articles profiled Rosset and Grove in the 1950s and 1960s, providing useful snapshots of both the company and the times: see "Advance Guard Advance," *Newsweek*, 3 March 1953, 94–98; Fred Warshofsky, "Grove Press: Little Giant of Publishing," *Paperback Trade News*, March 1962, 10–17; Gerald Jonas, "The Story of Grove," *New York Times Sunday Magazine*, 21 January 1968, 28–29, 47–48, 52–53, 59; John Updike, "Grove Is My Press, and Avant My Garde," *New Yorker*, 4 November 1967, 223–38; Albert Goldman, "The Old Smut Peddler," *Life*, 29 August 1969, 49–53; and Martin Mayer, "How to Publish 'Dirty Books' for Fun and Profit," *Saturday Evening Post*, 29 January 1969, 33–35, 72–75. John Gruen has an informative section on the company in its early years (*The Party's Over Now: Reminiscences of the Fifties—New York's Artists, Writers, Musicians, and Their Friends* [Wainscot, NY: Pushcart Press, 1989], 40–49); and Al Silverman has a useful chapter on Grove (*The Time of Their Lives: The Golden Age of Great American Book Publishers, Their Editors and Authors* [New York: St. Martin's, 2008], 41–68). Also useful is Richard Seaver's posthumously published memoir, *The Tender Hour of Twilight: Paris in the '50s, New York in the '60s: A Memoir of Publishing's Golden Age* (New York: Farrar, Straus and Giroux, 2011). In addition, a film has been made about Grove: Neil Ortenberg and Daniel O'Connor, *Obscene: A Portrait of Barney Rosset and Grove Press* (Arthouse Films, 2008). There is one dissertation devoted to Grove's censorship battles: Brian McCord, *An American Avant-Garde: Grove Press, 1951–1986* (Ann Arbor, MI: UMI, 2002). Also useful is the chapter on Grove in Henry S.

Somerville's doctoral dissertation, *Commerce and Culture in the Career of the Permanent Innovative Press: New Directions, Grove Press, and George Braziller Inc.* (Ann Arbor, MI: UMI, 2009). Finally, Rosset conducted a series of interviews with Jules Geller with the intention of coauthoring a book to be called "Magnificent Maverick." The transcriptions from these interviews are housed in the Barney Rosset Papers recently acquired by Columbia University's Rare Book and Manuscript Library. They will hereafter be referred to as Rosset interview transcript.

2. Check of Records: Francis W. Parker High School, February 1944, BRP. In a startling sign of the casual anti-Semitism of the day, Smith also added, "In spite of the depth of his emotions and the fact that he has Jewish blood, he never obtrudes himself or his ways on his comrades and has none of the self-centered preoccupation with his own viewpoints that sometimes marks boys of Jewish extraction, who, like himself, have no physical characteristics to distinguish them."

3. Barney Rosset, "Henry Miller vs. 'Our Way of Life,'" *Nexus: International Henry Miller Journal* 2, no. 1 (2005): 1.

4. Ibid., 2, 4.

5. Ibid., 6.

6. Loren Glass, "Redeeming Value: Obscenity and Anglo-American Modernism," *Critical Inquiry* 32, no. 2 (Winter 2006): 341–61.

7. Steven Brower and John Gall, "Grove Press at the Vanguard," *Print*, March/April 1994, 61.

8. Barney Rosset Jr. to Barney Rosset Sr., 9 April 1951, BRP.

9. Rosset interview transcript, 44, BRP.

10. Ibid., 7.

11. Herbert Gold, "A Friend to Writers, Whatever the Cost," *San Francisco Chronicle*, 3 April 2012, F1.

12. "Military Intelligence?," *Review of Contemporary Fiction* 10, no. 3 (Fall 1991): 60.

13. In truth, US Army Intelligence had considerable difficulty characterizing Rosset. In one document he obtained through the Freedom of Information Act, his characteristics are listed as "boyish, unusual resources, keen and habitual analyst, impetuous, courageous, popular, melancholy, intelligent, well poised, well mannered, loyal, mild and quiet, retiring, sober, levelheaded, liberal, idealist." FOIA request, file no. LA-5880: IX-0/2-17756, BRP.

14. Fred Jordan, interview with author, 23 October 2010.

15. Jeanette Seaver, interview with author, 21 October 2010.

16. Herman Graf, interview with author, 25 October 2010.

17. Guenther Roth and Claus Wittich, eds., *Max Weber: Economy and Society* (Berkeley: University of California Press, 1978), 1113.

18. Warshofsky, "Grove Press," 1.

19. Gontarski, "Modernism, Censorship," 29.

20. James English, *The Economy of Prestige: Prizes, Awards, and the Circulation of Cultural Value* (Cambridge, MA: Harvard University Press, 2005), 13.

21. John Sutherland, in his contribution to an issue of *Critical Inquiry* devoted to the sociology of literature, asserts that the history of publishing is a "hole at the centre of literary sociology" and cites Robert Darnton, along with McGann and D. F. McKenzie, as scholars endeavoring to fill that hole ("Publishing History: A Hole at the Centre of Literary Sociology," *Critical Inquiry* 14, no. 3 [Spring 1988]: 574). Sutherland deprecates case studies as inherently unrepresentative and gloomily prophesies that "most future publishing history will be drudging, unexciting labour" (579), but I argue that he overstates his claims. In the case of the United States, John Tebbel's magisterial four-volume *History of Book Publishing in the United States* (New York: Bowker, 1972–81) has established itself as an authoritative reference work, providing the more quantitative and statistical overviews within which case histories like my own can comfortably position themselves without having to claim representativeness. Indeed, as this study reveals, Grove was in many ways the exception to most rules of the publishing business, which is part of what makes it so interesting.

22. Robert Darnton, "What Is the History of Books?," in *The Book History Reader*, ed. David Finkelstein and Alistair McCleery (New York: Routledge, 2002), 11.

23. "The Cult of the Colophon," *Publishers Weekly*, 6 August 1927, 384. Most modernist theories of the brand focus on industries whose products are uniform. Thus, W. F. Haug, in his landmark *Critique of Commodity Aesthetics* (Minneapolis: University of Minnesota Press, 1986), offers Chiquita bananas and Melitta coffee filters as examples of how "the trans-regional brand-names of large companies impose themselves on the public's experience and virtually assume the status of natural phenomena" (25). Naomi Klein, whose highly influential study, *No Logo* (New York: Picador, 2000), famously argues that, in our contemporary corporate world, "the product always takes a back seat to the real product, the brand" (21), still illustrates much of her argument with companies that mass-produce uniform commodities such as shoes and coffee. While Grove's acquisition of a counter-cultural constituency anticipates the "lifestyle marketing" increasingly characteristic of contemporary culture's brand-saturated public culture, it is also worth emphasizing that its effort to establish a colophonic identity recognizable by a discrete group of readers also hearkens back to the modernist publishing industry. For a sample of recent scholarship on branding and promotional culture, see Melissa Aronczyk and Devon Powers, eds., *Blowing Up the Brand: Critical Perspectives on Promotional Culture* (New York: Peter Lang, 2010).

24. "Cult of the Colophon," 384.

25. Ibid., 389.

26. Jason Epstein, "A Criticism of Commercial Publishing," *Daedalus* 92, no. 1 (Winter 1963): 64.

27. Pascale Casanova, *The World Republic of Letters*, trans. M. B. DeBevoise (Cambridge, MA: Harvard University Press, 2004), 87. Important engagements with Casanova's book include Christopher Prendergrast, "Negotiating World Literature," *New Left Review* 8 (March–April 2001): 100–121; Alexander Beecroft, "World Literature without a Hyphen: Towards a Typology of Literary Systems," *New Left Review* 54 (November–December 2008): 87–100; Jerome McGann, "Pseudodoxia Academica," *New Literary His-*

tory 39, no. 3 (Summer 2008): 645–56; Frances Ferguson, "Planetary Literary History: The Place of the Text," *New Literary History* 39, no. 3 (Summer 2008): 657–84; and Aamir R. Mufti, "Orientalism and the Institution of World Literatures," *Critical Inquiry* 36, no. 3 (Spring 2010): 458–93.

28. Serge Guilbaut, *How New York Stole the Idea of Modern Art: Abstract Expressionism, Freedom, and the Cold War*, trans. Arthur Goldhammer (Chicago: University of Chicago Press, 1985), 5.

29. Ibid., 143.

30. The two most significant studies of the avant-garde are Renato Poggioli, *The Theory of the Avant-Garde*, trans. Gerald Fitzgerald (Cambridge, MA: Harvard University Press, 1968); and Peter Burger, *Theory of the Avant-Garde*, trans. Michael Shaw (Minneapolis: University of Minnesota Press, 1984). Poggioli's theory is the more general one, asserting that "the avant-garde is a law of nature for contemporary and modern art" (225), while Burger's Marxist approach is far more precise, seeing avant-garde movements as historically specific efforts "to negate those determinations that are essential in autonomous art" (53). Poggioli's more catholic definition is far closer to that endorsed by the editors at Grove; indeed, he concludes by offering Grove authors Alain Robbe-Grillet, Samuel Beckett, Jean Genet, and Eugène Ionesco as contemporary avatars of the avant-garde.

31. Barney Rosset, interview with author, 23 October 2010.

32. Tebbel, *History of Book Publishing*, vol. 4, *The Great Change, 1940–1980*, 105–282. See also Charles Madison, *Book Publishing in America* (New York: McGraw-Hill, 1966), 403–557; André Schiffrin, *The Business of Books* (New York: Verso, 2000); and John B. Thompson, *Merchants of Culture: The Publishing Business in the Twenty-First Century* (Cambridge: Polity, 2010), 100–187.

33. See Tebbel, *History of Book Publishing*, vol. 3, *The Golden Age between Two Wars, 1920–1940*. See also Jay Satterfield, *"The World's Best Books": Taste, Culture, and the Modern Library* (Amherst: University of Massachusetts Press, 2002); and Catherine Turner, *Marketing Modernism between the Two World Wars* (Amherst: University of Massachusetts Press, 2003).

34. Kenneth Davis, *Two-Bit Culture: The Paperbacking of America* (Boston: Houghton Mifflin, 1980), xii. See also Thomas L. Bonn, *Heavy Traffic and High Culture: New American Library as Literary Gatekeeper in the Paperback Revolution* (New York: Meridian, 1989); Tebbel, *History of Book Publishing*, 4:347–412; and Madison, *Book Publishing in America*, 547–57.

35. For Epstein's account of his career and his relationship with Rosset, see Jason Epstein, *Book Business: Publishing Past Present and Future* (New York: W. W. Norton, 2001).

36. David Dempsey, "Quality (Culture) Plus Quantity (Readers) Pays Off," *New York Times*, 3 June 1956, 18.

37. Samuel Beckett to Barney Rosset, 6 April 1957, BRP. Extract from Samuel Beckett's letter to Barney Rosset of 6 April 1957 reproduced by kind permission of the Estate of Samuel Beckett c/o Rosica Colin Limited, London. © The Estate of Samuel Beckett. Beckett's relationships with his publishers, and with the literary marketplace more gen-

erally, have been the subject of two recent books: Stephen John Dilks, *Samuel Beckett and the Literary Marketplace* (Syracuse, NY: Syracuse University Press, 2011); and Mark Nixon, ed., *Publishing Samuel Beckett* (London: British Library, 2011).

38. Barney Rosset, "Remembering Samuel Beckett," *Conjunctions* 53 (Fall 2009): 10.

39. Barney Rosset to Samuel Beckett, 18 June 1953, quoted in Rosset, "Remembering Samuel Beckett," 10.

40. Seaver, *Tender Hour of Twilight*, 25.

41. For Seaver's account of his initial meeting with Rosset, see ibid., 200–207.

42. Richard Seaver, "Samuel Beckett: An Introduction," *Merlin* 2 (Autumn 1952): 73.

43. Alexander Trocchi, "Editorial," *Merlin* 2 (Autumn 1952): 55.

44. Richard Seaver, "Introduction," in Alexander Trocchi, *Cain's Book* (New York: Grove Press, 1992), xii.

45. Richard Seaver, "Revolt and Revolution," *Merlin* 3 (Winter 1952–53): 172, 184.

46. For a history of the Olympia Press, see John de St. Jorre, *Venus Bound: The Erotic Voyage of the Olympia Press and Its Writers* (New York: Random House, 1994); and James Campbell, *Exiled in Paris: Richard Wright, James Baldwin, Samuel Beckett and Others on the Left Bank* (Berkeley: University of California Press, 2003), 36–80, 122–80. See also Maurice Girodias's rambling autobiography, *The Frog Prince* (New York: Crown, 1980); and Seaver, *Tender Hour of Twilight*, 179–94.

47. Seaver, *Tender Hour of Twilight*, 286.

48. On the complex relations between modernism and obscenity, see Adam Parkes, *Modernism and the Theater of Censorship* (New York: Oxford University Press, 1996); Allison Pease, *Modernism, Mass Culture, and the Aesthetics of Obscenity* (New York: Cambridge University Press, 2000); and Florence Dore, *The Novel and the Obscene: Sexual Subjects in American Modernism* (Stanford, CA: Stanford University Press, 2005). The prominent role of Jews in this history is frequently noted but rarely analyzed. Two exceptions to this significant oversight are Jay Gertzman, *Bookleggers and Smuthounds: The Trade in Erotica, 1920–1940* (Philadelphia: University of Pennsylvania Press, 1999); and Josh Lambert, *Unclean Lips: Obscenity, Jews, and American Literature* (New York: New York University Press, forthcoming).

49. Seaver, *Tender Hour of Twilight*, 249.

50. S. E. Gontarski, "Don Allen: Grove's First Editor," *Review of Contemporary Fiction* 10, no. 3 (Fall 1991): 133.

51. Donald Allen to Barney Rosset, 10 July 1956, GPR.

52. Kenneth Rexroth, "San Francisco Letter," *Evergreen Review* 1, no. 2 (1957): 11–12.

53. Donald Allen to Barney Rosset, 14 July 1957, GPR.

54. "Cody's Salutes Evergreen Books," *Daily Californian*, 14 April 1958, 9.

55. Barney Rosset, interview with author, 5 October 2009.

56. *Evergreen Review* news release, n.d., 1, GPR.

57. On the rise of paperback bookstores in the postwar United States, see Laura Miller, *Reluctant Capitalists: Bookselling and the Culture of Consumption* (Chicago: University of Chicago Press, 2007), 42–44.

58. Grove Press spring 1958 catalog, 1, GPR.

59. "An Experiment in Book Publishing That Worked!," display ad, *New York Times Book Review*, 19 October 1958, 29.

60. Raymond Walters Jr., "Market Report: Trends of a Year," *New York Times*, 14 January 1962, 22.

61. Barney Rosset, "Paperbacks: Does Good Taste Cost More?," speech presented at "The Popular Arts in American Culture," University of California, Berkeley extension, Summer 1962, 2–3, GPR.

62. Rosset interview transcript, 6.

63. Gontarski, "Don Allen," 133.

64. Jacques Barzun, "Three Men and a Book," foreword to *A Company of Readers: Uncollected Writings of W. H. Auden, Jacques Barzun, and Lionel Trilling from the Readers' Subscription and Mid-Century Book Clubs*, ed. Arthur Krystal (New York: Free Press, 2001), x.

65. Marshall Best, "In Books, They Call It Revolution," *Daedalus* (Winter 1963): 36. Tebbel affirms that "book clubs by 1960 were an important part of the publishing scene," adding that, in 1958, "90 percent of adult books distributed in America had gone through book clubs or paperback outlets" (*History of Book Publishing*, 4:363–64).

66. Louis Menand, *The Marketplace of Ideas: Reform and Resistance in the American University* (New York: Norton, 2010), 64.

67. Ibid., 66.

68. Ibid., 73.

69. *Digest of Education Statistics*, "Earned Degrees in English Language and Literature," http://nces.ed.gov/programs/digest/d96/d96t281.asp.

70. *Digest of Education Statistics*, "Earned Degrees in Modern Foreign Languages and Literatures," http://nces.ed.gov/programs/digest/d96/d96t282.asp.

71. Stephen Schryer, *Fantasies of the New Class: Ideologies of Professionalism in Post–World War II American Fiction* (New York: Columbia University Press, 2011), 1–28.

72. Davis, *Two-Bit Culture*, 2–3.

73. Fredric Jameson, *A Singular Modernity: Essay on the Ontology of the Present* (New York: Verso, 2002), 164, 209.

74. Ibid., 210.

75. Philip Beidler, *Scriptures for a Generation: What We Were Reading in the '60s* (Athens: University of Georgia Press, 1994), 7. My main reservation about Beidler's fascinating study is that he doesn't include enough Grove Press titles.

76. "Your Black Cat 'Kit,'" GPR.

77. Warshofsky, "Grove Press," 13.

Chapter 1

1. Thornton Wilder, "Goethe and World Literature," *Perspectives USA* (1952): 134.

2. David Damrosch, *What Is World Literature?* (Princeton: Princeton University Press, 2003), 5.

3. Ibid., 4.

4. Casanova, *World Republic of Letters*, 47.

5. Mark McGurl, *The Program Era: Postwar Fiction and the Rise of Creative Writing* (Cambridge, MA: Harvard University Press, 2009), 56.

6. UNESCO, *Basic Texts* (Paris: UNESCO, 2004), 7.

7. Luther Evans, *The United States and UNESCO* (Dobbs Ferry, NY: Oceana Publications, 1971), 1.

8. William Preston, Edward Herman, and Herbert Schiller, *Hope and Folly: The United States and UNESCO, 1945–1985* (Minneapolis: University of Minnesota Press, 1989), 70.

9. Robert Escarpit, *The Book Revolution* (London: Harrap, 1966), 9.

10. Christopher E. M. Pearson, *Designing UNESCO: Art, Architecture and International Politics at Mid-Century* (Burlington, VT: Ashgate, 2010), xv.

11. Ibid., xiv.

12. Evans, *United States and UNESCO*, 39.

13. Ibid., 115.

14. Lawrence Venuti, *The Translator's Invisibility: A History of Translation* (New York: Routledge, 2008), 177.

15. Paul Blackburn, "The International Word," *Nation*, 21 April 1962, 357. Grove, of course, was not alone in this postwar "sack of world literature," arguably inaugurated by New American Library's important series New World Writing, first issued in 1952. Nevertheless, it rapidly established a reputation for providing the most avant-garde examples of international writing.

16. Ibid., 358.

17. "Evergreen Books for World Literature and Humanities," n.d., GPR.

18. News release, "Khushwant Singh Wins Grove Press India Contest Award," 15 March 1955, GPR.

19. The judges were Wallace Fowlie, Alfred Kazin, Mulk Raj Anand, and V. K. Krishna Menon. Rosset later discovered, from documents obtained through the FOIA, that the political sympathies of the Indian judges brought the prize to the attention of the Department of State.

20. Khushwant Singh to Barney Rosset, 3 February 1955, GPR.

21. Barney Rosset to Luther Evans, 8 February 1955, GPR.

22. Singh to Rosset.

23. Barney Rosset to Richard Howard, 8 January 1959, GPR.

24. Richard Howard to Barney Rosset, 29 January 1959, GPR.

25. Ibid., n.d., GPR.

26. Barney Rosset to Samuel Beckett, 31 August 1955, GPR.

27. Leo Bersani, "No Exit for Beckett," *Partisan Review* 33 (1966): 262.

28. Martin Esslin, "Introduction," in *Samuel Beckett: A Collection of Critical Essays*, ed. Martin Esslin (Englewood Cliffs, NJ: Prentice-Hall, 1965), 4.

29. Bersani, "No Exit for Beckett," 262.

30. Esslin, "Introduction," 10–12.

31. Karl Ragnar Gierow, presentation speech for the Nobel Prize in Literature, 1969, http://nobelprize.org/nobel_prizes/literature/laureates/1969/press.html.

32. Samuel Beckett, "Three Dialogues on Painting," in Esslin, *Samuel Beckett*, 21. Grove published the dialogues in 1958 with lavish illustrations, including twelve color plates, under the title *Bram Van Velde* in its short-lived Evergreen Gallery series.

33. Hugh Kenner, *Samuel Beckett: A Critical Study* (New York: Grove Press, 1961), 205.

34. Barney Rosset to Samuel Beckett, 18 June 1953, GPR.

35. Samuel Beckett to Barney Rosset, 25 June 1953, in *The Letters of Samuel Beckett*, vol. 2, *1941–1956*, ed. George Craig, Martha Dow Fehsenfeld, Dan Gunn, and Lois More Overbeck (New York: Cambridge University Press, 2011), 385.

36. Seaver, *Tender Hour of Twilight*, 252.

37. Paul Auster, "Editor's Note," in *Samuel Beckett: The Grove Centenary Edition* (New York: Grove Press, 2006), 1:viii.

38. Alain Robbe-Grillet, *For a New Novel: Essays on Fiction*, trans. Richard Howard (New York: Grove Press, 1965), 8.

39. Georges Borchardt to Judith Schmidt, 23 April 1957, GPR.

40. Robbe-Grillet, *For a New Novel*, 24.

41. Roland Barthes, "Objective Literature: Alain Robbe-Grillet," in *Two Novels by Robbe-Grillet*, trans. Richard Howard (New York: Grove Press, 1965), 13.

42. "Robbe-Grillet," Talk of the Town, *New Yorker*, 9 January 1965, 24.

43. Barney Rosset to Georges Borchardt, 17 April 1964, GPR.

44. Alex Szogyi, "The Art of the Philosopher and Thief," *New York Times*, 29 September 1963, 303.

45. Gerard Genette, *Paratexts: Thresholds of Interpretation*, trans. Jane Lewin (New York: Cambridge University Press, 1997), 269.

46. Bernard Frechtman to Barney Rosset, 14 January 1953, GPR.

47. Ibid., 13 November 1956, GPR.

48. Donald Allen to Donald Keene, 9 February 1953, GPR.

49. Donald Keene to Donald Allen, 17 February 1953, GPR.

50. Quoted in Donald Keene to Donald Allen, 11 March 1953, GPR.

51. Donald Keene, *Chronicles of My Life: An American in the Heart of Japan* (New York: Columbia University Press, 2008), 31.

52. Donald Keene, ed., *Modern Japanese Literature* (New York: Grove Press, 1956), 8.

53. Ibid., 13.

54. Ibid., 28.

55. Ibid., 14.

56. Glen Baxter, Review of *Anthology of Japanese Literature*, ed. Donald Keene, *Literature East and West: The Newsletter of the Conference on Oriental-Western Literary Relations of the Modern Language Association of America* 3, no. 4 (Spring 1957): 60.

57. J. L. Cranmer-Byng, "The Wisdom of the East Series," promotional pamphlet, GPR.

58. D. T. Suzuki, "Aspects of Japanese Culture," *Evergreen Review* 2, no. 6 (Autumn 1958): 40.

59. Ibid., 41.

60. Ibid.

61. Frank O'Hara, "Franz Kline Talking," *Evergreen Review* 2, no. 6 (Autumn 1958): 58.

62. Ibid., 61.

63. Gary Snyder, "Cold Mountain Poems," *Evergreen Review* 2, no. 6 (Autumn 1958): 69.

64. Ibid.

65. "Kenzaburo Oe," *Publishers Weekly*, 3 June 1968, 55.

66. Kenzaburo Oe, *A Personal Matter* (New York: Grove Press, 1968), 2–3.

67. Kenzaburo Oe, answers to Grove Press publicity questionnaire, GPR.

68. Oe, *A Personal Matter*, 214.

69. Kenzaburo Oe, "How I Am a Japanese Writer," n.d., 2, GPR.

70. Barney Rosset to Amos Tutuola, 13 June 1953, GPR.

71. Selden Rodman, "Tutuola's World," *New York Times Book Review*, 20 September 1953, 5.

72. Janheinz Jahn, *Muntu: The New African Culture*, trans. Marjorie Grene (New York: Grove Press, 1961), 11.

73. Ibid., 154.

74. Ibid., 25.

75. Janheinz Jahn, *Neo-African Literature: A History of Black Writing*, trans. Oliver Coburn and Ursula Lehrburger (New York: Grove Press, 1968), 16.

76. Octavio Paz, *The Labyrinth of Solitude*, trans. Lysander Kemp (New York: Grove Press, 1961), 194. Both titles sold modestly well in Evergreen editions, with *Muntu* selling around fifteen thousand copies and *Labyrinth of Solitude* almost thirty thousand.

77. Paz, *Labyrinth of Solitude*, 184.

78. Octavio Paz to Barney Rosset, 9 January 1961, GPR. The spelling is Octavio Paz's.

79. Paz, *Labyrinth of Solitude*, 172–73.

80. José David Saldivar, *The Dialectics of Our America: Genealogy, Cultural Critique, and Literary History* (Durham, NC: Duke University Press, 1991), 20.

81. Press release, Formentor Prize, n.d., DAP.

82. Ibid.

83. Barney Rosset to Alfred Kazin, 16 December 1960, DAP.

84. Seaver, *Tender Hour of Twilight*, 313.

85. Quoted in Edmund Wilson, "The Vogue of the Marquis de Sade," *New Yorker*, 18 October 1952), 163. According to Seaver, it had an analogous effect on Grove's global reputation; as he says, the meeting "had hoisted us overnight to a level of international importance" (*Tender Hour of Twilight*, 314).

86. Anthony Kerrigan, translator's introduction to *Ficciones*, by Jorge Luis Borges (New York: Grove Press, 1962), 9.

87. Ibid.

88. Jorge Luis Borges, *Labyrinths*, ed. Donald Yates and James Irby (New York: New Directions, 1964), 180, 184.

89. Borges, *Ficciones*, 15.

90. Jason Wilson, *Jorge Luis Borges* (London: Reaktion Books, 2006), 13.

91. Ben Belitt to Donald Allen, 13 May 1952, GPR.

92. Ben Belitt, *Adam's Dream: A Preface to Translation* (New York: Grove Press, 1978), 23.

93. Ibid., 79.

94. Emir Rodríguez Monegal, ed., *The Borzoi Anthology of Latin American Literature*, vol. 2, *The Twentieth Century—from Borges and Paz to Guimaraes Rosa and Donoso* (New York: Knopf, 1977), 611.

95. Ben Belitt, translator's foreword to *Selected Poems of Pablo Neruda* (New York: Grove Press, 1961), 32–33.

96. Belitt, *Adam's Dream*, 10.

97. The 1966 PEN conference, the first in the United States in forty years, was also attended by Carlos Fuentes and Mario Vargas Llosa and was itself a benchmark in the cultural and diplomatic relations between the United States and Latin America. According to Deborah Cohn, "The conference serves as both a model and a touchstone for hemispheric American studies" ("PEN and the Sword: U.S.–Latin American Cultural Diplomacy and the 1966 PEN Club Congress," *Hemispheric American Studies* [2008]: 220).

98. Belitt, *Adam's Dream*, 48.

99. Ben Belitt to Barney Rosset, 6 April 1955, GPR.

100. "Contributors," in "The Eye of Mexico," special issue, *Evergreen Review* 2, no. 8 (Winter 1959): 8.

101. James Schuyler, review of *Anthology of Mexican Poetry*, ed. Octavio Paz, in "The Eye of Mexico," 221.

102. Ibid.

103. S. E. Gontarski, ed., *On Beckett: Essays and Criticism* (New York: Grove Press, 1986), 4.

104. Octavio Paz, "Todos Santos, Dia de Muertas," in "The Eye of Mexico," 37.

105. Donald Allen, ed., preface to *The New American Poetry* (New York: Grove Press, 1960), xi.

106. Ibid., xii.

107. Rosset interview transcript, 63.

Chapter 2

1. For an excellent performance history of this play, see David Bradby, *Beckett: Waiting for Godot* (Cambridge: Cambridge University Press, 2001).

2. W. B. Worthen, *Print and the Poetics of Modern Drama* (Cambridge: Cambridge University Press, 2005), 15.

3. Ibid., 8.

4. Antonin Artaud, *The Theater and Its Double*, trans. Mary Caroline Richards (New York: Grove Press, 1958), 73, 76.

5. Ibid., 60.

6. James Harding, ed., *Contours of the Theatrical Avant-Garde: Performance and Textuality* (Ann Arbor: University of Michigan Press, 2000), 4.

7. Julie Stone Peters, *Theatre of the Book 1480–1880: Print, Text and Performance in Europe* (New York: Oxford University Press, 2000), 311.

8. Wallace Fowlie, *Dionysus in Paris: A Guide to Contemporary French Theater* (New York: Meridian Books, 1960), 18.

9. Martin Esslin, *The Theatre of the Absurd* (New York: Vintage, 1961), 403.

10. Barney Rosset to Samuel Beckett, 18 June 1953, GPR.

11. Barney Rosset to Alexander Trocchi, 18 June 1953, GPR.

12. Barney Rosset to Jerome Lindon, 11 November 1953, GPR.

13. John Lahr, "The Fall and Rise of Beckett's Bum: Bert Lahr in Godot," *Evergreen Review* 13, no. 70 (September 1969): 30.

14. Barney Rosset to Samuel Beckett, 6 January 1956, GPR.

15. Samuel Beckett to Barney Rosset, 2 February 1956, in Craig et al., *Letters of Samuel Beckett*, 602.

16. Michael Myerberg to Samuel Beckett, 8 June 1956, GPR.

17. Barney Rosset to Dramatists Play Service, 1 November 1956, GPR.

18. Sommerville, *Commerce and Culture*, 294.

19. Samuel Beckett to Barney and Loly Rosset, 14 December 1953, in Craig et al., *Letters of Samuel Beckett*, 431.

20. "Read It before You See It," display ad, *New York Times*, 4 February 1958.

21. Vivien Mercier, "How to Read *Endgame*," Readers' Subscription catalog, GPR. See also Jack Frisch, "*Endgame*: A Play as Poem," *Drama Survey* 3 (Fall 1963): 257–63.

22. Judith Schmidt, boilerplate letter (Samuel Beckett), GPR.

23. Jules Geller to Donald Allen, 10 October 1967, DAP.

24. Ruby Cohn, ed., *Casebook on "Waiting for Godot"* (New York: Grove Press, 1967), 7.

25. Barney Rosset to Claude Gallimard, 19 May 1958, GPR.

26. Ibid., 25 May 1962, GPR.

27. Richard Coe, *Eugene Ionesco* (New York: Grove Press, 1961), 43.

28. Grove promotional flyer, *The Bald Soprano*, n.d., GPR.

29. Grove press release, *The Bald Soprano*, n.d., GPR.

30. Fred Jordan to Marshall McLuhan, 10 February 1967, GPR.

31. "Four Plays," display ad, *New York Times*, 21 January 1958, 27.

32. Eugène Ionesco, *Notes and Counternotes*, trans. Donald Watson (New York: Grove Press, 1964), 9.

33. Ibid., 210.

34. Quoted in Edmund White, *Genet: A Biography* (New York: Vintage, 1993), 349.

35. Bernard Frechtman to Barney Rosset, 3 March 1952, GPR.

36. Barney Rosset to Bernard Frechtman, 11 July 1952, GPR.

37. Jean-Paul Sartre, Introduction to *The Maids* (New York: Grove Press, 1954), 17.

38. Judith Schmidt, boilerplate letter (Jean Genet), 15 January 1959, GPR.

39. Ibid., 19 January 1960, GPR.

40. Sartre, Introduction to *The Maids*, 18.

41. Barney Rosset to Bernard Frechtman, 25 November 1959, GPR.

42. Bernard Frechtman to Barney Rosset, 27 November 1959, GPR.

43. Richard Seaver to Bernard Frechtman, 2 December 1959, GPR.

44. Jean Genet, *The Blacks*, trans. Bernard Frechtman (New York: Grove Press, 1960), 18.

45. Ibid., 35.

46. Norman Mailer, *The Presidential Papers* (New York: Bantam Books, 1964), 202.

47. Lorraine Hansberry, "Genet, Mailer, and the New Paternalism," *Village Voice*, 1 June 1961, 12.

48. Ibid., 15.

49. Genet, *The Blacks*, 4.

50. Jerry Tallmer, "Theater: The Blacks," *Village Voice*, 11 May 1961, 11.

51. Ibid., 12.

52. Ibid.

53. Harold Pinter, "Writing for the Theatre," introduction to *Complete Works: Volume 1* (New York: Grove Press, 1976), 9.

54. Ibid., 9.

55. Worthen, *Print and the Poetics of Modern Drama*, 80.

56. Esslin, *Theatre of the Absurd*, 261.

57. Martin Esslin, *The Peopled Wound: The Work of Harold Pinter* (New York: Anchor Books, 1970), vii.

58. Pinter, "Writing for the Theatre," 10.

59. Varun Begley, *Harold Pinter and the Twilight of Modernism* (Toronto: University of Toronto Press, 2005), 6.

60. Harold Pinter, *The Birthday Party & The Room* (New York: Grove Press, 1961), 9.

61. Ibid., 104–105.

62. Kenneth Tynan, preface to *The Connection*, by Jack Gelber (New York: Grove Press, 1960), 8.

63. Donald Allen to Barney Rosset, 2 June 1958, GPR.

64. "Seven Plays," display ad, *New York Times Book Review*, 2 April 1961, 19.

65. Eric Bentley, ed., introduction to *Seven Plays by Bertolt Brecht* (New York: Grove Press, 1961), xxxii.

66. Esslin, *Brecht: The Man and His Work*, 103.

67. Bentley, introduction to *Seven Plays*, xxxii.

68. Ibid., xiii.

69. Ibid., xxxiii.

70. Bentley, acknowledgments to *Seven Plays*, vii.

71. Grove published the following Brecht plays as mass-market paperbacks: *The*

Threepenny Opera (1964); *The Mother* (1965); *The Jewish Wife and Other Short Plays* (1965); *The Visions of Simone Machard* (1965); *The Jungle of Cities and Other Plays* (1966); *Mother Courage and Her Children* (1966); *Galileo* (1966); *The Caucasian Chalk Circle* (1966); and *The Good Woman of Setzuan* (1966). Fred Jordan was responsible for the rapidity with which these plays were issued. Doubting Bentley's abilities as a translator, he told me he requested a tight time line that would force Bentley to find others to perform the task. And these were the titles that sold. Although *Seven Plays* sold only about ten thousand copies in hardcover over the course of the 1960s, the Black Cat versions of *The Caucasian Chalk Circle, The Good Woman of Setzuan,* and *Galileo* sold more than twenty thousand copies each in 1966–67 alone.

72. Bentley, introduction to *Seven Plays*, xxxi.

73. Bertolt Brecht, "On the Experimental Theater," trans. Carl Richard Mueller, *Tulane Drama Review* 6, no. 1 (September 1961): 6.

74. Erwin Piscator, "Introduction to *The Deputy*," in *The Storm over "The Deputy*," ed. Eric Bentley (New York: Grove Press, 1964), 14.

75. Bentley, foreword to *Storm over "The Deputy*," 8.

76. Ibid.

77. Grove tended to issue the work of its German-language dramas on this "epic" scale. Friedrich Durrenmatt's *Four Plays*, which includes his lengthy preface, "Problems of the Theater," is 350 pages long.

78. "The Deputy," display ad, *New York Times*, 12 March 1964, 33, GPR.

79. Rolf Hochhuth, *The Deputy*, trans. Richard Winston and Clara Winston (New York: Grove Press, 1964), 14.

80. Barbara Garson, *MacBird!* (New York: Grove Press, 1967), 3.

81. Ibid., 8.

82. Ibid., 99.

83. Ibid., 41–42.

84. Ibid., 85.

85. Ibid., 93.

86. "Rosencrantz and Guildenstern Are Dead," press release, n.d., GPR.

87. "A Study Guide for the Play—*Rosencrantz and Guildenstern Are Dead* by Tom Stoppard," 11, GPR.

88. Thomas O'Brien, "Hamlet and the Player," 2, GPR.

89. Ibid.

90. Ibid.

91. Worthen, *Print and the Poetics of Modern Drama*, 20–21.

Chapter 3

1. Charles Rembar, *The End of Obscenity* (New York: Bantam, 1968), 483. The complex and constitutive relations between literature and obscenity in the modern era have been the subject of a number of important studies. In addition to Pease, *Modernism, Mass Culture*; Parkes, *Modernism*; and Dore, *The Novel and the Obscene*, see

also Elisabeth Ladenson, *Dirt for Art's Sake: Books on Trial from "Madame Bovary" to "Lolita"* (Ithaca, NY: Cornell University Press, 2006); Paul S. Boyer, *Purity in Print: Book Censorship in America from the Gilded Age to the Computer Age* (Madison: University of Wisconsin Press, 2002); Felice Flanery Lewis, *Literature, Obscenity, and the Law* (Carbondale: Southern Illinois University Press, 1976); and Edward de Grazia, *Girls Lean Back Everywhere: The Law of Obscenity and the Assault on Genius* (New York: Random House, 1992). Somewhat surprisingly, none of these texts deal centrally with Grove Press or the period Rembar chronicles in his account. For a useful discussion of Grove's battles in the 1960s, particularly in relation to the publishing industry, see Richard Ellis, "Disseminating Desire: Grove Press and 'the End[s] of Obscenity," in *Perspectives on Pornography*, ed. Gary Day and Clive Bloom (New York: St. Martin's, 1988), 26–43.

2. Barney Rosset, "A Few Steps from the Long March," BRP.

3. Rosset affidavit, *Grove Press, Inc. v. Robert K. Christenberry*, 10 June 1959, GPR.

4. Rosset affidavit, *Franklyn S. Haiman et al. v. Robert Morris*, n.d., GPR.

5. Frederick F. Schauer, *The Law of Obscenity* (Washington, DC: Bureau of National Affairs, 1976), 277. These developments were closely paralleled in England, where passage of the Obscene Publications Act in 1959 provided statutory support for expert testimony, which in turn precipitated legal cases over many of the same texts. Indeed, there was a transatlantic circuit running from Girodias's Olympia Press to Calder and Boyers in Britain and Grove in the United States, and out into the Anglophone world and beyond (there were also trials of *Lady Chatterley's Lover* in Japan and India), making the "end of obscenity" a truly transnational phenomenon.

6. De Grazia, *Girls Lean Back Everywhere*, xii.

7. Ibid., 686.

8. Quoted in Boyer, *Purity in Print*, 227.

9. Quoted in Michael Moscato and Leslie LeBlanc, eds., *The United States of America v. One Book Entitled "Ulysses" by James Joyce: Documents and Commentary: A 50-Year Retrospective* (Frederick, MD: University Publications of America, 1984), 189.

10. Felice Flanery Lewis affirms that "the most significant aspect of the *Ulysses* opinions was the classification of that novel as a modern classic" (*Literature, Obscenity, and the Law*, 133).

11. Rembar notes that "censorship and copyright have closely connected origins" (*The End of Obscenity*, 5) but doesn't pursue this connection. There is remarkably little legal or literary scholarship on this crucial intersection. One exception is David Saunders, who makes no mention of *Ulysses* ("Copyright, Obscenity, and Literary History," *English Literary History* 57, no. 2 [Summer 1990]: 431–44). For a fascinating discussion of the history of the American copyright in *Ulysses*, see Robert Spoo, "Copyright and the Ends of Ownership: The Case for a Public-Domain *Ulysses* in America," *Joyce Studies Annual* 10 (Summer 1999): 5–60.

12. Bennett Cerf, *At Random: The Reminiscences of Bennett Cerf* (New York: Random House, 1977), 94.

13. Susan Stewart, *Crimes of Writing: Problems in the Containment of Representation* (Durham, NC: Duke University of Press, 1991), 3.

14. The story of Grove's publication of *Lady Chatterley's Lover* has been told many times in many places. The most thorough and reliable account, on which my own is based, can be found in Raymond T. Caffrey, "*Lady Chatterley's Lover*: The Grove Press Publication of the Unexpurgated Text," *Syracuse University Library Associates Courier* 20, no. 1 (1985): 49–79.

15. Ephraim London to Barney Rosset, 10 March 1954, GPR.

16. Barney Rosset to Mark Schorer, 24 March 1954, GPR.

17. Barney Rosset to Karl Menninger, 17 May 1954, GPR. Bennett Cerf refused to provide testimony, writing to Rosset on 24 June,

> I would like to be helpful, but in all good conscience, I can't think of any good reason for bringing out an unexpurgated version of LADY CHATTERLEY'S LOVER at this late date. In my opinion, the book was always a very silly story, far below Lawrence's usual standard, and seemingly deliberately pornographic. It's precisely this kind of book, in fact, that provides ammunition for the people who are hollering for censorship. ULYSSES was a landmark in literature and we fought and won our battle over it with a good conscience, but I can't help feeling that anybody fighting to do LADY CHATTERLEY'S LOVER in 1954 is placing more than a little of his bet on getting some sensational publicity from the sale of a dirty book. (GPR)

18. Barney Rosset to Laurence Pollinger, 15 June 1954, GPR.

19. Laurence Pollinger to Barney Rosset, 23 June 1954, GPR.

20. Barney Rosset to Alfred Knopf, 30 August 1954, GPR.

21. Barnet Rosset, interview with author, 5 October 2009.

22. "Excerpts from Transcript for the Hearing Held 14 May 1959 at US Post Office Building, New York, New York," 4, GPR. Extensive testimony from the trial is also available in Rembar, *The End of Obscenity*.

23. "Excerpts from Transcript," 210.

24. Ibid., 212–13.

25. Ibid., 37.

26. Ibid., 39.

27. Ibid., 45.

28. Ibid., 122.

29. Quoted in Rembar, *The End of Obscenity*, 74.

30. Ibid., 94.

31. Departmental decision in the matter of Grove Press, Inc., 11 June 1959, 4, GPR.

32. "A Digest of Press Opinions," 8, GPR.

33. "Excerpts from Transcripts," 380.

34. "Signet Gram," 24 July 1959, GPR.

35. "Lady Chatterley's Lover," Grove press release, 29 July 1959, GPR.

36. "The Regrettable Plight of 'Lady Chatterley's Lover,'" *Publishers Weekly*, 17 August 1959, 28.

37. Ibid.

38. Rosset interview transcript, pt. 2, 6.

39. Cited in George Wickes, ed., *Henry Miller and the Critics* (Carbondale: Southern Illinois University Press, 1963), 26.

40. Robert Ferguson, *Henry Miller: A Life* (New York: W. W. Norton, 1991), 149.

41. Cited in Wickes, *Henry Miller and the Critics*, 76.

42. Ibid., 82.

43. Ibid., 119.

44. Henry Miller, *Black Spring* (New York: Grove Press, 1963).

45. Trial transcript, *Attorney General v. A Book Named "Tropic of Cancer,"* 345 Mass. 11 (1962) at 89.

46. Ibid., 88–90.

47. Ibid., 218.

48. Trial transcript, *Franklyn S. Haiman v. Robert Morris,* No. 61 S 19718 (21 February 1962) at 15.

49. Rosset interview transcript, 16.

50. "Opinion of the Honorable Samuel B. Epstein," *Franklyn S. Haiman v. Robert Morris* at 14.

51. "Statement in Support of the Freedom to Read," *Evergreen Review* 6, no. 25 (July–August), GPR. Miller had himself used the phrase "freedom to read" in his letter protesting the Norwegian ban on *Sexus*, "Defence of the Freedom to Read," published in *Evergreen Review* 3, no. 9 (Summer 1959): 12–20. While the rights of readers had been a concern for obscenity law from its nineteenth-century beginnings, prominent usage of the phrase "freedom to read" dates from the postwar era, beginning with the official statement "The Freedom to Read," adopted by the American Library Association and the American Book Publishers Council in May 1953.

52. "Petition for a Writ of Certiorari to the District Court of Appeal, Third District, State of Florida," October 1963, 4, 11, GPC.

53. *Jacobellis v. State of Ohio*, 84 S. Ct. 1676 (1964) at 195.

54. Ihab Hassan, *The Literature of Silence: Henry Miller and Samuel Beckett* (New York: Knopf, 1967), 35. In his acknowledgments, Hassan specifically offers his appreciation to "the farsighted publishers New Directions and Grove Press" (xiii).

55. Ibid., 30, 37.

56. Ibid., 4, 17.

57. Trial transcript, *Attorney General v. A Book Named "Naked Lunch,"* 218 N.E. 2d 571 (1966) at 32.

58. William Burroughs, *Naked Lunch: The Restored Text*, ed. James Grauerholz and Barry Miles (New York: Grove Press, 2001), 199. The deposition was not published in the Olympia edition and appears as an introduction to the first Grove edition.

59. Frank McConnell, "William Burroughs and the Literature of Addiction," *Massachusetts Review* 8, no. 4 (Autumn 1967): 668.

60. Trial transcript, *Attorney General v. A Book Named "Naked Lunch"* at 52–53.

61. Quoted in Michael Barry Goodman, *Contemporary Literary Censorship: The Case History of Burroughs' "Naked Lunch"* (Metuchen, NJ: Scarecrow Press, 1981), 235.

62. *Attorney General v. A Book Named "Naked Lunch,"* in de Grazia, *Censorship Landmarks*, 581.

63. "Naked Lunch," letter to booksellers, n.d., GPR.

64. "*Naked Lunch* on Trial," in William Burroughs, *Naked Lunch* (New York: Grove Press, 1959), xiii, xv.

65. Trial transcript, *Attorney General v. A Book Named "Naked Lunch"* at 203.

66. "*Naked Lunch* on Trial," xxxiv.

67. Rosset interview transcript, 75.

68. "News from *Evergreen Review*," GPR.

69. "*The Moderns*," display ad, *Evergreen Review* 8, no. 32 (April–May 1964): 4.

70. In this sense, Grove's strategy can be understood as a confluence and apogee of the two principal grounds of legal defense whose genealogy Elisabeth Ladenson provides in *Dirt for Art's Sake*: the "art for art's sake" argument that "art exists in a realm independent of conventional morality" and the "realism" argument that "the function of the work of art may legitimately include . . . the representation of all aspects of life, including the more unpleasant and sordid" (xv).

71. Although I did not borrow it from him, my use of the term "vulgar modernism" is similar to T. J. Clark's use of it to describe abstract expressionism, which he sees as "the style of a certain petty bourgeoisie's aspiration to aristocracy, to a totalizing cultural power. It is the art of that moment when the petty bourgeoisie thinks it can speak . . . the aristocrat's claim to individuality. Vulgarity is the form of that aspiration" (*Farewell to an Idea: Episodes from a History of Modernism* [New Haven, CT: Yale University Press, 1999], 389). The Grove Press canon can be understood as expressing a similar aspiration on the part of a similar class fragment. The term has also been used by film critic J. Hoberman, in a somewhat different sense, to designate experimental innovations in the so-called popular arts of cinema, television, and comics ("Vulgar Modernism," *Artforum* 20 [February 1982]: 71–76).

72. In *Miracle of the Rose*, Genet affirms that he was particularly drawn to "books with heraldic bindings, the Japanese vellum of deluxe editions, the long-grained Moroccan copies" (trans. Bernard Frechtman [New York: Grove Press, 1966], 257).

73. Michael Davidson, *Guys like Us: Citing Masculinity in Cold War Poetics* (Chicago: University of Chicago Press, 2004), 13. See also Barbara Ehrenreich, *The Hearts of Men: American Dreams and the Flight from Commitment* (New York: Anchor Books, 1983), 52–68.

74. John Rechy to Richard Seaver, 25 January 1963, GPR.

75. Ibid., 7 March 1963, GPR. Marcel Margin, reviewing *City of Night* for the "homophile" magazine *One* (August 1962), agreed, claiming, "This book is to a far greater degree the story of degenerate heterosexuals than it is of homosexuals" (25).

76. Peter Buitenhuis, "Nightmares in the Mirror," *New York Times*, 30 June 1963, 68.

77. David Carter, *Stonewall: The Riots That Sparked the Gay Revolution* (New York: St. Martin's, 2004), 163.

78. Edmund White, *Genet: A Biography* (New York: Vintage, 1993), 317.

79. Hubert Selby, *Last Exit to Brooklyn* (New York: Grove Press, 1964), 25.

80. Ibid., 56.

81. Ibid., 67.

82. Ibid., 122–23, 198–99.

83. *United States v. Ginzburg*, 338 F. 2d 12 (1964) at 465. Ginzburg had aggressively marketed his magazine *Eros* through a direct-mail campaign. The justices were particularly irked that he had sought mailing privileges from the postmasters of Intercourse and Blue Ball, Pennsylvania. For his account of his experience, see *Castrated: My Eight Months in Prison* (New York: Avant-Garde Books, 1973); see also Charles Williams, "*Eros* in America: Freud and the Counter Culture" (PhD diss., University of Iowa, 2012). Mishkin had, like Girodias, directly solicited authors to write pornographic texts, providing specific guidelines and paying in cash; he had also instructed the printer not to use his name as the publisher. Thus, it was the behavior of the defendants, more than the content of their wares, that led to their convictions being upheld.

84. William Lockhart and Robert McClure, "Censorship of Obscenity: The Developing Constitutional Standards," *Minnesota Law Review* 45, no. 5 (1960): 5–121. See also Marjorie Heins, *Not in Front of the Children: "Indecency," Censorship, and the Innocence of Youth* (New York: Hill and Wang, 2001), 66–88.

85. "Join the Underground," display ad, *New York Times*, 13 March 1966, 21.

86. Richard Seaver to Harry Braverman, 14 January 1966, GPR.

87. "'Evergreen' Digs into Underground Appeal, Finds 'Sold Out' Types Really Dig Its Copy," *Advertising Age*, 25 July 1966.

88. "Do You Have What It Takes to Join the Underground?," display ad, *New York Times*, 29 January 1967, 273.

89. Ironically, Grove's editions of these titles have now become collectible.

90. Edmund Wilson, "The Vogue of the Marquis de Sade," *New Yorker*, 18 October 1952, 176.

91. "Marquis de Sade," press release, n.d., GPR.

92. Austryn Wainhouse to Richard Seaver, 5 March 1966, GPR.

93. Richard Seaver to Maurice Girodias, 16 September 1966, GPR.

94. Richard Seaver, "An Anniversary Unnoticed," *Evergreen Review* 9, no. 36 (June 1965): 54.

95. "Sade Promotional Letter," n.d., GPR.

96. Jean Paulhan, "The Marquis de Sade and His Accomplice," in *The Marquis de Sade: "The Complete Justine," "Philosophy in the Bedroom," and Other Writings*, trans. Richard Seaver and Austryn Wainhouse (New York: Grove Press, 1965), 10.

97. Maurice Blanchot, "Sade," in Seaver and Wainhouse, *The Marquis de Sade*, 38.

98. Simone de Beauvoir, "Must We Burn Sade?," in Seaver and Wainhouse, *The Marquis de Sade*, 40.

99. Pierre Klossowski, "Nature as Destructive Principle," in Seaver and Wainhouse, *The Marquis de Sade*, 66.

100. Austryn Wainhouse, "On Translating Sade," *Evergreen Review* 10, no. 42 (August 1966): 51.

101. "Foreword," in Seaver and Wainhouse, *The Marquis de Sade*, xii.

102. "Publisher's Preface," in Seaver and Wainhouse, *The Marquis de Sade*, xxii.

103. Wilson, "Vogue of the Marquis de Sade," 173.

104. Albert Fowler, "The Marquis de Sade in America," *Books Abroad* 31, no. 4 (Autumn 1957): 355.

105. John Durham Peters, *Courting the Abyss: Free Speech and the Liberal Tradition* (Chicago: University of Chicago Press, 2005), 86.

106. Alex Szogyi, "A Full Measure of Madness," *New York Times Book Review*, 25 July 1965, 4, 22.

107. Seaver, "An Anniversary Unnoticed," 54.

108. Ladenson, *Dirt for Art's Sake*, 229.

109. Ibid., 234.

110. "Publisher's Preface," in Seaver and Wainhouse, *The Marquis de Sade*, xviii.

111. John Clellon Holmes, "The Last Cause," *Evergreen Review* 10, no. 44 (December 1966): 31.

112. Legman, "Introduction," in *My Secret Life*, by Anonymous (New York: Grove Press, 1966), xxi.

113. Ibid., xlviii.

114. "Publisher's Preface," in *My Secret Life*, xvi.

115. Ibid., xviii.

116. J. H. Plumb, "In Queen Victoria's Spacious Days," *New York Times*, 1 January 1967, 26.

117. Goldman, "The Old Smut Peddler," 50.

118. Rosset, nevertheless, took exception to the *Life* profile and wrote a letter to the editor accusing the author of "innuendo, insinuation, falsehood, libel, and malicious distortion" (Barney Rosset to the editors of *Life* magazine, 29 August 1969, BRP).

119. Michel Foucault, *The History of Sexuality*, vol. 1, *An Introduction*, trans. Robert Hurley (New York: Vintage, 1978), 34.

Chapter 4

1. Edgar Snow, "Author's Preface to the 1944 Edition," *Red Star over China* (New York: Grove Press, 1961), vi–vii.

2. "Book Reviews," *Chicago Daily Defender*, 11 July 1961, 9.

3. Jahn, *Muntu*, 19.

4. Donald Franklin Joyce, *Gatekeepers of Black Culture: Black-Owned Book Publishing in the United States, 1817–1981* (Westport, CT: Greenwood Press, 1983), 78–79.

5. Jahn, *Muntu*, 25.

6. Jahn, *Neo-African Literature*, 278, 282.

7. S. E. Anderson, "Neo-African Literature," *Black Scholar* (January–February 1970): 76.

8. Ibid., 78.

9. Jean-Paul Sartre, "Preface," in *The Wretched of the Earth*, by Frantz Fanon, trans. Constance Farrington (New York: Grove Press, 1965), 14, 26.

10. "Wretched of the Earth," press release, n.d., GPR.

11. "Books—Authors," *New York Times*, 12 April 1965, 32.

12. "Wretched of the Earth," display ad, *New York Times Book Review*, 25 April 1965, 44.

13. Lewis Nichols, "What the Negro Reads," *New York Times Book Review*, 16 April 1967, 5.

14. Mel Watkins, "Black Is Marketable," *New York Times Book Review*, 16 February 1969, 3.

15. Gail Baker Woods, "Merchandising Malcolm X: Melding Man and Myths for Money," *Western Journal of Black Studies* 17, no. 1 (1993): 45.

16. "The Bibliography of Malcolm X," Los Angeles Public Library, n.d., GPR.

17. "A Discussion Guide for *The Autobiography of Malcolm X*," 1968, GPR. The guide lists no author, but it is fair to assume that Geller and Braverman both had a hand in its design.

18. Nat Hentoff, "Uninventing the Negro," *Evergreen Review* 9, no. 38 (November 1965): 35.

19. Ibid., 68.

20. Hentoff, "Applying Black Power," *Evergreen Review* 10, no. 44 (December 1966): 47.

21. Ibid., 64.

22. Julius Lester, "The Black Writer and the New Censorship," *Evergreen Review* 14, no. 77 (April 1970): 19.

23. Ibid., 19, 20.

24. Earl Caldwell, "Black Bookstores Creating New Best-Seller List," *New York Times*, 20 August 1969, 49.

25. Julius Lester, *Look Out, Whitey! Black Power's Gon' Get Your Mama!* (New York: Grove Press, 1969), 19.

26. Ibid., 92.

27. Ibid., 138.

28. Ibid., 140.

29. Rosset interview transcript, 83.

30. Margaret Randall, "Notes from the Underground," *Evergreen Review* 11, no. 49 (October 1967): 20.

31. Michael Casey, *Che's Afterlife: The Legacy of an Image* (New York: Vintage, 2009), 128.

32. Michel Bosquet, "From *The Last Hours of Che Guevara*," trans. Richard Seaver, *Evergreen Review* 11, no. 51 (February 1968): 33.

33. Fidel Castro, "El Che vive!," *Evergreen Review* 11, no. 51 (February 1968): 35.

34. Ernesto Che Guevara, *Reminiscences of the Cuban Revolutionary War*, trans. Victoria Ortiz (New York: Monthly Review, 1968), 254.

35. Joseph Hansen, "Preface," in *Che Guevara Speaks*, ed. George Lavan (New York: Grove Press, 1968), 7.

36. Julius Lester, *Revolutionary Notes* (New York: Grove Press, 1969), 6.

37. "The Che Guevara Sweepstakes," *Publishers Weekly*, 5 August 1968.

38. The details of Liss's trip to Bolivia are wonderfully recounted in an unpublished report, "Notes for the Bolivian Trip on a Day to Day Basis: A Diary in Search of a Diary," BRP.

39. "Che Guevara's Bolivian Campaign Diary," trans. Helen Lane, *Evergreen Review* 11, no. 57 (August 1968): 33.

40. Leo Huberman and Paul Sweezy, "Foreword," in *Revolution in the Revolution?*, by Régis Debray (New York: Grove Press, 1967), 9.

41. Ibid., 7, 8.

42. Fredric Jameson, "Periodizing the Sixties," in *The Ideologies of Theory* (New York: Verso, 2008), 508.

43. Debray, *Revolution in the Revolution?*, 98.

44. Jean Genet, "A Salute to 100,000 Stars," *Evergreen Review* 12, no. 61 (December 1968): 51.

45. Ibid., 52, 88.

46. Jerry Rubin, "A Yippie Manifesto," *Evergreen Review* 13, no. 66 (May 1969): 42.

47. Ibid., 83.

48. Tuli Kupferberg and Robert Bashlow, *1001 Ways to Beat the Draft* (New York: Grove Press, 1976), 1.

49. Abbie Hoffman, *Steal This Book* (New York: Pirate Editions, 1971), iii.

50. Carl Oglesby, "The Idea of the New Left," in *The New Left Reader*, ed. Carl Oglesby (New York: Grove Press, 1969), 18.

Chapter 5

1. *United States of America v. A Motion Picture Entitled "I Am Curious, Yellow"* ended up being the only significant obscenity case that Grove lost, when the appeal made it to the Supreme Court in 1970. Justice William Douglas, who had published an excerpt from his recent book in the *Evergreen Review*, recused himself, and the vote was split 4 to 4, allowing the district court's ban to be upheld.

2. Seaver, *Tender Hour of Twilight*, 327.

3. Mark Betz, "Little Books," in *Inventing Film Studies*, ed. Lee Grieveson and Haidee Wasson (Durham, NC: Duke University Press, 2008), 319–52. Very little has been written about Grove's film division. The best resource I could find is an unpublished undergraduate thesis written at Harvard University by Rachel Whitaker, "Beyond Books: Film Production and Distribution at the Grove Press Publishing House" (2008).

4. "*Hiroshima mon amour*: A Round-Table Discussion with Eric Rohmer, Jean-Luc Godard, Jacques Doniol-Valcroze, Jean Domarchi, Pierre Kast, and Jacques Rivette," trans. Liz Heron, Criterion Collection, prod. Issa Clubb (2005), 13 (originally published in *Cahiers du cinéma* 97 [July 1959]).

5. Ibid., 15.

6. Ibid., 19–20.

7. Marguerite Duras, "Synopsis," in *Hiroshima mon amour*, by Marguerite Duras and Alain Resnais, trans. Richard Seaver (New York: Grove Press, 1961), 9.

8. Duras and Resnais, *Hiroshima mon amour*, 17.

9. Barthes, "Objective Literature: Alain Robbe-Grillet," 13. Barthes's essay was reprinted in translation in the *Evergreen Review* in 1958, and then again reprinted as one of three introductory essays for Grove's Black Cat version of *Two Novels by Robbe-Grillet* (*Jealousy* and *In the Labyrinth*) in 1965.

10. Alain Robbe-Grillet and Alain Resnais, *Last Year at Marienbad*, trans. Richard Howard (New York: Grove Press, 1962), 8.

11. François Thomas, "The Myth of Perfect Harmony," in *Last Year at Marienbad*, Criterion Collection, 36.

12. Robbe-Grillet and Resnais, *Last Year at Marienbad*, 18.

13. Samuel Beckett, *Film: Complete Scenario / Illustrations / Production Shots* (New York: Grove Press, 1969), 57.

14. Ibid., 63.

15. Rosset interview transcript, 11.

16. François Truffaut, *The 400 Blows* (New York: Grove Press, 1969), 6.

17. Robert Hughes, "A Note on This Edition," in Jean-Luc Godard, *Masculin Féminin* (New York: Grove Press, 1969), 6.

18. Ibid., 6–7.

19. "The Starting Point of the Film," in Godard, *Masculin Féminin*, 219, 221.

20. "The 'Script,'" in Godard, *Masculin Féminin*, 224.

21. Philippe Labro, "Godard Directing," in Godard, *Masculin Féminin*, 226–27.

22. Georges Sadoul, "Godard Does Not Pass," in Godard, *Masculin Féminin*, 250.

23. Pauline Kael, Review for *The New Republic*, in Godard, *Masculin Féminin*, 282.

24. "Grove Press Script Books," *Film Quarterly* 23, no. 1 (Autumn 1969): 58–59.

25. Adrian Martin, "A Young Man for All Times," in Godard, *Masculin Féminin*, 3.

26. Betz, "Little Books," 324.

27. "Suggested Courses Using Books and Films," Grove Press college catalog (1968), 97, GPR.

28. "Why Wait for Godard?," display ad, *Evergreen Review* 13 (December 1969): 73.

29. Quoted in Gontarski, introduction to *Grove Press Reader*, xxxvi.

30. There is some uncertainty about the amount Rosset paid for the rights. In Albert Goldman's article quoted later, the cost is given as $25,000. Rosset told Rachel Whitaker in an interview that he paid $100,000, a figure affirmed in the interview transcripts in his archive; it is also the figure Seaver states in his memoir. The film *Obscene* cites an article stating it was $160,000. Whatever the cost, it represented far more than Grove usually paid in advances or rights for book publication.

31. Jon Lewis, *Hollywood v. Hard Core: How the Struggle over Censorship Saved the Modern Film Industry* (New York: New York University Press, 2000), 192–229.

32. Goldman, "The Old Smut Peddler," 49. In an additional sign of Rosset's pre-science, Grove attempted to release *Evergreen* as a "video magazine" for home consumption in this same year, but, as Rosset lamented, "there was nowhere to play it" (Rosset interview transcript, 28).

33. "Dear Member," Evergreen Club mail-order offer, n.d., GPR.

34. "Dear Collector," Evergreen Club mail-order offer, n.d., KI.

35. "Private Invitation," Evergreen Club mail-order offer, n.d., KI.

Chapter 6

1. "Prospectus: Grove Press, Inc.," Van Alstyne, Noel, and Co., 25 July 1967, 3.

2. Ibid., 9.

3. "Notes from the Publisher," Grove Press annual report, 1967, BRP.

4. Seaver, *Tender Hour of Twilight*, 408.

5. "Women Have Seized the Executive Offices of Grove Press Because:," 13 April 1970, HFA.

6. Robin Morgan's account of the takeover can be found in *Going Too Far: The Personal Chronicle of a Feminist* (New York: Random House, 1978), 132–33, and in her more recent autobiography, *Saturday's Child* (New York: Norton, 2001), 289–96. A more comprehensive version can be found in S. E. Gontarski's pamphlet, *Modernism, Censorship*, 15–19. For an earlier and highly informative discussion of the occupation in terms of developments in the publishing industry more generally, see Powers, "Pride and Prejudice," *More* magazine 5, no. 1 (January 1975): 17–19, 26. For Seaver's account, see *Tender Hour of Twilight*, 414–30.

7. Ellis, "Disseminating Desire," 40.

8. Catharine MacKinnon, *Feminism Unmodified: Discourses on Life and Law* (Cambridge, MA: Harvard University Press, 1987), 147.

9. Jacques Pauvert to Richard Seaver, 6 December 1960, GPR (my translation).

10. Richard Seaver to Jacques Pauvert, 1 October 1964, GPR (my translation).

11. William Kristol to Richard Seaver, 25 December 1965, GPR.

12. Aury's authorship was revealed in an article for the *New Yorker* (1 August 1994) by John de St. Jorre. His account can also be found in *Venus Bound*, 202–36. Not until the release of the documentary film *Writer of O* in 2005 was Aury's real name publicly acknowledged. For Seaver's account, see *Tender Hour of Twilight*, 353–65. Grove had in fact published a translation of Aury's essays, *Literary Landfalls* (New York: Grove Press, 1961), as an Evergreen Original. The original French title was, significantly, *Lecture pour tous*, and in her foreword Aury provocatively asserts that "each one reads for himself, but also for others; all reading is for everyone" (3).

13. The admission can be found in Seaver's *New York Times* obituary of 7 January 2009. St. Jorre does opine that "'Sabine d'Estrée' is, almost certainly, the unmistakably masculine figure of Richard Seaver" (218). Seaver's widow, Jeanette, whose middle name is "Sabine," told me that her husband had loved such anagrams and word games (interview with author, 23 October 2010). Such pseudonymous shenanigans were popular

during this era, testifying to their transitional significance for the sexual politics of literary publishing. In addition to the sequel to *Story of O*, Grove also published *The Image*, written by Catherine Robbe-Grillet under the pseudonym Jean de Berg (with a preface by Pauline Réage), as well as *Emmanuelle*, written by Marayat Rollet-Andriane under the pseudonym Emmanuelle Arsan. As with Réage, the authors' real identities were closely guarded secrets at the time of publication. Also in the 1970s, Régine Deforges, herself a controversial publisher and writer of erotica, conducted a series of interviews with "Pauline Réage," which Seaver translated as Sabine d'Estrée and published as *Confessions of O* under his new Viking imprint, Seaver Books.

14. Réage, *Story of O*, trans. Sabine D'Estrée (New York: Grove Press, 1965), xii. "A Girl in Love" was added as front matter in the 1970s.

15. Ibid., n.p.

16. This analogy is further ballasted by the irony that the Evergreen Club's alternate selection to *The Story of O* was *The Autobiography of Malcolm X*.

17. Jean Paulhan, "Happiness in Slavery," in Réage, *Story of O*, xxv.

18. Réage, *Story of O*, ix.

19. "Albert Goldman in the *New York Times Book Review* (20 March 1966)," *Evergreen Club News* 1, no. 2, 5, 6.

20. Ibid., 7.

21. "Eliot Fremont-Smith in the *New York Times*," *Evergreen Club News* 1, no. 2, 7.

22. Ibid., 9.

23. Ibid., 8.

24. Thus, it is fitting that Grove's Sade became a key source text for the feminist engagement with pornography in the 1970s and 1980s. See, for example, Andrea Dworkin, *Pornography: Men Possessing Women* (New York: Plume, 1989), 70–101; and Angela Carter, *The Sadean Woman and the Ideology of Pornography* (New York: Pantheon, 1978).

25. Morgan, *Saturday's Child*, 107.

26. Quoted in Paul Meskil, "Grove Press Seized by Gals," *New York Daily News*, 14 April 1970.

27. "Women Have Seized the Executive Offices."

28. Quoted in Mike Golden, "The Women's Lib Takeover of Grove Press," http://smokesignalsmag.com/ISSUE0/Non-Fiction/womenlibtakeover.htm.

29. Julius Lester to Barney Rosset, 14 April 1970, BRP. The charges were, in fact, dropped, and Lester stayed on for another year.

30. "Women's Lib Occupation: An Exchange of Letters," *Evergreen Review* 14, no. 80 (July 1970): 16.

31. Ibid.

32. Ibid., 69.

33. Ibid., 70.

34. *Grove Press Election Bulletin*, no. 1 (28 April 1970), HFA. Other supporters included New York mayor John Lindsay, who praised the FLM for its "constructive role in the political life of our city"; labor activist Cesar Chavez, who expressed "undying grati-

tude" to the FLM board for "its support of our consumer boycott"; and Congresswoman Shirley Chisholm, who claims that the FLM "will always be remembered with gratitude and respect by the underprivileged and oppressed people of our nation."

35. *Grove Press Election Bulletin*, no. 2 (29 April 1970), HFA.

36. Committee for the Survival of Grove, "What It's Really All About," n.d., HFA.

37. Ibid.

38. Quoted in Powers, "Pride and Prejudice," 19.

39. Claudia Menza, interview with author, 21 October 2010.

40. Ibid., 26 October 2010.

41. Ibid.

42. Gontarski, *Modernism, Censorship*, 22.

43. Quoted in Golden, "The Women's Lib Takeover of Grove Press."

44. Tebbel, *History of Publishing*, 4:727.

45. Menza, interview with author, 21 October 2010; Seaver, *Tender Hour of Twilight*, 424.

46. Menza, interview with author, 21 October 2010.

47. "Grove Fires Union Activists, Women's Lib Seizes Offices," *Publishers Weekly*, 20 April 1970, 38.

48. Committee for the Survival of Grove, "What It's Really All About."

49. Menza, interview with author, 21 October 2010. I borrow the term "counter-canon" from S. E. Gontarski's introduction to the issue of the *Review of Contemporary Literature* dedicated to Grove, "Dionysus in Publishing."

50. Ellen Krieger to Judith Schmidt, 13 May 1969, GPR.

51. Judith Schmidt to Henry Miller, 14 May 1969, GPR.

52. Theodore Solotaroff to Grove Press, 23 June 1969, GPR.

53. Emily Jane Goodman to Judith Schmidt, 29 July 1969, GPR.

54. Kate Millett, *Sexual Politics* (New York: Avon, 1970), xii.

55. Lionel Trilling, *The Liberal Imagination: Essays on Literature and Society* (New York: Doubleday, 1953), 22.

56. Quoted in "Who's Come a Long Way, Baby?," *Time*, 31 August 1970, 16.

57. Millett, *Sexual Politics*, 303.

58. Ibid., 295.

59. Ibid., 22.

60. Ibid., 17.

61. Ibid., 343.

62. Ibid., 349.

63. Ibid., 356.

64. "Who's Come a Long Way, Baby?," 16.

65. Julius Lester, "Woman—the Male Fantasy," *Evergreen Review* 14, no. 82 (September 1970): 71.

66. "Jean Genet and the Black Panthers," *Evergreen Review* 14, no. 82 (September 1970): 36–37.

67. Kent Carroll, "Grove in the '70s," in Gontarski, *The Grove Press Reader*, 280.

68. Kathy Acker, *Blood and Guts in High School* (New York: Grove Press, 1984), 133, 137, 138.

Index

Page numbers in italics indicate illustrations.

Milton Keynes UK
Ingram Content Group UK Ltd.
UKHW010423250424
441649UK00004B/75/J